Pacific

W · E

S

Midway Island

Hawaii

Equator

Phoenix Islands

Marquesas Islands

Tokelau Islands

Western Samoa

American Samoa

Tuamotu Archipelago

Tahiti

Tonga

Cook Islands

French Polynesia

Austral Islands

Pitcairn Island

Easter Island

New Zealand

Tradewinds
&
Coconuts

A Reminiscence & Recipes
from the Pacific Islands

Tradewinds
&
Coconuts

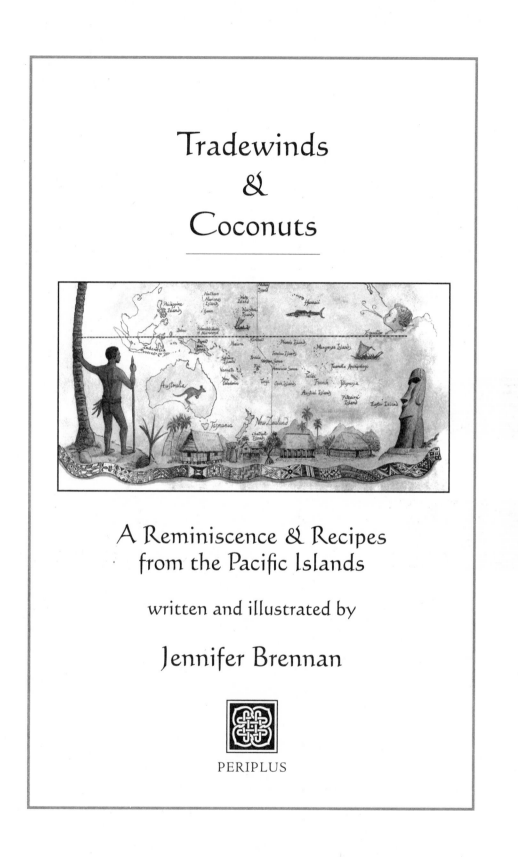

A Reminiscence & Recipes
from the Pacific Islands

written and illustrated by

Jennifer Brennan

PERIPLUS

First published in 2000 by Tuttle Publishing, an imprint of Periplus Editions (HK) Ltd, with editorial offices at 153 Milk Street, Boston, Massachusetts 02109.

Library of Congress Cataloging-in-Publication Data
Cataloging in progress

ISBN: 962-593-819-2

Distributed by

North America
Tuttle Publishing
Distribution Center
Airport Industrial Park
364 Innovation Drive
North Clarendon, VT
05759-9436
Tel: (802) 773-8930
Tel: (800) 526-2778
Fax: (802) 773-6993

Japan
Tuttle Publishing
RK Building, 2nd Floor
2-13-10 Shimo-Meguro,
Meguro-Ku
Tokyo 153 0064
Tel: (03) 5437-0171
Fax: (03) 5437-0755

Asia Pacific
Berkeley Books Pte Ltd
5 Little Road #08-01
Singapore 536983
Tel: (65) 280-1330
Fax: (65) 280-6290

First edition
1 3 5 7 9 10 8 6 4 2   06 05 04 03 02 01 00

Design by Graphic World Publishing Services/Rita Naughton
Printed in The United States of America

Contents

To Art

The ocean supporting my boat
The wind filling my sails
And the star guiding me to my destination

Acknowledgments

The decade it has taken to formulate, research and write *Tradewinds and Coconuts* has enriched me with a veritable army of friends, associates and helpful Samaritans all over the Pacific and the encircling rim. I count myself proud and lucky to know so many gifted and generous people. All their names would fill another book so I can list only the special few hereunder.

Firstly, I acknowledge an enormous debt to Kikkoman Corporation, particularly to Tadeo Kondo and Keiko Aono for their foresight, generosity and help in setting my feet in the right direction through the South Pacific and in providing me with valuable contacts and associates along the way; especially Charles Zisou in Papeete, Tahiti, who wiped his calendar to be able to open doors for my research through the labyrinths of French governmental bureaucracy.

Next, my longtime friend, Dr. Dirk Ballendorf, Professor of Micronesian Studies and Director of the Micronesian Area Research center, whose interest and assistance inspired me many years ago on Guam.

My most heartfelt gratitude goes to Dr. George Staples, Botanist and Acting Collections Manager in the Botany Department of the Bishop Museum in Honolulu. George—and his network listed below—has shown such immense patience, helpfulness and precision in proofing substantial sections of the manuscript, checking my mistakes, suggesting publications, sending relevant documents to me in Japan and putting me in touch with scholars and experts in every field I needed. Foremost are two of his colleagues in Hawai'i, Arnold Suzumoto, Collection Manager, Ichthyology (with expertise not exclusive to fishes and invertebrates, but with charm and kindness elaborated on almost all invertebrate organisms' entries) and Dr. Lucius Eldridge, Executive Secretary of the Pacific Science Association (invertebrate zoology). Together, they masterminded my mollusks, browsed through my bony fish and edited out my silly errors and demonstrable stupidity. The entire staff of the Department of Natural Sciences, Bishop Museum has lent their considerable help and input to whatever patina of erudition you may find herein. With my sincerest gratitude, I would like to acknowledge the contributions of the following scholars in the Department: Dr. Scott E. Miller, Chairman (insects); G. Allan Samuelson, Entomologist (insects); Karla Kishinami, Collection Manager, Vertebrate Zoology (reptiles, amphibians, birds, mammals); Dr. Robert Pyle, Collections Technician, Zoology (birds); Jack Fisher, Collections Technician, Botany (algae specialist); Dr. Isabella Abbott, Wilder Professor of Botany at the University of Hawai'i, Manoa campus (marine seaweeds).

Then, through the same network, I was also introduced to Dr. Helen Larson, Assistant Curator of Fish for the Northern Territory Museum of Arts and Sciences in Darwin, Australia, who assisted me in tracking down the true barramundi. I also wish to thank Dr. Diane Ragone, chair of the Plant Science Department, National Tropical Botanical Gardens in Lawai, Hawai'i, and Dr. Daniel F. Austin, Professor of Biology in the Department of Biological Sciences, Florida Atlantic University in Boca Raton, Florida. I am indebted to Dr. Julie Bailey-Brock of the Department of Zoology of the University of Hawai'i, who helped me locate the truth about the *palolo* and confessed envy that I had actually sampled them.

Moving quickly through the Pacific, my gratitude to Dr. Moi Seneka in Papua New Guinea, who guided me through Port Moresby and gave me an insider's view on the islanders' nutrition today. In Fiji, my thanks to Charlotte Thomas of *Pacific Islands Monthly*. She showed me through the *Fiji Times* newspaper's morgue, procured numerous publications and introduced me to the best little restaurant in Suva.

Thanks also to at least 25 good friends in Vanuatu, whom we shall see again next year. Also thanks to Tépoé of the Hibiscus in Moorea, Teina Hosking in Rarotonga, Bill Guinan in Honiara and Grant Waldref of the Hotel Tahiti in Papeete.

The warmth and hospitality of those I met in New Zealand were phenomenal. My gratitude goes to Annabel Langbein, Lauraine Jacobs, Jan Bilton, Jill Brewis, Scott Ashton and John Hughes of Auckland; also to Peter Stanaway in Rotorua, who toured me through the main centers and sites of Maori culture.

Nearing the end, but by no means least, to my beloved aunt, Gery Diamond in Canberra, who pointed out or took me to wherever there was aboriginal culture, and to Karla Mahanna in Melbourne, who introduced me to so much of Victoria and consented to eat my marinated kangaroo steaks with good grace and even enjoyment. To Audrey Albanese, who thoroughly researched the markets of Los Angeles for Pacific foodstuffs, and to my other, much-loved "wingnut," student, friend and supporter, Claudette Rees, who welcomed and encouraged this offering as she generously had done with all the predecessors.

A loving thank you to Adam and Kristine for their help and faith.

My everlasting appreciation to all who helped and contributed but, in fairness to those scholars and experts, I am obliged to remind the reader that I alone inherit the responsibility for any conclusions I gleaned from the scientific data. The mistakes are mine but the Pacific belongs to you.

Preface

From a cook's point of view, the first thing you notice in the Pacific Islands of Oceania is that food seems to be growing everywhere, without pattern or design. Every yard and plot is producing vegetables and fruit for its family. Flowers are incidental; happy but unintended explosions of blossoms on hedges or trees. The little villages are surrounded by individually owned patches of cultivation. Banana, papaya and breadfruit trees or spiky pandanus plants hug the walls of houses and cluster around wooden huts. Coconut palms dominate every vista.

On the drive from the airport into Papua New Guinea's capital, Port Moresby, my attention was caught by a sign proclaiming the "Six-Mile Police Station." Without the notice, I would have thought it an agricultural station since the building was almost obscured by a front yard full of large-leafed taro plants. Farther on at a crossroads, a corner market was in full swing under the hot sun. It looked like a party in progress. Bright umbrellas shaded the vendors and heavyset women in brilliantly flowered cotton dresses bunched around pyramids of fruit and vegetables, piled on grass mats or arranged in rows on banana leaves spread over the bare earth. Gossiping, laughing and bargaining, everyone was having a great time.

In the center of Port Moresby, I stepped onto my balcony for a glimpse of the sea, but focused instead on a lone woman toiling on the slopes surrounding a dirt football field directly below the hotel. Utilizing every inch of bare earth, she was digging little terraces and planting vegetables.

Growing and harvesting food is integral to the Oceanian daily rhythm of life, a never-ending occupation for the islanders. Vegetables are planted, fruits and nuts are picked, game is hunted, animals are raised, fish are caught.

From Tahiti to the Solomon Islands, from Guam to the Samoas, the fishing boats are always at work. By daybreak they are gone, paddled silently through the coral breaks in the lagoons, or launched from steep beaches through crashing breakers. As night falls on the shores of the islands, strings of twinkling lights define the dark horizon of the seas. They pinpoint the locations of the boats. They are the flaming torches or kerosene lanterns used to lure the nocturnal catch of fish.

Like so many before me, I was enchanted with the Pacific Islands upon first acquaintance. The magic has remained. Whilst living on Guam in the Marianas, at multicultural feasts and fiestas, I tasted and marveled at the wide variety of regional dishes from the rest of Micronesia. I sampled meats unfamiliar to me, unusual seafood, exotic vegetables and fruits, and rejoiced in the new, fresh combinations of flavors. From those beginnings, fifteen years ago, came the inspiration for this book.

Observing that culinary traditions were changing under the pressure of modernization within the islands, I was seized by a sense of urgency. "Talk to the old people!" the islanders advised, "Collect their recipes."

So I began, exploring the regions of Oceania, traveling through the remainder of Micronesia, heading out from Hawai'i into the vast triangle of Polynesian Islands and, finally, to Melanesia. I wanted to capture the basics of the island cuisines before they disappeared under the deluge of fast food franchises. What I found was both reassuring and alarming. Original and traditional feast foods, and everyday dishes are still prepared. However, the islanders are succumbing to the easy availability of packaged products. Then I got to know cooks and chefs throughout Oceania who are dedicated to reviving and celebrating the traditional cuisines. At the same time, in many instances, island chefs are challenging culinary creativity with modern techniques and ingredients. Retrospective attention is given to the influx of foreign cuisine elements, historically introduced by explorers, merchants, planters and imported laborers. The meld of cuisines has resulted in inspired fusions of ingredients and a cross-pollination of cooking techniques and influences.

My piles of scribbled recipes mounted. Each time I returned home, my luggage was overweight with books on the history of the Pacific. The testing and cooking began. I was pleasantly surprised to find that I could locate many of the foodstuffs of the islands. Taro and sweet potatoes, yams and coconuts—I located them all, together with Pacific fish and seafood. As I recreated dishes that I experienced, they reaffirmed that the traditional foods and eating patterns of the islanders are healthy—fish and shellfish, sea vegetables, large helpings of green and root vegetables, small portions of meat and a bounty of fresh fruit.

Starch dishes are the centerpiece of island diets. Subsidiary dishes provide flavor and variety. Everyday meals are simple not lavish. Feasting, and the inferred invitation to overeat, is reserved for the special occasions that mark the milestones of island life.

Living in Oceania is addictive. The easy, relaxed lifestyles, the friendly and outgoing peoples, their feasts and festivals, the fruits and flowers, the bounty of freshly caught seafood, the stunning beauty of the islands and the Pacific Ocean itself. Above all, there is the endless fresh and unpolluted air, the pearled and damp daybreaks, the breathtaking sunsets. You live in a cliché. But when your initial infatuation is replaced by respect, you realize that Oceania and its beloved Pacific occupies one-third of the earth's surface. It is a territory and a water land unto itself—a fragile network of islands and peoples, and one of the world's greatest and most fertile resources.

Jennifer Brennan
San Diego, California

Introduction

Think of the South Pacific and your imagination usually beckons images of the fabled South-Sea Islands. For over 300 years, their peoples, cultures and scenery have been popularized by discoverers' journals, missionaries' notebooks, sailors' yarns and romanticized in novels, poetry, paintings and film. We have their dazzling, white coral sands, turquoise lagoons and craggy, verdant peaks through the eyes of Cook, Loti, Stevenson, Gauguin, Grimble, Brooke, London, Melville, Wendt and Michener. Lithe, brown, flower-bedecked bodies have undulated across Hollywood's silver screens; plaintive, haunting notes of slack-key guitars have impressed their melodies upon our mass subconscious.

However, the South Pacific Islands are only a part of Oceania—the term that refers to all the islands within the vast basin of the Ocean. Over 12,000 islands are scattered across the tropical waters, both above and below the Equator. Look at a map. You will find them clustered between the horizontal lines representing the Tropic of Cancer and the Tropic of Capricorn. These are the "Coconut Isles," lands of fruits and flowers, of flashing bright birds, of lagoons teeming with reef fish and seafood. These are the islands of music and dance, of feasts and fiestas, and the home of the healthy and bountiful cuisines of Oceania. This book celebrates these cuisines.

The Regions of the Water Lands

To give a sense of order and location to specks of land sprinkled over the Pacific like stars across the heavens, anthropologists have divided Oceania into three principal ethnic regions: Melanesia, Micronesia, Polynesia. The

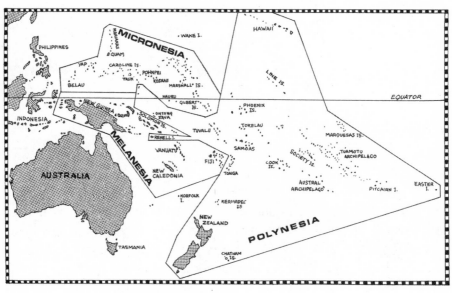

Approximate ethnic divisions in Oceania

names are based on the Greek root word for islands, *nesia*. Therefore, Melanesia means "black islands" and refers, geographically, to the islands of the southwest Pacific, from New Guinea east to Fiji. Micronesia is, literally, "region of small islands," accurately describing the myriad of tiny dots of land lying north of the Equator and west of the International Date Line. Polynesia, "many islands," outlines the archipelagoes situated within an enormous triangle of the Pacific settled by the Polynesian race. The triangle stretches from Hawai'i south to Easter Island and west to Fiji.

Some scholars referenced a fourth region, Australasia, the islands of which I would like to include, if only for their historic import. The name recognized Australia and New Zealand, not only as Pacific nations, but because they are, respectively, the first and last homelands populated by the immigrants from the Pacific. The Australian aborigines filtered south out of New Guinea into the southern continent and the Polynesian race of Maoris sailed their long, twin-hulled canoes over hundreds of miles of open water to settle in the islands of New Zealand. These two peoples—the aborigines and Maoris—became both the vanguard and rearguard of arguably one of the most substantial (in terms of difficulty and distance) migrations in the history of man. This sometimes slow but inexorable migration began to take place over some 30,000 years before the islands and their inhabitants were discovered by the West.

Signs of land

Island Fare

Traditional, everyday village meals in most of Oceania are based on starch foods, such as breadfruit, yams, sweet potatoes, taros, plantains, sago and/or cassava. This filling fare will usually have a leafy green or other vegetable side dish. Seafood and sea vegetables are frequently included for balance and, occasionally, chicken or other meats. Pacific Islanders do not consider they have eaten a "real" meal unless its basis is a starch; just as most Asians seldom contemplate an everyday meal without rice. Indeed, in times of hardship, one of the starches may well constitute the entire meal, served with a soupçon of grated coconut or a splash of sea water.

Desserts are reserved for feasts, not for ordinary meals. Fruit is generally eaten as a snack. To appease a sweet tooth, both children and adults like to suck and chew on lengths of sugar cane.

Coconut milk is the almost universal cooking liquid. The meat of the nut is an ingredient of both relishes and main dishes, as well as a primary ingredient in festive desserts. Coconut water is an everyday drink: the top of the nut is lopped off with a machete and the remaining shell, with its fluid, provides both container and beverage.

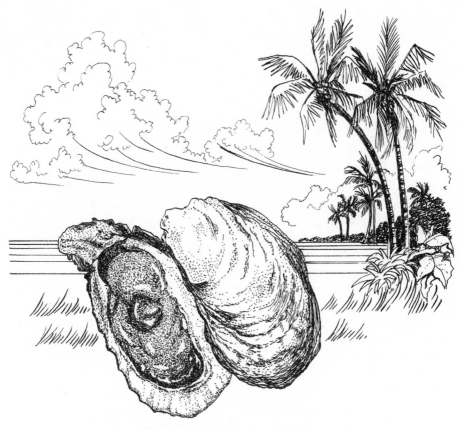

The large oyster, Grassostrea gigas

The women of the village usually perform the daily cooking. A favored method of preparation is to boil food in coconut milk (or sea water) in a convenient container. (In remote areas, a dried gourd or pottery bowl will suffice.) The vessel is placed on the glowing embers of a wood or charcoal fire, or nestled among preheated stones.

Another basic cooking technique is steaming, accomplished by wrapping and baking the food item in its own moisture. The food is wrapped in leaves of taro, banana, breadfruit or ti plants, according to the island's location and local flora, and the packages are securely tied with vegetable fiber. The bundles are then either buried inside an earth-pit oven or are placed within a mound of heated fuel. In each case, hot stones provide the prolonged heat source.

Bivalves are left in their shells for cooking; small fish and land creatures are wrapped in leaves. Large cuts of meat, whole fowl and entire pigs are either cooked in a large, communal earth-pit oven or are spitted and suspended from stout branches over an open fire. This is ceremonial food for feasts. Like our barbecues, it is a "guy" thing, traditionally the province of the men of the village. As is customary in some parts of Asia, in Oceania, fish can be eaten raw or cooked. Sometimes a facsimile of "cooking" is achieved through acidic marination.

The foregoing is a sketch of primitive island food and cooking. However, even at this tribal level, simple dishes can shine. Although the traditional preparation and cooking techniques are crude, the resultant flavors stand out, like the fresh aromas and incomparable textures of newly picked vegetables from your garden, or fish you've freshly caught and grilled over a fire by a stream or on a beach. Leaf-enclosed foods steam slowly to achieve a blend of their mingled essences. When root and leaf vegetables are combined with fish and/or fowl and blessed with a benediction of creamy coconut, the amalgam attains a culinary nirvana of its own. (In Oceanian cooking, the leaf wrappers frequently contribute their own individual flavors.) Add to these dishes the smoky hint from a wood or charcoal fire and you have a unique taste sensation.

As so often happens in isolated cultures where meals are prepared from a limited range of ingredients, the cook's own ingenuity becomes even more important. For instance, techniques of fermentation have been used in the Pacific Islands for hundreds of years. Together with sun drying, they are still used to preserve foods in areas without refrigeration, or to create an additional palette of novel and piquant flavors. Fermented coconut meat is recombined with freshly grated coconut and its cream for sauces. (In ancient Polynesia, fermented breadfruit was mixed with the freshly cooked starch as a base for main dishes.) Sun-dried seaweeds, prized for their nutty accent and tang of the sea, are crumbled and mixed with chopped nuts and sea salt for a dry seasoning dip. The acidity of local citrus fruits provides a complementary marinade for ocean-fresh cubes of raw fish. Wild herbs, green onions and other vegetables are added after the fish has firmed and become opaque. Then the collation is dressed with coconut cream and sea salt. The resultant salad/main dish triumphantly showcases the best of Pacific fare.

Even the basic starches can undergo surprising and pleasing culinary transformations. They are cooked, then mashed, or baked whole and stuffed. They can be steamed in chunks or boiled and sauced, even deep-fried as chips. Frequently they are dried and ground into flour. Occasionally local nuts are pounded into a paste and combined in a dough with the starch flour. This dough is then pressed out as a wrapper for savory vegetable, fish or meat-filled dumplings or pasties. These Oceanian equivalents of our pies and turnovers are steamed or baked, and either reserved for food on-the-go, or as special dishes for the numerous feasts held throughout the Pacific year. These composite preparations, which obviously represent special time and effort to produce, are also prized food gifts in the cultural rounds of inter-village visiting and the return of hospitality.

Traditional domestic meals are very informal affairs. After the food is prepared, individual family members may help themselves when they are hungry. Therefore, most dishes are presented at room temperature.

At larger or more important meals, all the dishes are presented and eaten together, in the same way we pile our plates at a buffet. Traditionally, banana or other large leaves serve as platters. Fingers are eating utensils. (The only historical instance of the use of eating utensils in Oceania was in Fiji, where skillfully carved wooden forks were employed in the ceremonial consumption of man meat.)

These patterns of culinary life and culture remained intact throughout Oceania prior to its discovery by the West. With the exception of the above-mentioned cannibalism, they still exist, virtually unchanged, in the remote tribal villages. The basic dishes and cooking styles continue to be featured in the traditional feasts of the islanders as well as in their meals at home.

The Great Oceanian Culinary Melting Pot

From that first historic moment in 1591 when the Spaniard, Ferdinand Magellan, sailed across the Pacific to eventually anchor off Umatac Bay in Guam, life and foods changed inexorably for the peoples of Oceania. As succeeding waves of foreigners introduced their own plants, animals and agricultural methods into the previously pristine cultural network of islands, diets and customs were altered. In the developing centers of west-ernization, a veritable culinary melting pot evolved.

The redoubtable Yorkshireman, Captain James Cook, during his three voyages through the Pacific, probably affected the cuisines of Oceania more profoundly than any other individual. While he carefully observed, recorded and respected the customs and lifestyles of the Pacific Islanders, as part of a pioneering nature that probably sprang from his hardy origins, he could not resist improving the islanders' ways of life; the botanists accompanying him yearned to experiment with the fecundity of the soils in the hospitable climates they encountered. In the interests of "science" and possible profit, livestock and plants began a two-way traffic so the Westerners could discover what would grow and flourish in which areas of the world. (It was, after all, the 18th century and the age of experimentation and exploration.)

Captain Cook in 1776, aged 48. (Sketched from a painting by John Webber, artist on Cook's last voyage.)

The Westerners stepped up the agricultural and mercantile trade between Oceania and their various home countries. In the ensuing century or so, carrots, tomatoes, cucumbers, beans, lettuces, mangoes, watermelons and any other edible botanical items that would adapt and flourish in the rich volcanic or coralline soils of many of the Pacific Islands, were imported and cultivated. If they grew successfully then intensive farming was implemented in anticipation of a huge profit.

Then the foreign settlers arrived in Oceania, whether as missionaries or planters. Together with the merchants, they brought in a wealth of additional foodstuffs from their home countries. It sustained them during their island sojourns and, occasionally, made money. Coffee was grown in the highlands of New Guinea and pineapples flourished in the Hawaiian Islands. Existing sugarcane was improved and grown in large-scale operations both in Fiji and Hawai'i.

The invasion of foods from the outside world eventually enriched and broadened the scope of the existing cuisines in Oceania. Today, at a weekend party on Guam or Saipan, a Chamorro (local islander) may load his plate with cooked shrimp in a marinade of Japanese soy sauce, chili peppers (originally from Southeast Asia, courtesy of the Portuguese; now growing wild on Guam) and lemon juice from Florida. He might then choose a helping of pork *adobo* (a Filipino stew soured with vinegar). This would be accompanied by rice—virtually unknown in the Marianas before the Japanese arrived. Hamburgers, barbecued American style, could be next. Then the meal could be topped off with a hearty portion of flan (a Spanish dessert introduced to Guam via the Philippines).

A Tahitian in Papeete or a New Caledonian in Nouméa will be most upset of they cannot purchase their daily *baguettes*. After her weekly marketing, a Fijian housewife will be happy to snack on *tandoori* chicken and *roti* (Indian unleavened bread) from a food stall in the center of Suva.

Honolulu is probably the best-known and most concentrated example of pan-Pacific and pan-Asian culinary influences. It is the city where Chinese chicken long-rice (actually, mung-bean noodles) is served with *sushi*; where *mahi mahi* may just as easily be served with a sauce based on coconut cream as one with a foundation of French wine and herbs.

The cuisines of Oceania open up new culinary horizons for us all, and break new ground with unfamiliar ingredients and cooking techniques. Therefore, instead of organizing the recipes in this book by their regional characteristics, I have ordered them using Western meal component labels. This should more closely conform to our familiar cooking and eating patterns, and comfortably fit into our menus. Thus, you can select a dish and seamlessly incorporate it into your Western meals. However, for those readers who seek authenticity, I have provided menus and recipe lists with regional or island-group headings.

Because of the different cultural approaches to eating and cooking there are, inevitably, island dishes that defy Western categorization. At the same time they can behave as appetizers, salads, main dishes, etc., depending on the quantity of the dish prepared and the meal occasion. Take advantage of their versatility and use them where you like.

Enjoy cooking and eating the incredibly diverse bounty of Oceania!

Chapter *1*

The Oceanian Kitchen

Descriptions, Utensils, Sundries and Basics

I remember with pleasure the extraordinary neatness of my friend Tino's cookhouse, beautifully constructed and thatched. It was divided into two equal parts by a coconut log, the cooking section covered with neatly raked white sand, the eating section covered with pandanus mats over a cushioning layer of sweet grass. All of his well-scrubbed utensils were hanging in order in an easily available place. . . .

Across the street there was another family, as well-to-do, as prominent, even larger than Tino's. But the cookshed was old and dilapidated, with great gaps in the roof through which the sunlight showed and rain could pour. No separation was made between eating and cooking place. Sloppiness prevailed, and the shack was full of unpleasant odors. Dogs, cats, and chickens skittered about and the family pigs looked on from the side.

Donald Marshall, 1961, *Ra 'ivavae*

Unassuming Cookeries and Rustic Hearths

The style of the home cook place in the Pacific Islands varies according to the particular culture, to wealth and position and to a household's proximity to an urban center. It may be a home-built kitchen with wooden shelves and a tiled counter within a modern house of cement or timber in a town—simple but functional, with amenities such as running water and electricity. The water may be cold and from a single tap, and the current may power a small refrigerator or support a single bulb or fluorescent strip in the ceiling but, to the cooks, it is modern technology. In contrast, only a few miles away but back in as many centuries in time, the cook place in a small village dwelling may be: an area set aside at one end of a large family hut; a corrugated-iron lean-to;

Cooking pot from Zumin Village, Papua New Guinea

a separate thatched structure with open sides; a mere patch of ground in the open air, covered by a palm-thatched canopy in the rainy season. Within the enclosure, an ancient, treasured and much used metal cooking pot and a few kitchen knives will provide the only traces of Western civilization.

In many places within Melanesia, including Fiji, the traditional dwellings are large enough to accommodate an extended family. Their roofs are sharply peaked to facilitate water runoff and are thickly thatched with pandanus or coconut palm leaves. Their floors are beaten earth. The kitchen area, or place for the hearth, is either in the center of the dwelling (if it is spacious) or at one end, maximum distance from the sleeping area. Caroline Mytinger, in her *Headhunting in the Solomon Islands—Around the Coral Sea,* describes it perfectly:

Carved, inlaid food-offering bowl, Solomon Islands. (From the author's collection.)

The central fireplace was used for cooking only during the rainy season, but it was also kept going every night with damp wood to smoke out the mosquitoes. And as there was no chimney nor any hole for the escape of the smoke, the thatching and cross saplings were dark with soot. The interiors of these huts were not handsome, but they were adequate. They reduced housekeeping to a minor chore. All the personal belongings were kept in the framework of the roof: spears, bows and arrows, paddles, banana leaf bundles (packages of sago "pudding" which can be kept indefinitely), perhaps a wicker fish trap, and any number of plaited dilly bags and sections of bamboo for drinking water or gnali nuts (looking like yellow rice and tasting like nothing else in the world so delicious), dozens of gourds, all with stoppers, and sometimes a carved wooden food bowl. And every one of these objects was ornamented in the same way as the huts; only incidental to the making.

Carved wooden food hooks often hang from the rafters. Sometimes they are in the form of primitive figures. All have large, movable wooden disks or collars at their tops to prevent rats and other marauders from scaling down from the ceiling to reach the suspended food. Bags of grain, dried fish and root vegetables are stored in this manner.

A separate, freestanding cookhouse, such as the one I visited in the Solomons, may have pebbles set into its hardened mud floor if the village is close to a beach—most are. That same cookhouse was constructed with half walls made of woven palm mats. The open spaces above allowed the breeze to dissipate the smoke from the fire. Overlapping strips of pandanus thatch formed the ceiling. There was a high narrow wooden bench—more of a leaning rail—at one end of the kitchen to accommodate the inevitable bunch of children, friends and

Food hook, Papua, New Guinea. (From the author's collection.)

neighbors. A slight depression in the floor at the opposite end of the hut was the site for the aboveground earth oven and the fire stones around it were blackened from constant use. There was also a rudimentary stove alongside, improvised from an empty kerosene can. A selection of scratched enamel pots and large calabashes was stacked on a rickety wood table, above which were hanging several pairs of cooking tongs. These were hand crafted from bamboo strips, heated in the center and folded to form and retain the shape of large tweezers.

I watched the earth-pit oven cooking I had requested to see. It consisted of preheating the stones in a fire, clearing the fire away and placing the hot stones in the depression. The cook and her sister layered large leaves over these, then placed an array of sweet potatoes on top. They bedded the food down with a quilt of leaves and sealed the arrangement with an old sack, providing further insulation. Neighbors dropped by, standing in the doorways, squatting on the floor or perching on the bench, together with innumerable children. After a period of gossip and laughter, the food was declared ready and unveiled from the layers.

After a meal, any pots and utensils involved were cleaned at the single water tap that serves the village. (If a village does not boast that amenity, the dishes are sluiced in a stream or in the sea.) The villagers told me that their earth-pit oven is in use about once a day for the main meal; the leftovers (such as the yams and sweet potatoes they had baked for me) being consumed the next morning before the children leave for school. The Sunday meal is generally prepared on Saturday since, in much of Melanesia and Polynesia, the islanders follow the early Christian missionary injunction against working on the Sabbath.

Urban dwellers in the islands use either charcoal or kerosene for cooking fuel. In Tahiti, traditional meals are prepared only at the weekend when the earth-pit oven is lighted. Day-to-day cooking is carried out on kerosene stoves. Although most of the villages on that island have become suburban and modernized, the village housewives dislike and distrust the notion of cooking with containerized gas. One woman explained it to me, "If the kerosene stove catches fire, I can just throw it out of the house. *Mais le gaz? Zut alors!*" She rolled her eyes in horror.

Of Shell and Wood, of Leaf and Stone

In ancient times, the Oceanian kitchen battery of equipment included long-necked gourds as containers for liquids, with woven twine embroidered in collars around their necks and into loops for suspending them. Shells were implements for scraping, either the skins off root vegetables or for removing the obstinate bristles from the hide of a pig. Large flakes of stone or sharks' teeth (often embedded in wooden handles), or long slivers of bamboo with serrated ends acted as knives. Wood was carved into pestles; heavier pounders were chipped from stone. Thick lengths of wood with central, hollowed-out bowls became mortars. These were used for pounding pastes of breadfruit or taro, called *poi* (in Hawai'i). Sieves were fashioned from woven palm or pandanus fibers. Coconut shells became ladles, food containers or lunch boxes.

In Polynesia—and much of Micronesia—cooking pots and bowls were carved from wood or made out of large, dried gourds. Since these containers would burn if exposed directly to

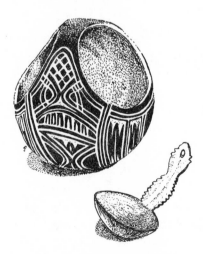

Carved coconut food bowl and spoon, Tami Island, Papua, New Guinea.

12

flames, boiling food within them was achieved by dropping preheated stones into the liquid. Pottery vessels for cooking were produced solely within Melanesia; not because of a superior culture, but because only the islands within that region yielded clays that could withstand firing.

Besides boiling, food was also broiled on or near hot coals, or was baked directly within their embers and ashes. Breadfruit, unpeeled plantains and root vegetables, small animals, reptiles, such as small turtles, mollusks in their shells and various foods in leaf-wrapped packages were all baked in this way.

The earth-pit oven (see page 127) was—and still is—the universal device of choice for baking/steaming food in large quantities. Encasing diverse items in individual leaf-wrapped packages, together with the inclusion of flavorings, such as coconut or herbs, meant that meat, fish and vegetables could all cook simultaneously yet retain their individual flavors.

Smoke on the Water

As on land, so at sea. The voyaging islanders designed safe, portable versions of both the earth-pit oven and the fire pit for cooking on the long journeys undertaken by their large, twin-hulled or outriggered canoes. Around the Fijian and Tongan Islands, smaller vessels often carried pottery fireplaces shaped like buckets. They lighted fires of coconut husks inside these and then placed a smaller, pottery container of food within the larger bucket, resting it on earthenware supports. The Fijians carved portable rectangular earth ovens. Hollowed from single large blocks of wood, these were often finished with pairs of long handles, by which the whole arrangement could be lashed to the deck. (To give an idea of the oven size, some were big enough to accommodate several pigs.) The classic earth-pit oven arrangement of the layering of earth, fire stones, leaves and food was repeated, but the tops were sealed from the sea that frequently swept the decks by a large mattress of woven leaves, securely tied down over the oven.

Keepers in the Pantry

One of the distinguishing features and abiding qualities of Pacific Island food derives from its unconditional freshness: it is newly picked, dug up,

Cooking on board. Tongiaki *voyaging canoe making toward Samoa, 1616. (Adapted from a print in the Fiji Museum.)*

caught, purchased from a local market in the cool, early morning before its use. (Seldom more than a few hours elapse between harvest and table.)

However, like any other region, cycles of plenty are episodic and sometimes unpredictable. Local catches of certain lagoon fish become depleted. In earlier times, the chiefs would place a taboo (*tapu*) or proscription on continued harvesting until stocks were replenished. A particularly harsh tropical cyclone season strips the trees and vegetation. The same storms cause heavy flooding, and roots and tubers rot in the soggy ground. Or a volcano erupts, smothering hillside vegetable plots forever beneath a bubbling blanket of lava. In favorable seasons with accelerated growth and harvesting, fruits and vegetables are supra-abundant. Bereft of electrical refrigeration, the Pacific Islanders adapted and created their own versions of preservation, born of necessity.

Fruits and vegetables were pounded into pastes, sometimes fermented. Frequently, both preparations were dried in the tropical sun, as were meat and fish. If humidity levels rose, then salt curing or smoking were the modes for food preservation. The resultant products were stored carefully for use in times of scarcity, or as hard rations onboard canoes during lengthy voyages.

Some of these early store-cupboard items were soaked and reconstituted as principal ingredients in dishes; others were used in small amounts as flavor accents for bland foods. Naturally sun-dried seaweeds, with their attendant salt, were prized for their piquancy. Sea salt itself was gathered from dried-out reef-and-rock pools.

Foreign influences—from all sides of the Pacific Rim—gradually affected the pristine core of island cultures. They brought with them their own legacies of favorite flavorings to spice the starch-dominated cuisines they encountered. These (once) alien sauces, spices and foods are now integrated, to a greater or lesser degree, into the cooking of Oceania: some only locally, due to historic anomalies that limited the influx of outsiders; others have spread into the cuisines of the entire Pacific region. As precious staples in cans, bottles or jars, they are purchased by the island women and placed on the shelves of their sparse kitchens like treasured possessions. Those sold in packets, such as dried spices and starch flours, are carefully rewrapped and sealed against the ravages of tropical humidity and insects. While they are mostly familiar and common to Westerners, they are a necessity to the preparation of the dishes of Oceania. First, let us examine the indigenous or historical store-cupboard items:

Turmeric (*Curcuma longa*) has ancient uses in Oceania. Called *'olena* or *malena* in Hawai'i and *rea* in Tahiti, it was originally used as a medicament (it is a powerful antioxidant), as a dye for *tapa* or *kapa*—beaten bark cloth—and in religious ceremonies. Immigrations of Indian workers and merchants into the West and Central Pacific spread the use of turmeric into the culinary arena for coloring and flavoring, and it has become a staple of island cuisines.

The annatto plant (*Bixa orellana*) is another coloring agent. The Fijians call it *kesa*, the Hawaiians, *'alaea la 'a*. In the Marquesas, annato is *mahiha, loa* in Samoa and the Guamanians call it *achiote* from the Spanish *achuete*. Ancient warriors infused a dye from its rusty red seeds, which look like small gravel; they then painted their bodies with it before going into battle. In Tonga and Samoa, the dye is still used to color *tapa* cloth. The Chamorros of Guam steep *achiote* seeds in hot water to prepare a rice dish, a staple at their year-round fiestas. Hawaiians tint cooking oil by heating the seeds in it. The oil's bright orange color awakens the appearance of stew-like dishes.

In Polynesia, particularly Hawai'i, sea or rock salt and red salt are derivatives from the ancient Oceanian custom of using sea water as a dip or condiment to enliven the bland starch foods. Hawaiian rock or sea salt is called *pa 'akai pu 'upu 'u* and takes the form of large, white crystals used to season dishes while cooking. (Our sea salt, ancient mineral salt or Kosher salt may be substituted.) Red salt is called *pa 'akai 'ula 'ula*, denoting salt mixed with an ocherous earth called *'alaea* in Hawai'i, *'araea* in Tahiti. In Hawai'i, red salt can be found in markets in one-pound bags of terra-cotta-colored crystals the same size as coarse, brown sugar. (The water-soluble red clay is found on Kaua'i, Moloka'i and Maui, as well as in Tahiti.) This "red earth" was traditionally eaten by the islanders as an iron tonic and is beneficial in small quantities. The Hawaiians use *'alae* salt as an after-cooking seasoning for fish and as an ingredient in dry dips, such as the traditional *'inamona* with roasted *kukui* (candle nut) kernels. Red salt is included also in the classic collection of condiments, such as dried octopus, chili peppers, onions, green onions and tender tips of tree fern; all presented on a ti leaf at an *'aha 'aina,* or feast.

Coconut requires mentioning here because of its function as a hallmark flavoring. For us, it is a store-cupboard item in its dried, flaked form (sweetened or unsweetened). Of course, in Oceania, the sobriquet "coconut islands" means exactly that; the nuts are always available.

Now on to those pantry "keepers" from without Oceania that the islanders have embraced wholeheartedly in their cuisines:

There is now no town nor city in Oceania where you cannot find "curried" dishes. The transplanted Indians within the Pacific, especially Fiji, naturally import the full range of spices for their native cuisine and employ them in the time-honored manner. But, for the rest of Oceania, curry is *curry powder.* Cans and jars of the ready-made mix can be found on the shelves of all the grocery stores and, since its spices blend so well in cooking with coconut milk, curry flavorings have insinuated themselves into all manner of Pacific dishes: rich melanges of fish or meats; fruits and vegetables in robust gravies. They deserve their own place in the pantheon of worldwide curries.

Both local and traditional in the Pacific, soy sauce occupies a special place in Oceanian cuisine. Wherever I traveled in the Pacific—east, west, north, south—bottles and gallon cans of the sepia liquid were lined up on the shelves of even the smallest shops. It has become the universal seasoning and staple in the island kitchen. Curiously enough, although Chinese soy is available, the Japanese *shoyu* from Kikkoman has achieved total market saturation. Within Oceania, Kikkoman is eponymous with soy sauce. In Micronesian cuisine, soy sauce is used in most gravies, relishes, condiments and main dishes. Whilst living on Guam and realizing the popularity and prevalence of the brand, I asked several local cooks about the phenomenon. "Why not use Chinese soy sauce?" "The food doesn't taste right!" was the reply, ". . . it's not the same." I received identical answers later on in Papua New Guinea, Fiji and Tahiti.

The historic Japanese presence in Oceania, particularly in Micronesia prior to and during World War II, is certainly one reason for *shoyu's* widespread popularity. After living in Japan, I realized two more compelling reasons for its universal appeal: flavor and standardization. Evolving from a 13th-century paste of fermented soy beans called *tamari,* commercial production really blossomed in the small town of Noda, outside Edo (now Tokyo) in the 16th century. At first it was a thick, strongly flavored sauce, similar to those being produced all over Japan and the salt concentration varied considerably. Through experimentation, wheat was added to the soy beans, salt and water. The individual family producers around Noda merged. The Noda Shoyu Company, because of its combined resources, improved and standardized its product, which then rose to national prominence. It became the sauce with an unmistakable flavor. In 1980, the company renamed itself Kikkoman. That sauce is the staple in the Oceanian larder.

No less popular than soy, chili pepper water or sauce—often homemade—can be seen on many kitchen shelves in the Pacific. Again, like *shoyu,* it is used as a condiment or flavoring agent to enliven the starches, grains and vegetables that form the traditional base of island meals. The tiny hot peppers are a fairly recent arrival in Oceania. The Spanish brought them into the Pacific in the late 16th or early 17th centuries. Don Marín, friend of Kamehameha I, planted them in Hawai'i prior to 1812 and chilies arrived in Micronesia by way of the Philippines.

At first, chili pepper water was prepared at home, and poured into whatever stoppered bottle was available. However, imported, commercial sauce has overtaken the home-bottled product. In 1868, the McIlhenny family produced it commercially in Louisiana, and now their bottles of scarlet Tabasco Brand Pepper Sauce can be found in stores and homes all over the Pacific Islands.

In Micronesia, Tabasco is so integrated into the diet of the Chamorros of Guam that they sprinkle it over almost everything savory. At the same time, they prepare a condiment of soy sauce, hot peppers and lemon juice or white vinegar that they call *finadene* (rhymes with "penny"). It is served as an accompaniment to traditional food. However, in an illustration of the Guamanian love of the hot and spicy, even when *finadene* is served, a bottle of the ubiquitous Tabasco will still be on the table.

Hawaiians—both at home and in restaurants—still prepare the traditional chili pepper water, combining freshly boiled water with a purée of chili peppers, Hawaiian sea salt and, occasionally, additions of garlic and vinegar. (This homemade product should be refrigerated between use.)

Last, there are two canned items stored in many Oceanian kitchens: corned beef and pork luncheon meat. Unless you are particularly fond of them, you need not stock them. However, they are both useful to and favored by the islanders, requiring no refrigeration and supplying meat protein in an inexpensive and easy fashion. (Corned beef is so popular in the Central Pacific that certain dishes have evolved in definition to the point where the islanders prefer to use the canned version of beef rather than the freshly-ground meat.)

Basic Preparations in Oceanian Cooking

Coconut Meat, Milk and Cream

The ground or flaked meat of the mature coconut is used in countless island dishes. The traditional island routine of husking fresh coconuts, cracking them open, extracting the liquid and grating the fresh meat looks disarmingly simple and picturesque to the casual spectator, but islanders have learnt the skill as children, practiced and exercised it, almost daily, for most of their lives. Their routine is almost impossible to imitate in a Western kitchen. In an effort to replicate freshly grated coconut, I have steeped dried, unsweetened coconut flakes in hot milk or water for an hour or so, squeezed the mixture to express the liquid and then used the resuscitated meat in recipes. This procedure approximates the product and is satisfactory for most recipes, but it is measurably inferior in flavor and texture to the creamy quality of freshly grated coconut. Here, then, is my method for preparing fresh coconut meat in a Western kitchen.

For the task, you will need the following tools and appliances: a hammer, a screwdriver (preferably Phillips head), a medium mixing bowl, a heavy cleaver, an oyster knife, a spice or coffee grinder (a food processor will accommodate larger volumes of coconut but may leave lumps).

Begin with a nut with its outer, fibrous husk removed. Pierce all three of the "eyes" with the screwdriver, striking the handle with the hammer. Turn the nut over and onto the mixing bowl to let the liquid drain. (Save and store the liquid for later use.)

Place the nut over the drain hole of your sink. Orient it so that the eyes are on your right or left and the midsection is centered, facing you. Using the blade of the cleaver to begin circumscribing the equator and striking the back of the blade with the hammer, rap the nut firmly. Rotate it slightly and repeat the blow. Continue rotating and striking until you have scored most of the nut's circumference. One last, vigorous blow should split the nut into two jagged hemispheres. (Points are not awarded for neatness.)

Insert the oyster knife between the meat and shell to prise out the coconut meat. (It will come away in pieces, which is desirable since you will need only small chunks for your grinder.) For cosmetic reasons, you may now want to remove the brown, outer skin from the meat. Use a paring knife or fixed-blade vegetable peeler. Chop the meat into coarse, one-inch chunks with the cleaver.

Place two or three pieces of the coconut into your grinder and grind the meat into fine flakes. (Alternatively, you may use your food processor, then remove any lumps and consign them to the spice grinder.)

Coconut milk is not the liquid sloshing around inside the mature nut. That is coconut water. In the islands, coconut milk is produced by steeping ground coconut meat (prepared as just described, for instance) in its own liquid or water. The resultant fluid is then squeezed out as coconut milk and behaves much the same as dairy milk. Thinner and lower-fat coconut milk can be obtained by macerating the same coconut meat in fresh batches of water for a second or third pressing.

Coconut cream is composed of the highly saturated and very stable fats that rise to the top of coconut milk during refrigeration. Treat it as dairy cream.

For those who are cautious about their intake of saturated fat but would still like to enjoy the richness of coconut-milk dishes, a slightly ersatz, but acceptable, coconut milk can be concocted by flavoring low or nonfat milk with coconut extract. (Taste the mixture after each drop of the extract has been added.)

Coconut milk is available in cans, frozen in plastic bags or as a powder in foil packets. These shortcuts are suitable as a backup but may have undesirable, slightly soapy overtones. For some years, I have used unsweetened, desiccated coconut flakes (available from health food stores and Asian markets) to make my own coconut milk. After soaking the flakes in hot dairy milk or water, the resultant liquid serves well for all cooking purposes. It is considerably less expensive than commercially-prepared products and usually quicker to make than a trip to the store. If I am producing coconut cream or rich coconut milk, then I use full cream (whole) dairy milk for the extraction. For thin coconut milk, I use nonfat dairy milk or water.

My recipe follows: Using a ratio of a generous half cup of dried coconut to two cups of liquid, the mixture should be heated to just under a boil and then allowed to cool to lukewarm. Line a sieve with a strong, thin cotton or muslin cloth. Strain the mixture through and then gather up the edges of the cloth; squeeze the bundle vigorously until all the liquid has been expressed. (The leftover coconut, known as trash, may be processed again for thinner coconut milk.) Homemade coconut milk freezes well. Pour it into two-cup measures, then into resealable, freezer-weight plastic bags, label, date and stack flat until frozen.

Leaf Wrappers

In the Pacific Islands, large leaves are used for wrapping foods to be cooked, and for lining and insulating earth-pit ovens. The preferred leaves are banana, ti, breadfruit, fig, papaya, taro and even sago palm. If you live in a warm climate, you may be able to grow or procure banana leaves. Asian markets are a good source for dried banana leaves and lotus or tiger grass leaves. Dried corn husks also make good food wrappers. Store all dried leaves, wrapped air tight, in a cool, dry cupboard. Revitalize them by soaking in warm water, then pat dry before using. We may also use many large, edible leaves from the produce sections of supermarkets or from our gardens. Choose collard, cabbage, Swiss chard, beet, kohlrabi or spinach.

For those of us blessed or cursed with Western kitchens, aluminum foil and cooking parchment are the useful all-purpose substitutes to leaf wrappers. Unfortunately, foods cooked in these sterile wrappings lack the distinctive flavors that the leaves contribute, therefore many recipes in this book call for an inner wrapping of leaves. However, leaf-wrapped dishes containing coconut milk as an ingredient, when further encased in foil, may accumulate an undesirable amount of liquid during cooking. This accumulation is almost impossible to predict or control because it depends on many variables: the latent water content of the ingredients, the cooking time, the internal temperature of the package, etc. The best way to solve the problem of surplus liquid, should it occur, is to drain it, or draw it off with a bulb baster.

Below is a quick guide to leaf wrappers, their uses and the preferred methods to make them pliant.

Size and Purpose	Leaves	Softening Method
Large outer wrappers	ti, banana, taro, papaya, breadfruit, large collard	Pass over an open flame until they soften and become limp. Excise their stems when cool.
Small outer wrappers (where their flavor and the blade may become a component of the dish)	cabbage, smaller taro, smaller collard	Blanch in boiling water for 30 sec. Excise their stems when cool.
All-purpose inner and outer wrappers (where their flavor may be needed)	Swiss chard, young taro, large beet, smaller collard	Microwave on high for up to 15 sec. Excise their stems when cool.
Inner wrappers (where their flavor is required)	small, young taro; kohlrabi; spinach	Excise the stem and microwave on high for about 5 sec., or until flexible.

Chapter 2

To Set the Mood

Pacific Appetizers, Hors D'oeuvres and Pupus

In the hour of the dusk, when the fire blazes, and the scent of the cooked breadfruit fills the air, and perhaps the lamp glints already between the pillars of the house, you shall behold them silently assemble to the meal, men, women, and children; and the dogs and pigs frisk together up the terrace stairway, switching rival tails. The strangers from the ship were soon equally welcome: welcome to dip their fingers in the wooden dish, to drink coconuts, to share the circulating pipe.

Robert Louis Stevenson, *1900, In the South Seas*

Sam, one of my two friendly, lovely, sturdy, Fijian giants, was husking a coconut upon a solid iron spike driven into the earth. He labored because the tip of the spike had been flattened. He bent over his self-imposed task—knee-length, droopy black shorts, loose printed shirt, sandal-shod feet planted firmly on the ground. Powerful shoulders and arms crashed the nut down again and again upon the spike. Each time he pulled off hunks of the wiry fibers. Behind him stretched the gray-blue waters of Suva bay and, beyond that, the hazy peaks of Tuvutau, Mount Voma and the Korosamba Sanga Mountain range. Lounging in a chair with my book, I watched him, a tall glass of freshly-squeezed lemonade at my elbow. He husked the nut, cracked it open and looked up. "Are you hungry? Would you like some coconut?"

I learned much about hospitality in the islands of the Pacific, the generosity of the islanders, their credo that food is to be shared. When you have abundance, no one in the vicinity will go hungry. If you only have a modicum, it will be shared, even with strangers.

Change the location to Guam in the Marianas. Two of us are walking along the beach at Tumon Bay. It is a weekend and 4WDs—sport utilities and pickup trucks—are parked in the tree line. Barbecues are lit. The islanders are celebrating the two-day holiday. As we reach our homestretch of beach, a voice hails us. It is Manny Perez, full of friendship and

Sam husking a coconut, Suva, Fiji.

Budweiser. "Eh! Howya doin'? You want some pork ribs? We got beer!'
Haven't seen you in a long time. Come on! Let's party!"

Islanders snack when they are hungry between meals: lengths of sugar
cane; fruit, such as bananas (but picked only from one's own trees); pieces
of coconut; leftover cooked breadfruit or yams. These could be called "little foods" as opposed to full meals.

The concept in the Pacific is that food is something to eat that fills the
vacancy. They are serious eaters. Food also equals hospitality; it is their
expression of giving in friendship. To share food and eat together confers
honor upon the guest, whose acceptance, in turn, lets the host enjoy his
generosity. Thus, the giving and taking of food completes the island circle
of fellowship. (Implicit within the bargain is the anticipation of reciprocity.)

This ritual of hospitality is ingrained in Oceania. However, when the
islanders refer to "little dishes" or "little bites," they are deliberately mis-
leading. Never expect a platter of meticulously prepared finger foods
you'd be served at the country club. The phrases are merely humble, self-
deprecating verbal conventions. "This is just a little piece of fish" actually
means that the seafood will not completely overlap your plate.

These attitudes about food generally apply to those Pacific Islanders
whose life is not urbanized; their existence remains relatively uncomplicated. In the towns and cities of Oceania, it is a different matter. The influx

of Western influences on food—its forms, manner of cooking and style of eating—has become more pronounced and pervasive over the past two centuries. As increasing numbers of plantation owners and merchants settled in the islands and prospered, so they began to entertain. Luncheons and dinner parties proliferated. Local celebrities and nobility adopted Western manners and meal service customs with alacrity. While they still gave lavish feasts in "island style," they also hosted social events to display their newly acquired knowledge of Western entertainment conventions: the eating surface rose from the ground to table level; chairs became de rigueur.

Flaming torches lighted the driveways to palaces and island mansions, their light flickering in long bars of yellow across manicured lawns. Plumeria and tiare blossoms perfumed the night air as chiefs in full tribal dress strode to the porticos; carriages debouched district commissioners in spotless white uniforms (albeit a little damp around their tight collars). Evening-gowned ladies, with plumes or flower blossoms in their hair and skins of both cream and coffee, were ceremonially escorted onto the wide verandahs.

Long banquet tables were just as easily covered with white linen as tapa cloth. Crystal stemware was set, cheek-by-jowl, with polished coconut bowls, silver trays with wooden platters along the surface strewn with fresh-cut flowers.

In the kitchens, island cooks labored to prepare Western hors d'oeuvres under the watchful eyes of missionaries' wives or school teachers who had been either impressed or volunteered for the duty. Local foods were remodeled into Western dishes. The fusions were always interesting, sometimes hilarious, when mutual misunderstandings arose about how certain dishes should be prepared or cooked.

Governors' ladies trained their domestic staff, cookbooks in hand. Substitutions were always necessary but, frequently, the imitations surpassed the Western originals. Hors d'oeuvres, as small dishes to start a meal, were generally the most successful transpositions and suited native table manners; fingers before forks.

Then, in the 1930s, when cocktail parties became fashionable in the West, a new genre of food fashion arose: canapés. Hawai'i led the Pacific in the creation of small foods; *pupus,* in the local language. Now, these miniature mouthfuls did not merely begin a full dinner, but starred in their own right at the cocktail party. (You recall it; where you stood and precariously balanced a glass of spirits and a plate of finger food in one hand, reserving the other for handshaking and gesturing.) The piquancy and assertive flavors of smoked fish complemented the astringency of a perfect martini. Succulent shellfish tidbits balanced champagne cocktails.

These "little dishes" were also featured at buffets or ladies' luncheons; set in sunlit island gardens overlooking the turquoise Pacific.

The *pupus* following reflect the wide variety of Pacific food, the bounty of the sea and the wealth of the islands, together with the stimulating influences of other cuisines upon classic island fare.

TOASTED COCONUT CHIPS (TUVALU)

Almost everywhere in the South Pacific, toward the end of my busy day, I would sit down in a friendly place, relax, perhaps have a drink and then, on the table before me, an islander would place a small wooden bowl of coconut chips. To a palate overexposed to salted and honey-roasted nuts (on commercial flights) or bar mix, these were a remarkably different snack. I came to expect them. If they were absent, I would feel disappointed, losing the special sensation that I really was in the South Pacific. (It's difficult to capture that sense of place when you are confronted by potato chips shaken out of a bag, even if they are, as proclaimed, from Maui potatoes.) The simple recipe below has my warmest endorsement. At first mouthful, I can hear the distant surf and see the tropical sunset in front of me.

1/2-**pound** (approximately) **ripe coconut, husked and the meat removed from the shell** *(see page 19)*	**3/4 teaspoon of salt** **a pinch of cayenne** **a pinch of curry powder**

1. Preheat your oven to 325° Fahrenheit.
2. Slice the coconut meat (skin included) into wafer-thin strips about 2 inches long with either a mandolin slicer or a sharp knife.
3. Thoroughly combine all the dry spices in a small mixing bowl. Arrange the coconut strips on a cookie or baking sheet. Sprinkle the spice mixture to evenly dust the coconut slices. Bake in your oven until the coconut is crisp and golden brown, about 20–25 minutes, stirring from time to time to distribute the spices and evenly cook the chips.
4. Remove from the oven and let stand to cool. Store in an airtight container until ready to serve.

COCONUT AND SAKE
DEEP-FRIED SHRIMP (GUAM)

Sometimes it is difficult to tell whether the Japanese influence in Guamanian food results from island history, from proximity to the archipelago of the Rising Sun or from a willingness to cater to the tastes of Japanese tourists. Whichever it is, the fusion is serendipitous when it results in snacks like these.

Serves 8

16 large (21- to 30-count per
    pound) raw shrimp,
    shelled with the tails left
    attached
1/4 cup of *sake*
2 tablespoons of soy sauce
1/2 cup of cornstarch

2 eggs, beaten
3/4 cup of dried, unsweetened
    coconut flakes
peanut oil for deep-frying
    (approximately 4–6 cups)
sprigs of parsley

1. Make several, short diagonal incisions on the underside of each shrimp to prevent them from curling too much during frying.
2. Pour the *sake* and soy sauce into a large (1 gallon) resealable plastic bag. Add the shrimp, seal and refrigerate for about half an hour, occasionally turning and massaging the bag to distribute the marinade.
3. Meanwhile, prepare and arrange your assembly line: place the cornstarch in a medium-sized paper bag; pour the eggs in a small, shallow bowl; put the coconut in a similar bowl. Line two plates or platters with paper towels and place them near the range top for use in Step 6.
4. Heat the oil in a deep-fryer or large saucepan to achieve a constant and mea-sured temperature of 365° Fahrenheit on a frying thermometer.
5. Remove and drain the shrimp from its marinade. Place them in the paper bag with the cornstarch. Fold the bag closed and shake it gently to evenly coat the crustaceans. Pluck out the shrimp by their tails, shaking them within the bag to shed any surplus cornstarch. In turn, dunk them first in the egg and then roll them in the coconut until they are jacketed with the flakes.
6. Working with 2 or 3 coated shrimp at a time, fry them until the coconut is golden, about 1–1 1/2 minutes. (Let the oil recover to frying temperature between each frying.) Drain the fried shrimp on the plates lined with paper towels.

7. Repeat the coating, dunking, rolling and frying until all the shrimp are fried and draining.

8. Arrange the shrimp decoratively on a platter and garnish with the parsley. Serve warm or at room temperature.

PALOLO

Reef Caviar on Toast (SAMOA)

While traveling in the South Pacific, I heard anecdotes about a small, but reputedly delicious, sea creature referred to as *palolo* or *balolo*. It so happened that I was in Apia, capital of Western Samoa, in mid-November, during the brief time that *palolo* fulfill their genetically programmed and lunar-inspired imperative to swarm to the surface of the sea to spawn. At this time, they are captured by swarms of larger creatures—Pacific Islanders.

The weekly newspaper, the *Samoa Observer,* had just been distributed. That morning, most of the town's population was off the cracked streets and in the coffee shops reading the *Observer.* Opening the paper, the first thing I noticed was an announcement. *Palolo* was the lunch special at the Apia Inn, a second-storey establishment just down Beach Road from the landmark Aggie Grey's Hotel.

It was Somerset Maugham's rainy season. As I walked down the street, the sun was blotted out by dark, steel-gray clouds. I ducked inside the building and was upstairs just as a powerful tropical squall battered the town. Jurgens, the friendly German chef, took my order whilst the wind lashed the rain horizontally against the windows of the empty restaurant; the canvas awnings outside cracked like pistol shots.

The *palolo* was brought, mounted on toast and garnished with carrot and cucumber julienne. It was dark and bluish-green with the appearance of seaweed. Then I tasted it. *Palolo* has an exquisitely delicate flavor of the sea, or malossol caviar. Jurgens hovered at my table, volunteering that he had sautéed the *palolo* with onion in a little butter. I dissected the ultramarine mass. Now I could see the little dark-brown threads that were the creatures themselves about one and one-half- to two-inches in length and the thickness of pencil lead.

Then Jurgens confessed he had bought them frozen and defrosted the blocks of *palolo* just before cooking. I was crestfallen. Later, I realized how valuable the confession was. It meant that the delicacy is exportable; it could become an exotic gourmet item in the not-so-distant future.

For now, gourmands on large budgets who wish to sample *palolo* firsthand must make travel arrangements to Fiji or Samoa during the tenth or eleventh months of the year. Consult your lunar calendars!

This simple recipe that recreates the dish I so enjoyed is given with the anticipation and expectation that you will soon be able to experience it as I did.

Serves 6

1/2-inch-long piece of cucumber, peeled and sliced into julienne matchsticks	1/2 cup of onion, peeled and minced
1/2-inch length of large carrot, peeled and sliced into julienne matchsticks	8 ounces of *palolo* (at room temperature)
12 slices of Melba toast	a pinch each of salt and white pepper
3 tablespoons of unsalted butter	6 thin wedges of lemon, seeded
	1 tablespoon of capers, drained

1.   Place the julienned cucumber and carrot into individual bowls of iced water.

2.   Spread the Melba toast thinly with butter and set aside for use in Step 7. Reserve the remaining butter for use in the next step.

3.   Place a medium frying pan over medium heat, add the butter and let it come up to frying temperature but not burning. Add the onion and sauté until it is soft, almost disintegrating.

4.   Introduce the *palolo* and gently stir-fry it for about 1 minute, or until the perfume of the sea hovers over the pan. Immediately remove from heat and set aside.

5.   Arrange 6 small serving plates and garnish the circumference of each with a lemon wedge and a few capers.

6.   Drain the cucumber and carrot from the iced water and arrange a few slivers of each beside the lemon wedges.

7.   Place 2 slices of Melba toast in the center of each plate and carefully deposit equal portions of the *palolo* on each slice. Present immediately with pride and satisfaction.

DALO, VAINAVIU, URA KEI VUAKA SA VAKAMASIMATAKI

Taro, Pineapple, Shrimp and Bacon (FIJI)

It seemed that all I was doing in Fiji was eating and doing a trencherman job of it! Not only was the food good, it was fresh, and the island of Viti Levu was blessed with more than its share of fine chefs (I can resist anything except temptation). At one stage I decided to refuse the services of the friendly but importunate Indian taxi drivers clustered outside the hotel and walk as much as I could. Unfortunately, the heat and humidity of Suva conspire to discourage exercise. Only in the early mornings is it pleasant to stretch your legs. On one such freshly-born morning, I walked all around the Thurston Botanical Gardens. I was immediately transported back to my childhood in India. Reflecting Fiji's long association with the British, it was the model of colonially-inspired parks in the tropics: perfect landscaping, curved walks, manicured lawns, the requisite lily pond and beautiful specimens of flora from all over the tropics, carefully signposted and described.

After a visit to the Fiji Museum—set like a gem in the center of the gardens— I decided to head for lunch. Among the many dishes on the buffet was this hot and surprising mixture of taro, fresh pineapple, seafood and bacon. It was delightful and here it it.

Serves 6

1 tablespoon of butter
1$^1/_2$ tablespoons of peanut oil
6 thin slices of Canadian
    bacon, cut into 1-inch-
    wide strips
1$^1/_2$ pounds of taro corms,
    peeled and boiled, cut into
    $^3/_4$-inch cubes
2 cups of fresh pineapple, cut
    into $^3/_4$-inch cubes
8 ounces of baby (Bay) shrimp
    (already peeled and cooked)

5 green onions, both white
    and green, sliced into
    $^1/_4$-inch lengths
1 tablespoon of freshly ground
    black pepper
1 tablespoon of parsley,
    minced
avocado, papaya, lettuce or
    other nontoxic leaves for
    decoration
2 or 3 edible flower blossoms
    (hibiscus, nasturtium, etc.)

1.   Place the butter and oil in a large skillet over medium-high heat. Quickly fry the bacon until it just begins to curl. Remove it from the skillet with a slotted spatula and place it in a large, non-reactive mixing bowl.

2.   While still on heat, carefully add the taro cubes. Stir-fry and sauté, shaking the skillet as necessary, until all the cubes are uniformly crisp and brown. As with the bacon, drain over the skillet and add to the mixing bowl.

3.   Now fry the pineapple cubes in the same oil until they begin to turn golden at the edges. Drain over the skillet and add to the other ingredients in the mixing bowl.

4.   Quickly stir and toss the shrimp in the skillet to just heat the crustaceans through. Remove, drain and add them to the mixing bowl.

5.   Add the green onions to the mixture in the bowl, season with the pepper, stir in the parsley and thoroughly combine all the ingredients.

6.   Line your serving dish with the leaves. Pile or mound the mixture from the bowl on the leaves. Decorate with the flowers and serve at once.

TUNA SASHIMI *ROLLS TUMON-STYLE*

(GUAM)

One of our special pleasures, when we lived on Guam, was to relax after the day's work and meet our friends in a gathering place in one of the island's luxury hotels overlooking Tumon Bay. The significant attraction was a "sundowner"; not a drink, but the Pacific preoccupation of witnessing the evanescent green flash; said to occur as the giant orange globe disappears below the horizon of the ocean.

Apart from the talented musicians who serenaded the sunset, another attraction was the platters of fresh tuna *sashimi* that were presented every evening as complimentary *pupus*. (The Japanese guests at the hotel were consistently amazed that this daily delicacy had no price tag.)

While the predominant foretaste of the traditional *wasabi/shoyu* dip was preferred by the tourists, Guamanians, who have adopted *sashimi*, liberally bathe their raw fish in **Finadene** sauce (see page 226).

3/4 cup of white vinegar

1/4 cup of sugar

3-inch piece of fresh gingerroot, peeled and grated into shreds *(see Note below)*

1 pound (approximately) of fresh skipjack tuna steak or slab about 4 inches wide × 1¹/2 inches thick (the length is determined by the weight)

1/3-inch piece of long, white radish *(daikon)*, peeled and grated into shreds *(see Note below)*

1/4 of a large head of iceberg lettuce, shredded

1. Pour the vinegar and sugar into a small, non-reactive saucepan and bring the liquid to a boil over medium heat, stirring to dissolve the sugar.

2. Add the ginger and reduce heat as necessary to maintain a simmer. Cook the ginger for 1 minute and remove the pan from heat. Let the ginger sit and the liquid cool for about 1 hour. Drain and reserve the ginger for use in Step 6.

3. Meanwhile, tightly wrap the tuna in plastic and place it in the freezer and chill it until almost frozen.

4. When firm enough to precisely slice, use a sharp knife to create tuna strips with the following dimensions: 1¹/2-inches wide × 4-inches long × 1/8-inch thick.

5. Line a serving dish or platter with the shredded lettuce.

6. Lay a strip of tuna flat and place a mixture of ginger and radish shreds across one end. Tightly roll the tuna into a small (1¹/2-inches long) column. Place the tuna rolls on the lettuce from the step above with the seam side down. Continue until all the tuna strips have been exhausted and they are decoratively placed on the bed of lettuce.

7. Serve at once accompanied by *Finadene.*

Note: The preferred method to achieve the proper dimensions for both the ginger and radish shreds is to use a mandolin shredder. Alternatively, you may slice the vegetables into the thinnest slivers and trim them to the width of the tuna, 1¹/2 inches.

HAWAI'I-THAI PORK AND SHRIMP DIM SUM

As in music, when certain harmonics strike a resonance, so, in eating, a particular combination of complementary flavors can become transcendent. The whole then surpasses the single-note taste of one of the main components.

This recipe produces one of those rare resonances: that of pork and shrimp, together with spices and *nam pla* (Thai fish sauce).

The composite flavor reminds me of when I lived in Thailand. This "Thai redux" occurred last year in Hawai'i when I tasted this Thai-Chinese-Hawaiian fusion. It is recreated for you here, together with its suggested, island-inspired dip (**Sweet and Hot Chili-Pineapple Sauce,** page 228).

Yield: 24 appetizers

24 black peppercorns, dry-roasted and ground to a powder in a spice grinder
4 cloves of garlic, smashed, peeled and minced
3 tablespoons of coriander roots and stems, minced
1/2 pound of ground pork
1 pound (before shelling) of small raw shrimp, shelled, deveined and coarsely chopped

2 tablespoons of Thai fish sauce *(nam pla)*
1 tablespoon of sugar
1 egg, beaten
rice flour as required
24 3-inch in diameter circular *wonton* wrappers

1.   Place all the ingredients except the rice flour and *wonton* wrappers in the bowl of a food processor and, using a steel blade, process to a coarse paste. Remove the paste with a rubber spatula to a medium, non-reactive mixing bowl, cover and refrigerate for use in Step 3.
2.   Place your steamer tray(s) alongside your working surface for easy access. Fill the base of the steamer with the requisite amount of water. Modulate the heat as necessary so the water reaches a full boil coincidental with the completion of your *dim sum* preparations in Step 4. Grease an ovenproof baking dish that will fit inside your steamer tray and set it aside for use in Step 4.

3.   Remove the mixing bowl from the refrigerator and test roll 1 tablespoon of the mixture into a small ball, dusting your hands with the rice flour. If the resultant ball is too soft, add just enough of the flour to stiffen the ball to the point where it can be easily molded and retains its shape. (Do not make the mixture too stiff and flour-laden.) Continue forming balls with rice flour as necessary until all the paste is exhausted. (Surplus balls may be frozen and later deep-fried for additional appetizers.)

4.   Place a *wonton* wrapper in the palm of your hand and partially cup your palm. Insert one of the balls into the center of the wrapper, then pinch, fold and pleat the wrapper around it, leaving the top slightly open and the wrapper forming an uneven frill at the top. Gently flatten the bottom, rounded section of the *dim sum* (so it will stand upright) and place it on the greased, ovenproof dish.

5.   Continue until all the *dim sum* are assembled and arranged on the greased plate. [Depending on the size (diameter) of your steamer, you may require more than 1 tray and, consequently, more greased plates to accommodate all the *dim sum*.] Place the plate(s) filled with *dim sum* into the steamer trays. Confirm the water is up to temperature and the volume is sufficient. Assemble the steamer and cover it. (If you are using a bamboo steamer, you may need to seal the top with a weight.) Steam the *dim sum* for about 30 minutes. (Replenish the liquid with boiling water as necessary to maintain the correct volume and so as not to disrupt the cooking.)

6.   Serve the *dim sum* warm or at room temperature.

Note: Accompany these savory appetizers with a dipping sauce, such as **Sweet and Hot Chili-Pineapple Sauce** (see page 228).

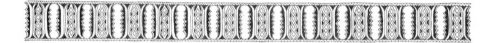

SWEET POTATO AND TARO CHIPS

(VANUATU)

One of the many pleasurable surprises I experienced in Oceania was discovering the superiority in flavor and texture of island root vegetables, freshly fried into thin, curling, crackly, crunchy and chewy wafers. Nothing out of a bag or canister from a supermarket can compare to these.

In this recipe, I include only sweet potatoes and taro. Plantains or coconut can be equally delightful.

For a double-dip of island sensations, serve the chips with *Miti* (see page 227) and **Spicy Banana-Ginger-Onion Dip** (see page 229).

Serves everybody

3 medium, uniformly shaped sweet potatoes, scrubbed	**1/2 teaspoon of freshly ground black pepper** (optional)
6–8 taro corms (maximum diameter 2 1/2 inches)	**1 teaspoon of curry powder** (optional)
Peanut oil for deep-frying (approximately 4–6 cups)	**1 teaspoon of garlic salt** (optional)

1.   Use a vegetable slicer (either hand-operated or electric) to slice the unskinned sweet potatoes into the thinnest possible potato chips. Immediately after slicing, drop them into iced water to prevent discoloration. Save for use in Step 5.

2.   Peel the taro and slice them in the same manner as the sweet potatoes above. Place them in a separate bowl of iced water. Let the vegetables soak for about 1 hour, changing the water in each bowl after about 30 minutes. Save them for use in Step 7.

3.   Fill a large saucepan or deep-fryer about one-half full with peanut oil and position a frying thermometer on the edge so the probe is immersed in the oil. Over medium-high heat, let the oil come up to a temperature of between 375°–380° Fahrenheit. Modulate the heat to maintain the temperature until Step 5.

4.   Turn your oven to its lowest setting (about 200° Fahrenheit) and, lining two large baking pans with a double layer of paper towels, place them in the oven. Line several plates with a double layer of paper towels and place them near the range top for use in the next step.

5.   Drain the sweet potato slices from the water and pat them dry. Using a wire basket and, working in small batches, slowly lower the potatoes into the oil and fry each lot, shaking to prevent them from sticking together, until golden brown. Drain the potatoes over the pan, then turn them onto the lined plates and continue until all are fried. (Let the temperature of the oil recover between each frying batch.) Transfer the drained potatoes to the lined baking pans in the oven. Continue this three-step process (frying, draining and heating) until all the potatoes are in the oven.

6.   While still on heat, inspect the frying oil. Remove any carbonized fragments or totally replace the oil if the color appears too dark.

7.   Repeat Step 5 with the taro chips and place them into the second, lined baking pan in the oven.

8.   When all the chips are cooked, remove them from the oven and sprinkle them with the optional pepper, curry powder and garlic salt, combined in a shaker, turning the chips to season them evenly. Return the chips to the oven until serving (no more than 15 minutes). Serve hot, warm or at room temperature.

MARCEL UKOY

Fish, Shrimp and Vegetable Fritters (GUAM)

The island version of this recipe is made with canned tuna (they do love it on Guam!). I prefer a firm, fresh white fish and baby (Bay) shrimp, which are already shelled and cooked. If you cannot find green (unripe) papaya, try chayote (sometimes called *choko* or vegetable pear).

Serves 6

1/4 cup of white vinegar	2 eggs, beaten
1 clove of garlic, smashed, peeled and minced	1 teaspoon of salt
1/2 teaspoon of salt	1/4 teaspoon of freshly ground black pepper
1 green chili pepper *(Serrano* or *Jalapeño),* minced (seeded optional)	1 medium onion, peeled and finely chopped
8 ounces of firm, white fish fillets, cooked	1 cup of green (unripe) papaya flesh, grated
4 ounces of baby (Bay) shrimp	1/2 cup of bean sprouts, trimmed of tails and
1/2 cup of cornstarch	coarsely chopped
1/2–3/4 cup of water	oil for deep-frying

1.   In a small serving bowl, thoroughly combine the vinegar, garlic, **2 table-spoons** of water, salt and chili pepper. Set aside to accompany the fritters in Step 7.
2.   Place the fish in a medium mixing bowl and break it into flakes with a fork. Add the shrimp and thoroughly combine the two seafoods and set aside for use in Step 4.
3.   In a large mixing bowl combine the cornstarch with the flour and stir. Gradually add enough of the 1/2–3/4 cup of water, stirring, to make a smooth cream. Whisk in the beaten eggs and season with the salt and pepper.
4.   Stir the onion, papaya, bean sprouts and the seafood (from step 2) into the batter. Set aside to rest for use in Step 6.
5.   Heat the oil in a deep-fryer or wok to achieve a constant and measured temperature of 375° Fahrenheit on a frying thermometer.
6.   When the temperature of the oil has stabilized, make individual fritters from about 2 tablespoons of the batter. Fry, 2–3 at a time, until they are golden and crisp. (Let the oil recover to frying temperature between each frying.) Drain the

cooked fritters on paper towels. Accumulate the fritters on a heatproof serving dish in a low oven.

7.   Serve the fritters hot accompanied by the vinegar sauce.

POLYNESIA

Tuvalu (Ellis) Wallis and Futuna, Western Samoa, American Samoa, Tonga, Niue, Cook Islands, French Polynesia [Tahiti (Society Islands), Tuamotus, Marquesas, Australs], Hawai'i (Sandwich Islands), Easter Island, etc., New Zealand—Maori

Of all the peoples of Oceania, the Polynesians are probably those with whom the Westerners are most familiar. After all, Polynesians populate the U.S.A.'s fiftieth state; American Samoa is an unincorporated U.S. territory; the Polynesians of the Society Islands, the Marquesas, the Tuamotus and Australs are all French citizens. The transplanted Polynesian Maori are New Zealanders, the independent Kingdom of Tonga is a member of the British Commonwealth and most South Pacific nations have close ties with Australia and New Zealand.

These are the peoples who gave taboo and mana to our vocabularies; who invented surfing and pioneered twin-hull catamaran construction. It was Polynesia that brought about the design fad for rattan and bamboo furniture decoration in the 1930s; that gave rise to the craze for Hawaiian shirts and *mu'umu'us* in the 1940s and 1950s; and, of course, inspired the fashion for exotic, tropical drinks.

The historical process of becoming acquainted and then familiar with the Polynesians has been helped by the unity of their (oral) language. (Strangely, in all of Polynesia, only Easter Islanders developed a written language, as their "talking boards" or artifacts carved with hieroglyphics demonstrate.)

New Zealand Maori carving

As in most of Oceania, the coconut—described by Stevenson as "the cocoa-palm, that giraffe of vegetables so graceful, so ungainly"—is also important throughout Polynesia, particularly in the low-lying atolls such as the Tuamotus. (Unfortunately for the emigrating Maori, it was one of the plants they eventually had to forsake in the colder climes of New Zealand.) It remains an incredible sight to watch a Polynesian youth with nothing more than a twisted length of cloth around his feet scale a 20-foot-tall coconut palm with more grace and speed than we can mount a step ladder. (And, once at the crown of the palm, either toss a coconut down with a precision and spin that causes it to land on its point and avoid splitting or, if more nuts are needed, lower them with a string.)

Breadfruit, yams, sweet potatoes and taro are still cultivated and enjoyed but not in the quantities of earlier days. On many islands giant circular or rectangular

(Continued.)

indentations in the earth mark the sites of former breadfruit fermenting pits. Taro patches, seemingly growing in the wild, proclaim the places where there was former habitation, now abandoned. Probably because of the large influx of Chinese to Hawai'i and Tahiti, Polynesians now eat rice on almost a daily basis. In Tahiti a housewife will mark it on her grocery list that she takes to the corner store—frequently owned by Chinese. Her list will also include lentils, sugar, green peas, potatoes, oil, soy sauce and salt, together with boxes of milk for the children. Corned beef is not particularly popular in Tahiti, unlike Fiji, for instance, therefore it may not be listed. Since all of the villages are near the sea shore (the interior of most of the Society Islands is steeply mountainous), the men will go fishing two to three times a week, bringing back reef fish, lobsters or even a local giant clam (*tridacna*), called *pahua*.

Life on the Polynesian atolls is much like atoll existence anywhere in the Pacific. Pandanus is ubiquitous, hardy and helpful. Its fronds are used for house walls and thatching—together with those of the coconut—for baskets, hats and almost anything that fertile imagination and nimble fingers can devise. The fruit is mostly reserved for subsistence food; the drupes being ground into flour and baked into cakes or bread. Bananas grow wild and, of course, coconuts, but the soil is thin and rainfall is mostly the only source of water. Hardier species of taro are nurtured together with breadfruit. Aside from a few chickens and the occasional festive slaughtering of a pig, the sea, with its almost endless variety of denizens, provides the main source of animal food. But, even with the narrow range of foodstuffs (including those that are imported), it is astounding the variations of dishes that can be produced through combinations and permutations of ingredients.

On the high, verdant islands, such as Rarotonga, Tahiti, Moorea, Bora Bora, Raiatea, Upolu, Tongapatu, Hawai'i, O'ahu, Maui, Kaua'i, Tutuila, etc., rainfall is plentiful and the edible vegetation, both indigenous and introduced, is varied and abundant. The cuisines are correspondingly more interesting and complex.

(The nicest sendoff I ever received at an airport was in Rarotonga. I was taking the night flight to Tahiti. After immigration check, I walked into a patio court where all the shops opened on to a grassy esplanade. At the gate area, a musician with ukulele, guitar and rhythm accompaniment, sat on a platform serenading everyone before they caught their planes. It was like a party. Passengers bought beers and wine, and then sang along to the island songs. It was more of a fiesta than a departure. I nearly missed my flight.)

These few words cannot really capture the awesome beauty and romance of Polynesia; the incredibly blue seas; the enthusiasm of the people; the fire and vivacity of the Maori; the sensuality of the French Polynesians; the general air of *joie de vivre*. My only recommendation is to sample some of their exciting food and then call your travel agent!

Chapter 3

From Island Kettles

Different Soups . . . Almost Stews

The preparation of soup requires the most strict attention
because the success of the meal depends very largely on the
impression it makes on the guests.

Auguste Escoffier, 1934, *Ma Cuisine*

A Sense of Soups

O ur personal preferences for particular soups often coincide with our
reaction to the weather. The pot of liquid nourishment always
promises—and usually delivers—immediate comfort and gratification,
whether served hot or chilled, depending on the pronouncements of the
local meteorologist.

Even in the tropical climes of Oceania, a rainy day can summon the
image of a kettle of hearty soup, perhaps a robust chowder of seafood or
one of the more chunky and fiery mulligatawnys. When the barometric
pressure increases, a brilliant sun back-lights fifteen different hues of green
in the foliage or reflects, unabated, off both water and white sand, we
instinctively become more languorous. Our culinary imaginations conjure
visions of perfectly chilled soups. These can be refreshingly astringent,
accented with salsa-like combinations of tomatoes, mint, cilantro, green
onions, chili peppers and cucumber (the epitome of cool), or they may take
the form of a silky purée of green, leafy island vegetables such as taro
leaves, *aibika,* watercress or *pit-pit* (an asparagus taste-alike). Then, of
course, there are the sophisticated cold bisques that delicately caress you
with the bouquet of fresh shellfish and slide over the palate leaving an
undernote of coconut cream.

"Cream poured onto velvet" describes the textures of soups created—
individually or in combination—from sweet potatoes, yams, plantains, taro,
sago and other starches. Cooked in coconut milk or stock (with judicious
additions of spices and herbs), they become refined creams assuming an

inviting range of pastels, from ivory, through beige, gold, orange to rose and mauve, depending on the root vegetable.

Fire Burn and Cauldron Bubble

The consumption of broth for its own sake is relatively new to Oceanian cuisines. It is interesting to explore this historic hiccup. Recall that most of the Pacific Islands were formed by the eruptions of volcanoes. (The Hawaiian chain is still spawning new islands.) The exceptions to these explosive origins are the islands nearest to Southeast Asia in the Western Pacific, New Guinea, for instance. Their geologic composition is similar to the Asian land mass, which means they separated from the larger land mass during the maelstrom that occasioned the birth of the Pacific Ocean.

Therefore, the earliest (and later) inhabitants of Oceania, with restricted contact and communication with the peoples of the Asian continent, never experienced the Bronze and Iron Ages. From Vanuatu (New Hebrides) eastward, there are no significant concentrations of mineral ore, nor the ability to mine and refine it. Metal utensils and weapons appeared in Oceania only after contact with the West. Without pots and pans, simple broths were not included in the traditional diet.

Soups of the Evening

Because the Pacific Islanders have a tradition of hearty consumption, there is a category of soups—almost stews—that they find universally appealing: those containing fish and seafood. Given the legendary fishing prowess of island men and the skills of women and children in gathering edible mollusks and crustaceans, is there any doubt that the bounty of Pacific waters lends itself to the production of soup/stews that rival provincial productions in the rest of the world? With the awesome variety of Pacific fish and seafood from which to choose, there are no restrictions nor conditions (except avoiding the toxic); merely marry the best of the catch of the day with a talented cook.

Having eagerly consumed trochus chowder on Guam and slurped a sensuous *bourride* in Tahiti that featured a vast selection from the fishermens' boats on the quay at Papeete, I can testify to unlimited possibilities of exquisite fish soups in the islands.

SOUPE DES POISSONS GAUGUIN
Fish Soup Gauguin (MARQUESAS)

In September 1901, Paul Gauguin embarked at Papeete on the steamship *La Croix du Sud* and arrived six days later at his last island, Hivaoa in the rugged Marquesas. Disillusioned by his lack of success in Tahiti, its modernization and narrow-minded colonialists, "the romantic savage" was still seeking the unspoiled paradise he had dreamed of for so long. Tragically, he was too late; both in health (he was ravaged by disease, frail from heart attacks and, finally, suffering from a broken leg) and in expectations. La Dominique, now Atuona, was then already populated by some one dozen European settlers, as many Chinese storekeepers, a Protestant missionary and a Roman Catholic enclave headed by a bishop.

However, with renewed hope, Gauguin bought land in the center of the village and built a large house that he named *Maison du Jouir* (House of Pleasure). He then took a 14-year-old *vahine*, Vaeoho Marie-Rose, from a mission school as his mistress and housekeeper. In a final creative frenzy he painted relentlessly, even the doors of his house. The beautiful, verdant valley that cradled Atuona and the awesome, jagged peak of Mount Heani, towering above, inspired him.

Marie-Rose ministered to his needs and cooked, when the morphine for his pain and the absinthe he drank allowed him an appetite. Catastrophe struck again. Marie-Rose, pregnant with his child (an anonymous daughter) was taken back by her parents. Gauguin died alone in May 1903; his body lies in the Catholic cemetery above Atuona.

Although the Marquesas islands have no reefs, being girt by sheer cliffs, the islanders are skilled fishermen. Barracuda was—and is—often caught. I would like to think that this Marquesan soup, with its added French fillip of Pernod, is something that Marie-Rose might have prepared for the suffering artist.

Serves 4 to 6

1/4 cup of olive oil	2 pounds of barracuda fillets,
2 small onions, peeled and	skinned and cut into
finely chopped	2-inch cubes
4 cloves of garlic, smashed,	1 teaspoon of salt
peeled and minced	1/2 teaspoon of freshly ground
2 bay leaves, torn into small	black pepper
pieces	3 tablespoons of parsley,
1/4 teaspoon of thyme	minced
1/8 teaspoon of celery seeds	3 tablespoons of butter
2 cups of bold red wine	3 tablespoons of flour
4 cups fish fumet or clam juice	1 tablespoon of Pernod

1. Place a large, non-reactive saucepan over medium-high heat and pour in the olive oil. When a haze just forms over the oil, add the onions and stir-fry for about 3 minutes. Drop in the garlic, continue stirring and frying for about 1 more minute.

2. Reduce heat to medium and add the bay leaves, thyme and celery seeds, stir and pour in the wine and fish fumet. Adjust the heat as necessary to bring the mixture to a boil.

3. Add the fish fillets and season with the salt and pepper. Let the mixture return to a boil and add the parsley. Immediately reduce heat to maintain a simmer, cover and cook for about 15 minutes.

4. While the soup is simmering, in a small bowl, use a fork and your fingers to work the butter into the flour to make a *beurre manié,* and form it into small balls.

5. Uncover the soup and reduce the heat so it is at or below a simmer. Thicken the mixture by adding the *beurre manié* balls, one at a time, stirring constantly. (Do not allow the soup to boil again.)

6. When the soup is satisfactorily thickened, stir in the Pernod and transfer it to a large tureen. Serve immediately.

Note: Accompany this **Fish Soup Gauguin** with a crusty French bread and a bottle of medium-bodied red wine.

FAI SUA A 'ULU I LE TALO

Breadfruit and Taro Soup (SAMOA)

The first things I really noticed in Upolu, Western Samoa, were the *fales* (generic term in Samoan for building, particularly a house). Here, though, I refer to the open-sided, half-walled structures that act as meeting halls and social centers. Wealthy families use their individual *fales* as drawing rooms or parlors, separate from their main dwelling—a place in which to welcome guests.

Their design captures the attention. Generally built on raised platforms of large lava stones or coral, their open floor plan is elongated but rounded; similar in shape to a circular dining table with about three leaves inserted. The roof is supported by many painted wooden poles, usually bi-colored—green and blue, green and dark red, blue and dark red—with the second, or contrasting, color beginning on the bottom one quarter of each. The roof echoes the design of the traditional thatched variety, having a central ridge with a shallow pitch. The ends appear molded by compound curves and, except for the ridge, look like an upside-down bathtub. Currently, the roofing material of choice is corrugated tin.

Through their open sides I observed high-backed wooden chairs lining the interior perimeter, facing inward; each placed precisely in front of a pillar or pole support. Some *fales* even contained beds and armoires with plastic sheets or blinds for protection from rain and insects. Small boys lounged on the front steps. Girls sat, slightly separated, facing the highway and appearing to concentrate on the sparse traffic. Porkers and their piglets gamboled on the grass amid the ever-present breadfruit trees.

Arriving at the renowned Aggie Grey's Hotel at the stroke of noon, I began my meal with this typical Polynesian soup.

Serves 6 to 8

2 tablespoons of peanut oil
1 boneless chicken breast,
  skinned and cut into
  1/2-inch chunks
1 cup of taro, peeled and cut
  into 3/4-inch cubes
2 cups of breadfruit, peeled,
  seeded and cut into
  3/4-inch cubes
1 large onion, peeled and diced
2 medium tomatoes, blanched,
  skinned and coarsely
  chopped
2 small carrots, peeled and
  diced

1/4 teaspoon of turmeric
2 small bay leaves, torn into
  small pieces
1 teaspoon of salt
1/2 teaspoon of freshly ground
  black pepper
6 cups of chicken stock or 3
  141/2-ounce cans of
  chicken broth plus
  enough water to make
  6 cups
1/2 cup of coconut cream
  (see page 19)

1.   Place a small frying pan over medium-high heat and add the oil. When the
fat comes up to frying temperature, add the chicken pieces and quickly stir-fry
until the exterior of the meat is golden. Drain the chicken and set aside for use
in Step 4.
2.   Place a large, non-reactive saucepan over medium heat and add all the
remaining ingredients **except** the coconut cream. Bring the mixture to a
boil, reduce heat to maintain a simmer, cover and cook for about 30
minutes.
3.   Uncover the pan and, working in batches (the quantities determined by
the volume of your blender), transfer the soup to a blender and purée on a
high setting. Accumulate the purée in a large mixing bowl for use in the next
step.
4.   Return the large saucepan from step 2 back to medium heat and pour in the
puréed soup. Drop in the fried chicken pieces. Pour in the coconut cream, stirring, and adjust the temperature to just heat the ingredients through but not
boil.
5.   Pour the soup into individual serving bowls taking care that some chicken
pieces are apportioned among each serving. Serve at once.

ROUROU SUPSUP

A Soup of Mixed Greens (FIJI)

Soups or vegetable dishes of taro leaves cooked in coconut milk are standard and favored fare in most of the Pacific Islands. This version is more complex (hence, I hope more interesting) than its more common relatives, with a compound bouquet of mixed greens.

In Fiji, the leaves of the taro plant are called *rourou* (pronounced "rooroo"); the tuber itself as *dalo*.

Serves 4 to 6

2 tablespoons of canola oil
1 medium onion, peeled and
    finely chopped
3 cloves of garlic, smashed,
    peeled and minced
2 cups of taro leaves, chopped
2 cups of green onions, both
    white and green, chopped
1 cup of snow peas (immature
    pea pods), **finely chopped**
1/2 cup of celery leaves, finely
    chopped

5 1/2 cups of chicken stock
1 tablespoon of soy sauce
2 tablespoons of ground
    coriander
1/4 teaspoon of cayenne
1/2 cup of coconut milk
the meat of one, whole chicken
    breast, cooked, boned and
    skinned, diced
1 heaped tablespoon of corian-
    der leaves, finely chopped
salt and pepper to taste

1.   Place a large saucepan over medium-high heat and pour in the oil. When a haze forms over the fat, add the onions and stir-fry for about 2 minutes. Add the garlic, continue stirring and frying for about 1 more minute.
2.   Deposit the taro, green onions, snow peas and celery leaves into the saucepan and continue to stir until the vegetables are wilted.
3.   Pour in the chicken stock and soy sauce, and bring the soup to a boil. Reduce and adjust the heat to maintain a simmer for about 10 minutes.
4.   Remove the saucepan from heat and allow the mixture to cool slightly. Using a slotted spoon, transfer about one quarter of the vegetables to a mixing bowl. Set it aside for use in Step 6.
5.   Pour the soup and remaining vegetables into a medium mixing bowl. Using your blender, purée the soup from the mixing bowl in repeated batches. After

each batch is blended to a uniform consistency, return it to the saucepan. When the puréeing is complete, place the saucepan back over medium-high heat and stir in the coriander and the cayenne.

6. Bring the soup to a boil, then return the reserved vegetables from Step 4 to the saucepan. Pour in the coconut milk and add the diced chicken meat.

7. Adjust the heat and allow the mixture to simmer for about 2 minutes. Stir in the coriander leaves, season to your taste and serve hot or warm.

Note: Spinach can be a perfect substitute for taro leaves. Vegetarians can replicate this robust soup by (a) substituting vegetable stock for chicken stock and (b) omitting the chicken meat.

TROCHUS CHOWDER (GUAM)

The meat of the foot muscle of the trochus or top shell is comparable in flavor to conch or abalone, as well as clam and mussels; indeed, most recipes are interchangeable between and among these meats.

Because the foot meat is exclusively musculature it can be tough, particularly in larger shells. So I prefer to cook shells with a maximum diameter of $2^1/_2$ inches. Trochus are generally boiled first in order to extract the creature. However, if overcooked, the meat becomes extremely leathery so, as a rule, allow 20 minutes of boiling time for a 2-inch diameter shell (as a baseline) and add 5 minutes more for each $^1/_2$-inch increase in the diameter of the shell (calipers, please!).

Following is the chowder I used to make on Guam from freshly caught mollusks. Crusty French bread and a bottle of chilled Chablis are recommended accompaniments.

Trochus or top shell

Serves 6

18 **trochus shells** (each approximately 2^1/$_2$-inches in diameter)

^{3}/$_4$ **stick of butter** (6 tablespoons) **at room temperature**

2 **large onions, peeled and finely chopped**

2 **cloves of garlic, smashed, peeled and minced**

4 **bacon slices, finely chopped**

^{1}/$_2$ **cup of celery, finely chopped**

1 **cup of dry white wine**

2 **bay leaves, torn into small pieces**

^{1}/$_4$ **teaspoon of thyme**

1 **green Serrano chili pepper, minced**

2 **cups of clam juice**

1^3/$_4$ **cups of chicken stock or 1 14^1/$_2$-ounce can of chicken broth**

1^1/$_2$ **cups of potato, peeled and diced**

1 **teaspoon of salt**

^{1}/$_4$ **teaspoon of white pepper**

2 **tablespoons of flour**

1 **cup of thick coconut milk** (*see page 19*)

^{1}/$_4$ **cup of parsley, minced**

1. Scrub the trochus shells thoroughly. Place a large saucepan almost filled with water over high heat and bring it to a rolling boil. Add the trochus shells and continue to boil for about 25 minutes. Remove the shells and rinse them under cold, running water to arrest the cooking. When the shells are cool enough to handle, extract the meat from the shell. (A darning needle, tweezers, corkscrew or curtain hook all work well for the extraction process.)

2. Cut off and discard all parts of the animal except the muscled foot. Coarsely chop the muscle and set aside for use in Step 7.

3. Place a large, non-reactive saucepan over medium heat. Add **4 tablespoons** of butter and, when it comes up to frying temperature, stir in the onion. Sauté it for about 2 minutes, then add the garlic, bacon and celery and continue frying and stirring occasionally for an additional 3 minutes.

4. Pour in the wine and add the bay leaves, thyme and chili pepper. When the mixture comes up to temperature, add the clam juice and chicken stock. Modulate the heat to bring the mixture to a boil.

5. Add the potatoes and season with the salt and pepper. Let the potatoes cook for about 10 minutes.

6. Pour the flour into a small mixing bowl and work the remaining **2 tablespoons** of butter into the flour to make an even paste (*beurre manié*). Gradually introduce small pieces or balls of the flour/butter paste into the liquid to thicken it, stirring constantly.

7.   When the stock has thickened, add the trochus meat. Reduce the heat as necessary to maintain a simmer and add the coconut milk. Let the chowder simmer for about 5 minutes and add the parsley.

8.   Ladle the chowder into a large soup tureen and serve immediately.

Note: As suggested in the introduction, you may substitute the meat from conch, abalone and, obviously, clam to make an equally satisfying chowder.

CARROT, MANGO AND PUMPKIN SOUP

(HAWAI'I)

The skill of combining fruit and vegetables in appetizing combinations is almost an Hawaiian trademark. Keep your guests healthy with this creamy collation; it contains a triple dose of vitamin A. Its flavor is, at once, distinctive and sensuous; the color is the sunset sky as seen from Diamond Head.

Serves 6 to 8

2 tablespoons of butter
1 large onion, peeled and
     finely chopped
1-inch piece of fresh ginger-
     root, peeled and minced
1 large carrot, peeled and
     finely chopped
4 cups of chicken stock or 2
     $14^1/_2$-ounce cans of
     chicken broth plus
     enough water to make
     4 cups

$1^1/_2$ cups of raw pumpkin,
     peeled and cut into
     1-inch cubes
a pinch of ground cardamom
1 cup of ripe mango, peeled
     and the flesh coarsely
     chopped
$^1/_2$ cup of coconut cream *(see
     page 19)* or whipping
     cream may be substituted
salt and pepper to taste
6 mint sprigs for garnish

1.   Place a large non-reactive saucepan over medium-high heat and add the butter. Let the fat come up to frying temperature but not burning and stir in the onion. Sauté the onion for about 3 minutes, or until it is limp and almost disintegrating. Add the ginger and carrot, continue to stir and fry for about 2 more minutes.

2.   Pour in the chicken stock and add the pumpkin and cardamom. Adjust the heat as necessary to bring the mixture to a boil. Reduce the heat to low, cover and simmer for about 20 minutes.

3.   Uncover and add the mango. Let the liquid return to a simmer and cook for 2 minutes.

4.   Transfer the contents of the pan to your blender and blend on a high setting for about 45 seconds to a smooth purée. Return the soup of the saucepan on medium heat, stir in the coconut cream and season with the salt and pepper. Let the soup heat through but not boil.

5.   Pour the soup into individual serving bowls and garnish each with a mint sprig. Serve immediately.

KANGAROO TAIL SOUP
(WESTERN AUSTRALIA)

For those who think of oxtail as . . . well, positively the last part of a bovine they would consider cooking, the robust flavor and melt-in-your-mouth texture of this sometimes maligned sequence of vertebrae has to be experienced to be believed.

Certainly of equal culinary stature are the tails from kangaroo and wallaby. In fact, Australia's kangaroo tail soup has become so popular that it is now canned and exported. Rich brown and aromatic, it's a worthy rival to the oxtail variety. In truth, I began to lust for this stew-like soup the moment I discovered fresh wallaby tails on display in the Gordon Market of Port Moresby, Papua New Guinea.

At this writing, I do not know the status of exportation with regard to Australia's kangaroo meats. Make it so, and soon. The soup never disappoints. Reserve it for a cold winter's day and serve it accompanied by one of Australia's premier red wines.

Serves 6 to 8

2 tablespoons of butter	1 large stalk of celery, diced
1 large onion, peeled and finely chopped	1 cup of canned tomatoes, coarsely chopped
1 large kangaroo tail, skinned and cut into vertebral segments (similar to oxtail)	1/2 teaspoon of bouquet garni
	1 tablespoon of all-purpose flour
4 pints (approximately) of water	2 tablespoons of butter
1 1/2 teaspoons of salt	1/4 cup of dry sherry
6 black peppercorns	1/4 cup of parsley, finely chopped
1 bay leaf	
1 large carrot, peeled and diced	

1.   Place a large saucepan over medium-high heat. Add the **first** 2 tablespoons of butter and let the fat come up to frying temperature; the butter stops bubbling but does not burn.

2.   Add the onion and stir-fry for about 30 seconds. Carefully add the kangaroo segments and brown them on all sides, stirring, for about 6 minutes.

3.   Pour in the water and season with the salt, peppercorns and bay leaf. Increase the heat to produce a boil and cover. Immediately reduce the heat to maintain a simmer and cook, covered, for several hours, or until the meat is tender. (A pressure cooker on a high setting can accelerate this process to reduce the cooking time to about 40 minutes.)

4.   When the simmering is complete and the meat is tender, add the carrots, celery, tomatoes and bouquet garni. Continue cooking on the simmer for about 30 minutes, or until the vegetables are tender and the tomato disintegrates.

5.   Using a sieve and cheesecloth, strain the stock into a medium mixing bowl, reserving the meat and vegetables for use in Step 6. (Wash and set aside the saucepan for use in Step 7.) Place the stock, uncovered, in your refrigerator to chill, let the fat come to the top and coalesce.

6.   Meanwhile, cut all the meat off the bones of the vertebrae and dice it. Reserve the meat and vegetables for use in Step 8.

7.   Remove and discard the collected fat on the top of the stock and return the liquid to the saucepan. Place the pan over medium heat.

8.   Place a medium-sized frying pan over medium heat and add the flour. Vigorously shake the pan to lightly brown the flour and add the **second** 2 tablespoons of butter, a teaspoon at a time. Use a wooden spoon to blend the butter and lift and rotate the pan to modulate the heat and prevent burning. After you have created a coarse *roux* or paste, add about 1½ cups of the simmering stock (from above), stir and continue cooking to produce a thick sauce. Pour the thickened sauce (*velouté*) back into the saucepan above.

9.   Add the reserved meat and vegetables. Adjust the heat and let the mixture come to a boil. Immediately reduce the heat to low and add the sherry.

10. Apportion the soup to individual serving bowls and sprinkle each with parsley. Serve immediately.

Chapter *4*

Crisp and Dressed or Marinated and Piquant

Tropical Salads of Meat, Fish, Fruit, Vegetables and Seaweeds

The produce of this island is Bread fruit, cocoa-nuts, Bananoes, Plantains, a fruit like an apple, sweet Potatoes, yams, a fruit known by the name of Eag melloa and reckond most delicious, Sugar cane which the inhabitants eat raw, a fruit of the Salop kind call'd by inhabitants Pea, the root also of a plant call'd Ether and a fruit in a Pod like a Kidney bean, which when roasted eats like a chestnut and is call'd Ahu, the fruit of a tree which they call Wharra something like a Pine Apple, the fruit of a tree call'd by them Nano, the roots of a fern and the roots of a Plant call'd Theve.

From the diaries of Captain James Cook, written in Tahiti, July, 1769

Salads, according to our definitions of them, were never a feature in conventional meals in the Pacific Islands. In distant times, vegetables were cooked and their temperature at the moment they were consumed was merely a matter of circumstance, not of deliberate design. Fruits were eaten raw and seldom prepared in any special manner; except for the use of a knife to cut the larger specimens into convenient pieces.

Even back then, however, there were many classic island dishes that we Westerners, nowadays, could construe as a *salad,* for want of a more precise category. (A common example could be the cooking of peeled chunks of breadfruit, taro, or sweet potato, and their subsequent dressing in coconut milk and salt—a rudimentary ancestor to our potato salad, particularly when consumed at room temperature.)

Ho! 'Tis the Time of Salads

Our Western preoccupation with healthy eating has nudged salad from its humble status as an ancillary course within a meal to a position of prominence, far beyond its nutritional contribution. The definition of salad has expanded. Salads may now be main dishes, side dishes or slide into categories of fresh relishes and salsas. Mixed salads perform well as cold entrées; simple salads can become artful compositions.

The ingredients may be presented raw, cooked, wilted (as in greens) or as combinations thereof. Salads can showcase fruits, meats, vegetables and fish—not to mention grains and their products, such as pastas—in endless juxtapositions. There is no limit to our saladarity!

The current evolution of *salad* now allows us to include many Pacific Island dishes that would previously be impossible to classify within our meal "course" structure.

Because of the increasing popularity of tourism in Oceania, the islanders have not only learned to cater to the tastes of their Western guests, but also to improvise and create new salads using the marvelous array of local produce, seafood and meat. They also include other elements of island flora in their ingredients, toppings, garnishes. Freshly-grated coconut, chopped green onions, crisp-dried and crumbled seaweeds, and innumerable tropical nuts are tossed in salads or liberally sprinkled over the top.

Dressed for the Occasion

Island salad dressings particularly showcase the ingenuity of the respective cooks. Fruit juices (pineapple, passion fruit, mango and all of the citrus family) can create excitement with nut oils and coconut milk. The latter can be the basis of an intriguingly tropical mayonnaise, particularly suited to grace seafood or coat precooked vegetables. Occasionally, these salad creams are enlivened with curry powder.

Thinner vinaigrettes are whipped into emulsions of lemon or lime juices, oils (usually peanut) and, surprisingly, soy sauce. The Hawaiian vinaigrette-based dressing that features the peppery spark of coarsely-ground papaya seeds is now so popular that it is commercially available in the United States.

The combination of soy sauce and lemon juice, together with chili peppers and onions, is the hallmark base of a series of dishes in the Mariana Islands called *kelaguens*. These feature seafoods or meats that are first lightly cooked and then marinated in this piquant and often fiery dressing. (Not only are these "pickled" dishes popular in the islands, but they can remain fresh for up to 24 hours without refrigeration. The chili peppers also induce perspiration that, in turn, tends to ameliorate the effect of tropical heat and humidity on the body.) Consumed merely as side dishes on Guam, they can become an interesting, spicy addition to our salad inventory.

Cooking without Heat

An Australian couple was standing next to me at a buffet-style feast served near a lagoon in Moorea. Most of the dishes had been ceremonially uncovered from the *ahima'a* (Tahitian earth-pit oven). Others had been prepared by Tahitian women close to the area of eating and celebration. (The feast was followed by fire dancing displays and foot-stomping, soul-stirring revelry to the insistent beat of Tahitian drummers and the haunting melody of nose flutes.) The sun had set. Tropical darkness lay softly upon us; flaming torches anchored in the sand provided illumination and, to complete the setting, we could hear the surf crashing on a distant reef.

The wife began speculating on the dishes before us. I could not resist. I named them. She looked at a giant clam shell heaped with the signature marinated seafood salad of Polynesia called, in French Polynesian, *"poisson crû."*

"What's that?" she asked.

I hesitated. "Er, fish—try it, it's very good."

She helped herself to a large portion. I felt obscurely guilty. Her husband glanced across at me and his eyes crinkled in amusement. He knew what it was but he said nothing.

From the next table, I watched her as she ate the salad with brio. When she finished, her husband leaned over and whispered something in her ear.

Her eyes grew. "Raw fish!" she exclaimed, "Oh no!"

"You ate it, though, didn't you?" he counseled.

"Actually, I liked it," she said, reluctantly. Her face broadened into a satisfied grin.

Our Tahitian hosts within earshot, who I am quite sure encountered this situation many times, flashed wide smiles.

Lime or lemon juice, together with salt, forms the basis of an ancient technique of "cooking" seafood. (The technique probably originated in Peru.) It is familiar to us as *Ceviche* or *Seviche*. The citric acid in the juice denatures the enzymes in the fish, firming the flesh and changing its appearance to white and opaque. It is a form of "cooking" that requires no heat.

Whether the technique was brought to Oceania by voyaging islanders, by the Spaniards, or spontaneously and independently invented by the islanders is obscure. However, the islanders have provided a major contribution that gives their autograph to the unique variation: after the initial marination, the seafood is drained and, together with inspired additions of certain vegetables, is subsequently dressed in rich coconut milk or cream. The acidity of the initial marination is then ameliorated and subsumed into a creamy dressing that echoes the flavors of the best of the Pacific.

The salads following encompass the full range of taste and texture; from assertive, piquant and spicy, they mellow to creamy and delicate. They can be crisp and crunchy or solid, smooth and satisfying. Overall, they should provide us with new dimensions when we contemplate the salad.

AVOCADO, MANGO AND ORANGE SALAD WITH HONEY-SESAME-LIME DRESSING

(HAWAI'I)

As with so many of Hawai'i's plants, the first avocado plants in Hawai'i were grown by Don Francisco de Paula y Marín, the premier Spanish horticulturist and friend of King Kamahameha. They probably emigrated from Central Mexico, because the Spanish terms for the plant, *ahuacate* or *aquacate,* come from the Aztec word *ahuacati.* Now three varieties are grown in Hawai'i, one from the West Indies, another from Guatemala and the third from Mexico.

Serves 6

3 large, ripe avocados, seeded,
    peeled and sliced crosswise
4 ripe mangoes, peeled and the
    flesh cut into 3/4-inch
    cubes
3 small, seedless oranges, peeled
    and the membranous pith
    pared away with a sharp
    knife, then sliced into thin
    disks (parallel to the equator)
2 green onions, both white
    and green, thinly sliced
    into disks

1 small hothouse (English),
    cucumber, peeled and
    thinly sliced into disks
1/4 cup of coriander leaves,
    coarsely chopped
Honey-Sesame-Lime Dressing
8 large leaves of red romaine
    lettuce, washed and
    drained
2 tablespoons of macadamia
    nuts, coarsely chopped

1. In a large, non-reactive mixing bowl, gently combine the avocados, mangoes, oranges, green onion, cucumber and coriander leaves. Pour the **Honey-Sesame-Lime Dressing** over and toss lightly.

2. Line a salad (serving) bowl with the lettuce leaves. Spoon the salad into the center. Sprinkle the top with the macadamia, cover and refrigerate until serving.

HONEY-SESAME LIME DRESSING

1/4 cup of honey
1/4 cup of freshly squeezed
    lime juice
2 tablespoons of sesame
    oil

1/2 teaspoon of hot Oriental
    sesame chili oil
1/4 teaspoon of salt
1/4 teaspoon of fresh ginger-
    root, peeled and minced

1. Combine all the ingredients in a small, non-reactive mixing bowl, stirring thoroughly.

Note: The dressing may be kept, refrigerated, in a tightly sealed container for several days.

KELAGUEN UHANG

Shrimp *Kelaguen* (GUAM)

Kelaguens are chopped meat or seafood salads or relishes, vividly alive with the bite of hot chili peppers and the tartness of lemon juice. Fiesta food on Guam is not considered complete without at least one or two of these spicy side dishes.

This dish, **Kelaguen Uhang,** is traditionally made with freshly-grated coconut meat. Failing that, dried, unsweetened coconut flakes may be used (see page 19).

Also please note that the shrimp are parboiled (Step 3) before being included.

Serves 4 to 6

1 quart of water (approximately)
1¹/₂ pounds of raw, medium (20–30 count per pound) shrimp
the juice of 2 lemons
¹/₂ cup of green onions, coarsely chopped
3 red Serrano chili peppers, minced (omit the seeds to reduce the heat of the dish)

¹/₂ teaspoon of sea salt
¹/₂ small, green bell pepper, cored, seeded and finely chopped (optional)
¹/₄+ of a medium coconut, meat grated or ¹/₂ cup of reconstituted dried, unsweetened coconut flakes
4 large lettuce leaves, washed and drained

1.   Place your kettle with about 1 quart of water on your range and bring the liquid to a full, rolling boil for use in Step 3.

2.   Shell (peel) and devein the shrimp under cold, running water. Finely chop the crustaceans for use in Step 3.

3.   Place the chopped shrimp in a medium mixing bowl. Pour the boiling water over the chopped shrimp and let them steep for several minutes. Drain off all the water.

4.   Add all the remaining ingredients (except the lettuce). Stir the mixture to thoroughly coat the shrimp, cover and refrigerate for about 30 minutes.

5.   To serve, line the salad bowl with the lettuce leaves, then mound the **Kelaguen** in the center. Serve cold or at room temperature.

CRAB AND NAMA SALAD (FIJI)

As would be expected, the shallow coastal waters of the Pacific abound with edible marine crabs, some curiously shaped, others graphically marked with spectacular colors. The most common is *Scylla serrata,* the swimming crab with a serrated shell or carapace. It turns up in Papuan markets, purple-blue and tied with twine so it cannot attack shoppers. Introduced to Hawai'i in the 1920s, it is known there as the Samoan swimming crab. Hawai'i is also the home of the Kona crab, *Ranina ranina.* It is red above, white below and about six inches across. Hawaiians call it *papaʻi kua loa.*

"Seven-Eleven" crab

Amongst the many crabs in the Marianas, Guam has a farcical, Disneyesque fellow that the Chamorros nickname Seven-Eleven (*Carpilius maculatus*) because of the seven large, dark red spots on its dun-colored shell. In Micronesia, box crabs (family Calappidae) often become entangled in the monofilament gill nets (intended for near shore and reef fishes) and the fishermen take them home to cook. These strange creatures are able to tuck their legs into their body, appearing like a toy tank.

Nama is the Fijian name for the seaweed we call sea grape (see Glossary, page 269). For this salad, you can substitute any other seaweed with a similar crunchy texture.

Serves 6 to 8

2 cups of fresh seaweed, coarsely chopped, rinsed thoroughly and drained	2 cups of cooked crab meat (preferably in chunks)
1 small onion, peeled and finely chopped	the juice of 2 lemons
	1 green chili pepper (*Serrano* or *Jalapeño*), seeded and minced
2 green onions, both white and green, finely chopped	1/4 teaspoon of salt
4 medium tomatoes, coarsely chopped	4–6 large lettuce leaves, washed and drained

1. Place the seaweed in a large, non-reactive mixing bowl. Add the onion, green onions, tomatoes and crab meat. Stir briefly to combine all the ingredients. Cover and refrigerate until needed.

2. Combine the lemon juice, chili pepper and salt in a small plastic or glass bowl. Stir until the salt dissolves and set aside. (Postpone dressing the salad until just before serving.)

3. Line your serving bowl with the lettuce leaves. Pour the lemon dressing (Step 2) over the seaweed/crab mixture from Step 1. Stir once and transfer the dressed salad to the lettuce-lined dish or bowl. Serve at once.

Note: Fresh seaweed needs to be picked over carefully in order to remove any sand and other foreign objects before rinsing thoroughly and repeatedly. Resist refrigerating the seaweed for longer than two hours.

AUCKLAND KIWI WALDORF SALAD WITH TROPICAL MAYONNAISE DRESSING (NEW ZEALAND)

If you think that the cutting edge of evolving cuisines resides on the European continent or ends at the West Coast of the United States, then a visit to the major city on New Zealand's North Island will be an eye-opener. The influx of Polynesians from all over the South Pacific, together with the spanking fresh bounty of homegrown and raised New Zealand food has been exploited by a core of enthusiastic and skilled young chefs, food stylists and writers to produce exciting innovations in cooking.

Serves 6 to 8

3 large, red apples, cored and diced (skin left on)

2 tablespoons of freshly squeezed lemon juice

3 stalks of celery, diced

1 cup of walnut pieces

2 tablespoons of dried, unsweetened coconut flakes

6 kiwi fruit, peeled, quartered lengthwise (similar shape to an orange segment), **and the quarters sliced crosswise 1/4-inch thick**

2 cups of Tropical Mayonnaise Dressing

58

1.   Place the apples in a large, non-reactive serving (salad) bowl and sprinkle in the lemon juice. Toss to thoroughly coat the apples. Add the celery, walnuts and coconut flakes, and continue to toss and coat.

2.   Add the kiwi slices, stir gently and spoon in the chilled **Tropical Mayonnaise Dressing.** Cover and refrigerate until ready to serve.

TROPICAL MAYONNAISE DRESSING

1 cup of sweetened condensed milk	1 teaspoon of salt
	1 teaspoon of white pepper
3/4 cup of malt vinegar	1 teaspoon of dry mustard
1/4 cup of thick coconut milk	
(see page 19)	

1.   Combine all the ingredients in a small, non-reactive mixing bowl. Beat until smooth. Refrigerate until thickened.

Note: The **Tropical Mayonnaise Dressing** may be successfully refrigerated for several days. However, if refrigerated, it may require whipping with a teaspoon or so of water to return it to dressing-like consistency.

KELAGUEN BENADO

Marinated Salad of Venison (GUAM)

After the Spanish expelled the Jesuits from Guam in 1769, the island economy and agriculture fell into disarray until a wise and humane gentleman, Don Mariano Tobias, was appointed as governor in 1771. He set the economy on an upswing, reestablished the balance of domestic animals, stocked the island with imported flora and fauna, planted gardens and avenues of coconut palms and breadfruit trees.

During Tobias's administration, a Lieutenant Crozet, a member of the expeditionary voyage of the famous French navigator, Captain Marion-Dufrense, landed on Guam with the remnants of the expeditionary force. (The force was leaderless at the time, because the unfortunate Marion-Dufresne had been invited on shore in New Zealand by the Maoris to attend a feast and ended up as the main dish.) Crozet was enchanted with the island and enthused about its governor. He wrote:

> Some time ago M. Tobias brought over from the Philippines some stags and hinds which have begun to multiply in the forests. These deer are as big as ours but their coat is different.

59

In fact, the bucks of the Benado deer (*Cervus nigricans*) could weigh up to 300 pounds and the does about 100 pounds less. By the mid-1800s, Tobias's imports had wreaked havoc on the islanders' crops and gardens so, when public possession of guns eventually became legal, the deer were enthusiastically hunted for food. On Guam, one can frequently overdo a good thing and the island deer are now endangered and protected by law. However, the Chamorro way of preparing venison is delicious and, though venison is rarely available nowadays, **Kelaguen Benado** can still be sampled on special occasions.

As a footnote: the Jesuit-educated Guillame-Thomas, Abbé de Raynal, the writer and propagandist who helped mold the anti-Royalist sentiment in France, wrote a very popular, six-volume history of the European colonies in India and America, in which he extolled the benevolent colonial policies of Don Mariano Tobias on Guam. This publicized championing, together with the affection the Chamorros gave the Governor, incurred the jealousy and, eventually, the enmity of the Augustine monks on the island. They persecuted Tobias for his "lack of piety" (a useful umbrella accusation that had been around since the Spanish Inquisition) and persuaded his wife to leave him. He was then ignominiously relieved of his position and sent as a mere Lieutenant Colonel to the Spanish garrison in Manila. In the Philippines, another renowned navigator, La Pérouse, encountered him and reported that Tobias had to pay all his income, except 26 dollars per month for his own subsistence, to his estranged wife for her support!

Plus ça change . . .

Serves 6 to 8

3 pounds of venison or flank steak	**3 green onions, both white and green, sliced into thin**
1 medium red onion, peeled and finely chopped	**disks**
2 teaspoons of soy sauce	**the exterior leaves of a head of**
4 hot, red chili peppers	**red romaine lettuce,**
(*Serrano* or *Jalapeño*),	**washed and drained**
minced	**1 hothouse** (English) **cucumber, thinly sliced**
the juice of 6 large lemons	

1. Wrap the venison or flank steak in plastic wrap and place it in your freezer for about one hour or until the meat is stiff but not frozen.
2. Slice the meat thinly, then cut the slices into narrow, approximately 2-inches long × 1-inch wide strips. Pat the meat dry with paper towels as you place it in a large plastic mixing bowl.
3. Stir the red onion, soy sauce, chili peppers and lemon juice into the meat.
4. Toss the mixture to distribute the ingredients, cover the bowl and let the meat marinate, refrigerated, for at least 2 hours.

5.   Just before serving, line a large serving platter or salad bowl with the lettuce leaves.

6.   At serving, uncover the meat and stir in the green onions. Mound the **Kelaguen** in the center of the leaves from Step 5. Circle the meat with the sliced cucumbers and serve.

Note: In beef, venison and chicken *kelaguens,* the raw meat appears to "cook" in the acidic marinade that denatures the surface proteins making the main ingredient appear more tender. This enzymatic arrangement also occurs with fish, most notably *Ceviche* and **Poisson Crú.** This dish, however, nods more toward steak tartare.

VILA CURRIED PAPAYA SALAD

(VANUATU)

When residents of "Vila" (Port Vila, the capital of the Vanuatuan archipelago on the island of Éfaté) want to meet for lunch or dinner, go sailing, or just relax and kick back, they say, "Let's meet at Rick's." By that, in fact, they mean the Waterfront Bar and Grill, owned by Rick Hogg (an engaging New Zealand expatriate), which is the unofficial headquarters of the Vanuatu Cruising Yacht Club and hosts an international set of global sailors. (The club's offices are actually across the parking lot but, for all intents and purposes, they are conjoined.)

The Waterfront is an enormous, circular, open-sided *nipa* hut with wooden pillars and a lofty, peaked, thatched roof. It overlooks the marina and a few hundred yards of intensely blue water to the Iririki Island Resort in the middle of the bay. Tables on the inside of the Waterfront also spill onto the grass outside, near all sizes and designs of exotic craft (both power and sail), tied up or moored beyond. "Yachties" from all over the world sit at the tables, under green and yellow umbrellas bearing the slogan (in Bislama) for the local brew, Bier Blong Yumi.

Rick provides lunches, dinners and a most sumptuous salad bar, managing his kitchen staff, bartenders, wait persons, office and an ever-changing—often joyously rowdy—crowd of customers with the greatest of ease and cheerful aplomb. The Waterfront is a kind of a South Seas version of the legendary Rick's Café Américain in Casablanca, Morocco (or was it the Warner Brother's lot in Burbank?), except nobody's trying to pay for letters of transit to Lisbon with their body, and many *are* forming "the beginning of a beautiful friendship."

At one luncheon buffet, Rick pointed out his curried papaya salad to me. "Try that," he said. I did. I fell in love with it. I was having such a rowdy-good time that I forgot to ask him for the recipe.

If you're ever in Vanuatu in the autumn, I may see you at Rick's. In the meantime, here is my adaptation of the salad.

1 tablespoon of butter
1 tablespoon of peanut oil
1 medium onion, peeled and
    finely chopped
1 clove of garlic, smashed,
    peeled and minced
2 tablespoons of curry powder
$1/4$ cup of pineapple (fresh or
    canned), crushed
1 banana, finely chopped
2 tablespoons of flour
$1^1/2$ cups of chicken stock
    (fresh or canned)
1 teaspoon of salt, or to taste
$1/4$ teaspoon of freshly ground
    black pepper

2 tablespoons of mango chutney (with the fruit finely
    chopped)
$1/2$ cup of thick coconut milk
    (see page 19)
5 cups of ripe papaya, peeled,
    seeded and diced
$1/2$ cup of celery, coarsely
    chopped
2 green onions, both white
    and green, thinly sliced
    into disks
$1/2$ cup of mayonnaise

1. Heat the butter and oil in a medium, non-reactive saucepan over a medium setting and fry the onion, stirring, until it is translucent. Add the garlic and stir for an additional 30 seconds. Spoon in the curry powder and, lowering the heat, stir for another $1^1/2$ minutes.

2. Add the crushed pineapple and chopped banana and stir to thoroughly mix all the ingredients. Now add the flour and stir vigorously for about 30 seconds, or until it is incorporated. Slowly pour in the chicken stock, stirring constantly, until the mixture thickens.

3. Season with the salt and pepper, add the mango chutney and coconut milk, stir, increase the heat and bring the mixture to a simmer. Modulate the heat as necessary to maintain a simmer and let the mixture cook, stirring occasionally, for about 30 minutes, or until it becomes a thick sauce. (If the sauce thickens too much, add water, a tablespoon at a time, stirring and checking the consistency. The sauce's consistency should be that of a thick, but fluid, custard.) Remove from heat and set aside to cool for use in Step 5.

4. Place the papaya, celery and green onions (reserving 1 tablespoon for garnish) in a large mixing bowl.

5. Blend the mayonnaise into the cooled curry sauce from Step 3. Spoon the sauce over the combined vegetables from the above step. Toss thoroughly to coat all the ingredients. Transfer to a serving bowl, sprinkle the

reserved green onions (from Step 4) over the top. Cover and chill until ready to serve.

Note: Vegetarians may want to substitute water or vegetable stock for the chicken stock in Step 2.

MAL

Purple Taro Salad (YAP)

Purple taro is becoming popular in Hawai'i and should be available on the mainland by the time you read this. Taro itself makes one of my favorite variations on potato salad but *purple* taro makes this dish a show stopper. (If you cannot locate the purple variety, petition your local greengrocer to order it.) Ordinary or true taro may be substituted but, of course, it will lack the visual impact of this recipe from Yap in Western Micronesia.

	Serves 6 to 8
3 hardcooked eggs, finely chopped	peeled, cooked and cut into 1-inch cubes (approximately)
1 cup of mayonnaise	
1 teaspoon of dried mustard	3 green onions, both white and green, finely chopped
1 teaspoon of Worcestershire sauce	1 green bell pepper, cored, seeded and diced
2 teaspoons of salt	1 dill pickle, finely chopped
1/2 teaspoon of freshly ground black pepper	
5 cups of large taro corms,	

1.   Place the eggs in a large, non-reactive mixing bowl and add the mayonnaise, mustard, Worcestershire sauce, salt and pepper. Stir to thoroughly combine all the ingredients and coat the eggs with the mayonnaise.
2.   Add the taro and all the remaining ingredients. Toss and stir to coat the taro.
3.   Transfer the *Mal* to a large serving bowl, cover and refrigerate until ready to serve.

CURRIED SWEET POTATO, BANANA AND BRAZIL NUT SALAD

(SAIPAN)

The fourteen islands comprising the Marianas lie in a gentle arc stretching northward from Guam. Most of them are tiny fragments of land, where the only animal life are seabirds. One of them, Pagan, contains a frequently angry volcano. (The volcanic grumblings would probably be recorded only by seismologists in Japan or California except that this island *is* inhabited by people.)

The second largest island in the chain, Saipan, is both beautiful and haunting, with towering perpendicular escarpments on three sides and sparkling, white sand beaches facing its western lagoon. (An area in the southeast quadrant of the island used to be the primary jungle training location for the CIA.) Haunting also describes the rusting World War II armament (both Japanese and Allied) almost buried in the thickets of *tangantangan* brush, but more appropriately refers to the stark and lonely Suicide and Banzai Cliffs at the island's northernmost point. Hundreds of Japanese civilians jumped to their deaths from these cliffs, some facing north to their mother country, Japan, many preferring to walk swiftly backwards so they would not know the fatal foot fall.

The past, as they say, is prologue. The present reveals Saipan as a mecca for tourists. Water sports, hiking, eating and dancing occupy their sun-filled days and tradewind-cooled Pacific nights.

Since Saipan is only a 35-minute flight from Guam, we would often fly over to day-trip or for a weekend, staying at our favorite beach-side hotel in Garapan, the island's capital. This locally inspired salad is from one of those lavish and tempting buffets at the hotel.

Serves 8

2 tablespoons of peanut oil	1 teaspoon of orange zest,
2 cloves of garlic, smashed,	grated
peeled and finely chopped	2 large sweet potatoes, cooked
1 heaped teaspoon of fresh	and cut into $3/4$-inch
gingerroot, peeled and	cubes
minced	$1/4$ cup of Brazil nuts, finely
1 tablespoon of curry powder	chopped
$1/2$ cup of mayonnaise	3 green onions, both white
$1/4$ cup of plain yogurt	and green, finely chopped
4 ripe bananas, peeled and	8 large lettuce (iceberg,
sliced into $1/2$-inch-long	Boston, Bibb) **leaves,**
disks	**washed and drained**
$1/4$ cup of freshly squeezed	1 tablespoon of coriander
orange juice	leaves, finely chopped

1.   Heat the oil in a medium frying pan over medium heat and quickly fry the garlic and then the ginger. Reduce heat to low and stir in the curry powder. Continue frying and stirring (to prevent sticking) for about 1 minute, or until the aroma changes and mellows. Remove from the heat and set aside to cool for use in the next step.

2.   Combine the mayonnaise and yogurt in a small, non-reactive mixing bowl and stir in the curry mixture from above. Beat and blend to thoroughly combine all the ingredients.

3.   Place the bananas in a large, non-reactive mixing bowl, add the orange juice and the zest and gently stir to coat the banana slices. Add the sweet potatoes. Scrape in the curry/mayonnaise from Step 2 and add the Brazil nuts and green onions. Toss to combine and coat all the ingredients.

4.   Line a large salad bowl with the lettuce leaves, spoon in the salad and sprinkle with coriander leaves. Cover and refrigerate until ready to serve.

POKE AKU

Fish, Seaweed and *Kukui* Nut Salad (HAWAI'I)

The ancient Hawaiians adored fish. They ate it raw or cooked. They salted, massaged and dried it, depending on the species.

During the season of violent storms in the Pacific, fishing was suspended. Against this contingency, when the catch was bountiful, a substantial proportion was dried and salt cured. Large fish were cut into pieces, bone-in, the pieces scored and rubbed liberally with sea salt. The pieces were further soaked in brine for up to three days before being laid on large stones; preferably on a hot, sunny beach. The drying process also took up to three days, after which the dried product could be stored for up to one year.

Aku, in Hawaiian, is the skipjack tuna or bonito (see table, "A Selection of Popular Bony Fish in Oceania," on page 103) and was much esteemed by the islanders, who considered its red flesh special. They consumed it raw but always added salt because to eat fish without salt was unthinkable. When the Hawaiians ate dried *aku,* they occasionally broiled it; more frequently, they consumed it directly from storage.

The classic *Poke Aku* is prepared from dried fish (available from most fish markets in Honolulu). However, in this recipe, we use fresh skipjack because it is more widely available. (It also produces a more moist and tender dish with a lower sodium content.)

For seaweed substitutions, please refer to the Glossary. Again, unless we're fortunate enough to live in our fiftieth state, we shall be using the *'Inamona* that substitutes macadamia for the *kukui* nuts.

Serves 8

1 pound of bonito, filleted, skinned and cut into ³/₄-inch cubes	1 green chili pepper *(Serrano* or *Jalapeño),* seeded and minced
¹/₂–1 teaspoon of sea salt	¹/₄ teaspoon of *'Inamona (see page 225)*
1 cup of *limu kohu* or 3 tablespoons of salted *limu manauea* or *limu mane 'one'o,* finely chopped	

1.   Combine all the ingredients in a large, non-reactive mixing bowl and toss to thoroughly mix.

2.   Cover and refrigerate for up to 12 hours. Transfer to a serving bowl and serve as a side dish at a *lu'au*.

KELAGUEN MANNOK

Marinated Salad of Chicken (GUAM)

While I would like to think I have eaten every version of *kelaguen* in the culinary lexicon of Guam, this was the first. And, we know, first loves are most precious. The occasion was a christening feast shortly after I first arrived on the island in 1981. Its assertive flavor can still seduce me.

	Serves me and a small party
4 whole chicken breasts, skinned, cooked and boned	**$1/2$ cup of freshly grated coconut or the equivalent in reconstituted dried coconut** *(see page 19)*
1 small onion, peeled and finely chopped	**$1/2$ teaspoon of salt**
the juice of 6 freshly squeezed lemons	**$1/4$ teaspoon of freshly ground black pepper**
2 green chili peppers *(Serrano* or *Jalapeño),* **minced**	

1.   Finely chop the chicken and place it in a large, non-reactive mixing bowl. Add all the remaining ingredients and thoroughly combine.

2.   Transfer to a serving bowl and present at once or refrigerate until ready to serve.

Note: *Kelaguen* is normally served as a side dish at an island buffet.

KOKODA

Marinated Fish and Shrimp Salad in Coconut Cream

(FIJI, VANUATU)

This hallmark marinated seafood salad—a cousin to the Latin American *Ceviche*—is repeated throughout the islands of the South Pacific, from Vanuatu and Fiji, through Tonga and Samoa, the Cook Islands to Tahiti in French Polynesia, and to the Marquesas and Tuamotus farther east. Many claim it as their own; specifically the Fijians, as **Kokoda,** and the Tahitians, their signature **Poisson Crû.** The fundamentals of the dish are almost universal—the difference lies in the details.

Ongoing debates about **Kokoda** continue among island cooks and chefs. There are interminable discussions as to whether the marinade should be lemon or lime juice? (It depends on what is currently and locally available.) Which fish is best to use? (Again, whatever firm-fleshed fish is local and fresh.) To mention the composition of marinated fish salads in any yacht club in the South Pacific is similar to polling the customers at Canter's famous delicatessen in Los Angeles about the proper ingredients for chicken soup.

After much research on the composition of this dish in several countries in the South Pacific (in hindsight, I wish I hadn't; I was inundated with recipes), I came to the conclusion that there are five basic elements: fish (shell and/or bony); citrus juice (in a pinch, you may substitute white vinegar); coconut cream; onions (green or globe); salt. Everything else is, as they say, showbiz, dictated by the vision and ingenuity of the individual chef.

The following recipe is commonly prepared in Fiji; it owes its regional flavor dialect to the addition of shrimp and turmeric. Also in Fiji, **Kokoda** is prepared equally with either tuna or *walu.* (For more information about suggestions and substitutions, please see table, "A Selection of Popular Bony Fish in Oceania," on page 98.

1 pound of fresh tuna
(Substitutions may include
walu, halibut, swordfish,
bonito, snapper, etc.), **cut
into** $1/2$- **to 1-inch cubes**
1 cup of freshly squeezed
lemon juice
1 pound of medium shrimp
(20–30 count per pound),
**cooked, shelled and
coarsely chopped**
1 medium onion, peeled and
finely chopped
3 medium tomatoes, seeded
and finely chopped
1 green bell pepper, cored,
seeded and diced

1 green chili pepper *(Serrano* or
Jalapeño), **seeded and
minced**
2 hardcooked eggs, shelled and
coarsely chopped
$1^1/2$ teaspoons of sea salt
$1/2$ teaspoon of freshly ground
black pepper
$1/2$ teaspoon of turmeric
1 cup of coconut cream *(see
page 19)*
5–6 lettuce leaves, washed and
drained
5 cherry tomatoes, washed and
stemmed (hulled)

1.   Place the fish in a large, resealable plastic bag and pour in the lemon juice. Seal and rotate the bag several times to distribute the lemon juice. Place the bag in the refrigerator to marinate for 1 to 3 hours. The fish chunks should firm slightly and become white or opaque as a result of the citric acid as it denatures the surface enzymes. (The length of time the fish will take to "cook" in the marinade depends on the Family/*Species* of the particular fish: snapper the shortest; swordfish the longest. You can press on the bag to determine the degree of firmness of the fish.)
2.   After marination, drain the fish through a sieve or colander and pat the pieces dry with a paper towel. Place the fish chunks in a large, non-reactive mixing bowl.
3.   To the bowl, add the shrimp, onion, chopped tomatoes, green bell pepper, chili pepper, and eggs. Stir to evenly distribute the ingredients and season with the sea salt and pepper.

4.   Place the turmeric in a small bowl and slowly add the coconut cream, stirring vigorously until the spice is blended. With a rubber spatula, scrape the mixture over the fish mixture and toss gently to coat all the ingredients with the coconut cream.
5.   Line a large (preferably chilled) salad bowl with the lettuce leaves, spoon in the **Kokoda** and decorate with the cherry tomatoes. Serve at once or keep in a cool place until you are ready to present it.

Note: Do not refrigerate the *Kokoda* because the coconut cream will solidify. Optional, additional ingredients include: chopped gherkins (6); halved, pitted olives (6); grated carrots (2).

POISSON CRÛ

Tahitian Marinated Fish Salad (SOCIETY ISLANDS)

There is something especially South Seas about this (usually) snow-white, creamy collation of fresh fish and citrus juice—particularly when it is served in a giant clam shell set amid green leaves by a palm-lined lagoon. Tuck a scarlet hibiscus behind your ear (this is gender neutral) and you step directly into a Gauguin painting.
   This is the **Poisson Crû** I ate in Moorea, one of the Windward Group (*Îles du Vent*) in French Polynesia, about 20 km northwest of Tahiti.

Serves 6 to 8

2 pounds of fresh tuna (substitutions include *mahi mahi*, bonito, halibut, etc.), **cut into 1-inch cubes**	**2 small carrots, grated**
	1 small, hothouse (English) **cucumber, thinly sliced into disks**
1½ cups of freshly squeezed lime juice (8–10 large limes)	**1½ teaspoons of sea salt**
	½ teaspoon of white pepper
4 green onions, both white and green, coarsely chopped	**½ packed cup of parsley, minced** (plus a few full sprigs for decoration)
2 medium tomatoes, seeded and diced	**1 cup of coconut cream**

1.   Place the fish in a large, resealable plastic bag and pour in the lime juice. Seal and rotate the bag several times to distribute the lime juice. Place the bag in the refrigerator to marinate for 1 to 3 hours. The fish chunks should firm slightly and become white or opaque. (The length of time the fish will take to "cook" in the marinade depends on the Family/*Species* of the particular fish: halibut the shortest; *mahi mahi* the longest. You can press on the bag to determine the degree of firmness of the fish.)

2.   After marination, drain the fish through a sieve or colander and pat the pieces dry with a paper towel. Place the fish chunks in a large, non-reactive mixing bowl.

3.   To the bowl, add the green onions, diced tomatoes, grated carrots and cucumber slices. Season with the sea salt and white pepper. Stir in the minced parsley.

4.   Pour and scrape the coconut cream over the mixture and toss gently to coat all the ingredients.

5.   Transfer the **Poisson Crû** to a large (preferably chilled) glass bowl or giant clam shell. Decorate the salad with the remaining sprigs of parsley and serve at once or keep in a cool place until you are ready to present it.

Note: Do not refrigerate the **Poisson Crû** because the coconut cream will solidify.

Chapter 5

Harvest from Coral Reefs, Lagoons and Estuaries

An Extravagance of Mollusk, Crustacean and Amphibious Reptile Recipes

All shell-fish were collected by women and not by men.
An old belief was that they are all descendants of Hine-
moana the Ocean Maid. Tuangi or cockles originated from
Te Arawaru and Kaumaihi. Kuku or mussels originated
from a relative of Hine-moana, from whom also sprang all
the different kinds of seaweed which were to form a shelter
for her descendants.

Makereti, 1938, *The Old-Time Maori*

Early on a serene Pacific morning, your long shadow precedes you down the slope of coral sand to the lagoon, coconut palms creaking slightly overhead. A scattering of tiny shells has been strewn across the beach by the retreating water. They appear stationary but stand still and, as the vibrations of your footfalls subside, some of them begin to move almost imperceptibly; drawn back to the magnet of the lagoon and survival before the full strength of the tropical sun condemns them to death.

Where the sand flattens and packs hard at the water's edge, you enter an environment of earth, water and sky that defies you to distinguish where one begins and another ends. The surface of the water close to you has disappeared and sea creatures lie on the bed of the crystalline lagoon like so many specimens suspended in acrylic resin. Reflection and refraction compete. The mirrored clouds above wrap the starfish below in white cotton fluff.

Two huge paces into the water and you are still only in a depth of four inches; water as warm as the air, so that your feet are unaware of a change in temperature. Fingernail-sized crabs, magnified into small monsters, scuttle away from your giant toes. Strands of seaweed drape over a chunk of dead, white coral, moving gently like mermaids' hair. Ahead, where the first zephyrs of breeze distort the liquid glass, dark logs of sea cucumbers lie supinely, ceaselessly filtering sand through their length to extract nourishment.

Sand drawing of a turtle from Ambrym Island, Vanuatu. (Imaged by Kristine Cole.)

From beyond the jungled headland to your right, the muffled roar of breakers signals the end of the lagoon. The beach is steeper there and, like the tracks of some amphibious vehicle, the trail of a sea turtle marks her laborious journey to lay her eggs in the warm sands. Swaths of brushed patterns betray her attempts to disguise the burial nest of her embryos.

Farther still, where the fresh water of a river pushes into the sea, a crocodile lurks in the shadows of a mangrove swamp; yawning jaws mimicking the opening of the estuary. A small crack echoes along the beach as a giant coconut crab hunkers down at the foot of a palm, demolishing the coconut husk and shell with its powerful claws to reach the sweet meat inside.

To the visitor to Oceania, this is a scene of unspoiled primordial beauty. To the islanders, it is a realm of gathering and hunting, a self-replenishing source of food.

Hunters and Gatherers of the Littoral

Much that is gleaned from this domain traditionally lay within the bailiwick of the females; particularly in Polynesia, where the hunting and catching of vertebrates, both marine and land, were *tapu* (taboo) to women—being the preserve of the males. So the women developed the skills of discerning the sweetest of the mollusks and echinoids, and where they were to be found. They learnt the sites of the best shallow-water seaweeds, their characteristics and use. The males speared or netted the reef fish, slaughtered the turtles, grappled with the crocodiles and wrestled the octopus that, although a mollusk, was deemed a worthy and tricky opponent, demanding both strength and skill to prize it from its watery home. The giant clam, reputed to catch the unwary diver and sever a limb, was also a food trophy for the men.

The separation of the sexes into gender-specific tasks regarding the harvesting of seafood is more relaxed today. Even so, the men primarily man the fishing boats, and the women and children confine their hunt to the shallow waters close to shore.

I witnessed the following scene in French Polynesia:

It was low tide on Moorea. The breeze had dropped, the ocean calming in the evening hush. I was sitting on a low bluff, gazing idly at the rose and amber seascape, when my attention was drawn to the distant sounds of voices and laughter drifting across the still air. A straggle of women and children were out on the exposed reef, silhouetted against the lambent sky. I watched. They meandered along the outcropping; motionless at times, then crouching so low I could barely discern their shapes before moving again. Curious now, I picked my way cautiously across the sharp and uneven coral—thongs are not the recommended footgear for reef walking.

Gaugin, with his profound sense of color and mystery, could have painted them: *pareus* hiked up around their thighs, hibiscus blossoms tucked behind their ears, skins golden-bronze in the sunset. The little boys ran about, sure footed, dripping wet shorts almost at half-mast. Everyone carried mesh bags and I realized they were hand-fishing the tide pools in the reef. The catch was mostly small mollusks and crustacens but one boy, older than the other children, triumphantly brandished a crayfish, holding it behind its head as the creature waved its legs and pincers in the air.

With variations, this scene is repeated across Oceania: the harvesting of reef fish, crabs, shrimp, crayfish and eels by women and children from tide pools at dusk. The hand-fished catch is cleaned at water's edge before being taken home for supper (some is preserved by smoking); seldom does any appear in the local markets.

The men also work the reefs, using harpoons of wood with single barbed tips of steel or trident-like spears with multiple prongs. Before the arrival of iron in the Pacific, spears were handcrafted completely of wood or bamboo. The spears are often designed for hunting octopus. I have watched the island men wait motionlessly on the reef, then with split-second timing and precision, transfix a passing prey. However, the most dramatic sight is to observe them spear-fishing at sunset and into the night—burning torch held aloft in one hand and spear in the other—standing like gods above the dark sea.

From abalone (*paua*) to coconut crab to turtle and trochus, a unique variety of delicious and unusual recipes is here presented. They feature marine creatures from the lagoons, reefs and estuaries of the Pacific Islands. (Pacific Ocean bony fish offerings follow in the next chapter.)

The majority of shellfish and seafood for dishes in this chapter can be found in better fish markets. A few recipes require specific and exotic denizens. They are included because they are authentic to the diets of the

Pacific Islanders. At this time, I only hope that many will travel to Oceania and sample these rare delicacies in their local surroundings. Eventually, if efforts at preservation are sustained and/or aquaculture has sufficiently increased their respective populations, they may become available in the West. It is my hope that popularizing rare species herein will also help to (a) focus attention on preservation and (b) hasten their importation. Where exotic seafood is already plentiful but popularity is regional, I anticipate that commercial shipping enterprises will soon bring them to our markets. Meanwhile, substitutions and replications are suggested; if only approximating the original while enjoying the spirit and intent of the island dishes.

Finally, with nostalgia in hand, in a tribute to the graciousness of Pacific ocean voyages of bygone years, I have included an extravagant buffet centerpiece. Considering the time-honored custom of pictorial representation with food, this recipe also salutes the infatuation that Hollywood has maintained with the South Seas.

BANANA-BUD PAELLA

(POHNPEI)

This recipe finds an interesting use for the banana bud. Although one can barely call it paella, that is the name under which I discovered it. The mixture of seafood, sausage and chicken puts it within hailing distance of the saffron-flavored Valencian original. But this *is* the Carolines in Micronesia and they have domain over their own cuisine. I suspect this dish emigrated to the Carolines via the Philippines.

Bananas and Blossom

Serves 6 to 8

1 tablespoon of annato
  (achiote) seeds
2 teaspoons of salt
6–8 trochus shells (optional),
  about 2 inches in diameter, well scrubbed
1 banana bud, outer petals
  removed
3 tablespoons of peanut oil
1/2 pound of boneless pork
  round, cut into 1/2-inch
  cubes
1 medium onion, peeled and
  finely chopped
2 cloves of garlic, smashed,
  peeled and minced
2 *lup cheong* (Chinese) dried
  sausages, sliced into
  1-inch-long disks
1 red bell pepper, cored,
  seeded and sliced into thin
  strips

1 large tomato, blanched,
  peeled and coarsely
  chopped
2 cups of long-grain rice
1 whole chicken breast,
  skinned, boned and cut
  into 1-inch chunks
3 cups of clam juice
1 bay leaf, torn into small
  pieces
1/2 teaspoon of freshly ground
  black pepper (Pohnpei's
  own local product is preferred)
1 pint of fresh clams (with their
  liquor)
14 medium (31- to 40-count
  per pound) raw shrimp,
  shelled with the tails left
  attached

1. Put the annato seeds in a 1-cup, ovenproof measuring cup, pour in 3 tablespoons of boiling water and let the seeds steep for about 5 minutes.
(Alternatively, using your microwave, place the same amounts of annato and
water in the measuring cup and microwave on a high setting for 1 minute.)
Strain the liquid and set aside for use in Step 7. Discard the seeds.
2. Almost fill a large, non-reactive saucepan with water, add **1 teaspoon** of salt
and bring to a boil over medium-high heat. Put in the trochus and boil for
about 5 minutes. Add the banana blossom and, when the liquid returns to the
boil, cook for a further 15 minutes. Drain off the water and set aside both the
trochus shells and the banana blossom to cool separately.
3. Remove the trochus meat from the shells with a large (darning) needle or
tweezers. Cut each into quarters and set aside for use in Step 9.
4. Slice the banana bud crosswise into disks of varying diameter that are about
1/2-inch thick. Cut each disk into quarters and set aside for use in Step 8.
5. Place a large wok over medium-high heat and pour in the oil. When a haze
forms over the oil, carefully deposit the pork cubes and stir-fry for several

minutes, or until they are lightly browned on all sides. Remove the cooked pork with a slotted spoon and set aside for use in Step 9.

6. While still on heat, add the onion and stir-fry for about 1 minute. Introduce the garlic and *lup cheong* and stir-fry for another minute. Add the bell pepper and tomato and continue to fry, stirring until the pepper softens.

7. Pour in the rice and the annato liquid. Add the chicken chunks and clam juice. Season with the bay leaf and the remainder of the salt and pepper. Bring the mixture to a boil, cover and modulate the heat to maintain a simmer for 5 minutes.

8. Uncover and stir in the banana bud. Add the fresh clams and their liquor. Re-cover the wok and continue on the simmer for an additional 5 minutes.

9. Now put in the trochus, the pork and shrimp. Do not stir. Cover the wok again and cook for about 2 minutes.

10. Uncover the wok for the last time and selectively remove about one-third portions each of the clams, trochus, pork and shrimp and set aside for use in the next step.

11. Transfer the paella to a large, heatproof platter and randomly replace the reserved pork and seafood on top. Serve immediately.

Note: You may substitute about 1 1/2 cups of clam meat for the trochus.

POINT CRUZ TIGER SHRIMP AND PAPAYA IN A PEANUT, GARLIC AND COCONUT SAUCE

(SOLOMON ISLANDS)

Down at the Point Cruz Yacht Club in Honiara, Jeff is known as the "shrimp man," not for his stature (which is husky), but because he breeds tiger shrimp. They are handsome monsters, 5 count per pound. He recounts that his business really took off when the Thai supply of tiger shrimp shrank because of pollution problems.

When he was younger, Jeff was a surfer. Story goes that he tried to persuade a light plane pilot in the Solomons to give him a tow on his surfboard. Jeff had this crazy idea that it would be a fun way to travel from island to island. Unfortunately, or perhaps fortunately for Jeff and the tiger shrimp business, the pilot emphatically refused. Now his enthusiasm is directed to breeding and selling oversized crustaceans.

This one's for you, Jeff.

Serves 4 to 6

12 **tiger shrimp** (sometimes called tiger prawns, about 5–8 count per pound)
1 **tablespoon of peanut butter**
shrimp stock from Step 1
1$^1/_2$ **tablespoons of low sodium soy sauce**
5 **cloves of garlic, smashed, peeled and minced**
1 **teaspoon of curry powder**
3 **tablespoons of peanut oil**
1-**inch piece of fresh ginger-root, peeled and minced**

3 **green onions, both white and green, sliced into** $^1/_2$-**inch-long sections**
2 **cups of firm, ripe papaya, peeled, seeded and cut into** $^3/_4$-**inch cubes**
$^1/_4$ **cup of coconut cream** (*see page 19*)
2 **teaspoons of coriander leaves, chopped**

1.   Peel and devein the shrimp, reserving the shells and tails. Refrigerate the shrimp and reserve for use in Step 5. Place the shells and tails in a medium saucepan. Cover with water, place over high heat and bring to a boil. Continue on the boil until the liquid is reduced by one-third. Remove from the heat, strain the liquid through a sieve (reserving the liquid for use in Step 2) and discard the solids.

2.   Place the peanut butter and about $^1/_4$ cup of the shrimp stock from above in a blender. (Reserve the remainder of the shrimp stock for use in Step 5.) Blend for about 30 seconds or until the mixture is smooth and creamy. Add the soy sauce, 1 **teaspoon** of the minced garlic and the curry powder. Blend again to a smooth, thick sauce, adding more of the reserved stock from above if necessary to achieve the proper consistency.

3.   Heat the peanut oil in a medium saucepan or wok over a medium-high setting. Add the remaining garlic, ginger and green onions, stir and fry for about 1 minute. With a rubber spatula, scrape the contents of the blender into the saucepan. Stir and let the mixture come to a simmer.

4.   Now add the papaya and continue to cook for about an additional 2 minutes.

5.   Add the reserved shrimp from Step 1, stir and cook until the crustaceans just begin to change color. Pour in an additional $^1/_2$ cup of the reserved stock from Step 2. Stir and continue on heat until the sauce just begins to bubble. Add the coconut cream and allow all the ingredients to heat through, **without** boiling.

6.   Transfer the shrimp/papaya mixture to a serving bowl, sprinkle the top with the coriander leaves and present, accompanied by rice.

PAUA STEAKS ROTORUA

(NEW ZEALAND)

Paua is the Maori name for local abalone. Makereti writes in her book *The Old-Time Maori*:

> Paua haliotis, generally called mutton fish, has a univalve shell. It is taken from the rocks by hand, and the inside is taken out and beaten to soften it before it is cooked on hot coals or in a ha[a]ngi.

Thus she describes the Maori method of mechanically tenderizing the abalone before cooking. Be sure to check if the abalone steaks that you purchase, usually trimmed, sliced and frozen, are already tenderized.

Serves 6

3 eggs, beaten
1 1/2 tablespoons of Worcestershire sauce
1 1/2 pounds (approximately) **of abalone steaks (6 steaks, minimum), tenderized**
1 1/2 cups of fine, white breadcrumbs
1/4 cup of parsley, minced
1/2 teaspoon of salt

1 teaspoon of black peppercorns, smashed and crushed
2 tablespoons of canola oil
3 tablespoons of butter
3 firm bananas, peeled, halved lengthwise and then halved again crosswise (effectively quartering each)
parsley sprigs to garnish

1.   Combine the eggs and Worcestershire sauce in a large shallow dish. Immerse the abalone steaks in the mixture and let them macerate for about 30 minutes, turning occasionally.
2.   Combine the breadcrumbs, parsley, salt and pepper in a shallow bowl. Using tongs, drain the steaks from the egg mixture and dip them in the breadcrumb combination, turning as necessary to coat them on all sides.
3.   Place a large, non-reactive frying pan over medium-high heat. Add the canola oil and **1 tablespoon** of the butter. When the fat comes up to frying temperature, fry the steaks, several at a time, no more than 1 minute per side, or until the coating is crisp and golden. Accumulate the steaks on an ovenproof

serving platter in your oven on its lowest setting. Continue until all the abalone is fried and collected for use in Step 5. (Leave the pan on heat but reduce the setting to medium.)

4.   Add the remaining **2 tablespoons** of butter to the pan and, when the butter stops foaming, add the banana quarters and sauté until they are golden.

5.   Remove the steaks from the oven and surround them with the fried bananas. Decorate with parsley and serve immediately.

Note: You may like to accompany the abalone with similarly-fried pineapple disks instead of the banana.

AVOCADO SEA FOAM WITH CUCUMBER OUTRIGGER CANOES AND A CARGO OF SHRIMP AND LOBSTER

(HAWAI'I)

No book on Pacific food would be complete for North Americans without one of those extravagant and ostentatious presentations representing the glamour and romance of ocean voyages to the Hawaiian Islands in the 1930s. This is for fun. This is the type of dish presented in a Matson Navigation Company's opulent buffet in those days when a cruise to Hawai'i was a fashionable adventure. It was a culture and time where lives were dominated by a quest for continuing gaiety, everybody was perpetually young; where horizons were unlimited, pastimes luxurious and sophisticated, and where your First Class bill of fare conjured visions of the exotic destination.

Imagine bobbed and marcelled hairstyles, bias-cut, frilly but unabashedly pretty dresses; your dance partner was either William Powell or Myrna Loy. When your ship (perhaps the S.S. *Lurline*) docked at pier 9, next to the ten-storey Aloha Tower, the hula dancers, ukuleles, and steel guitars were there to greet you on the quay. You smelled the fragrant *pikake* and ginger leis placed around your neck as you stepped off the gangplank onto Hawaiian soil. You booked into the Royal Hawaiian and experienced the gracious Honolulu of that time—swing bands, starlit nights, the booming surf of Waikiki Beach—and were convinced that this way of life would never end.

AVOCADO SEA FOAM

Serves a party

3 3-ounce packets of lime gelatin	1 teaspoon of salt
3 cups of hot water	1 cup of mayonnaise
6 tablespoons of freshly squeezed lime juice	2 cups of avocado purée
	1 cup of whipping cream

1. Dissolve **1 packet** of lime gelatin in **1 cup** of hot water. Chill the mixture until it just begins to thicken but not set. Pour the liquid gelatin in a thin layer onto a large, silver buffet tray. Refrigerate the lined tray to set the gelatin and for use in Step 3, **Avocado Sea Foam.**

2. In a large, non-reactive mixing bowl, dissolve the **remaining** packets of gelatin in the final **2 cups** of water. Let the mixture cool and thicken slightly. Stir in the lime juice, salt, mayonnaise and avocado purée. In a separate, medium mixing bowl, whip the cream to form stiff peaks. Fold the whipped cream into the gelatin mixture. Stir gently into a uniform, thick cream.

3. Spread the cream over the set gelatin leaving a 1+-inch margin around the perimeter. Use a frosting spatula or dinner knife to sculpt the cream into uneven waves. Replace the **Avocado Sea Foam** in the refrigerator to set until ready for use in **Assembly.**

OUTRIGGER CANOES

3 large cucumbers, halved lengthwise	several banana leaves, washed, drained and softened
several palm or banana leaf ribs (satay sticks may be substituted)	*(see page 21)*, stems removed

1. Take **5** of the cucumber halves and scoop out the seeds and flesh leaving walls of skin and flesh about 1/4-inch thick. (These will be the canoe hulls.) Scoop the seeds out of the **6th** cucumber half. Slice it lengthwise into 5 long, slivers. (These will be the outriggers.)

2. Split the ribs into slivers about 6 inches in length. (These will be the spars.) Split several more ribs into stouter slivers about 8–9 inches long. (These will be the masts.) Force 2 "spar" ribs into the side of each cucumber "hull," equally

spaced and at right angles to the "hulls." Impale the cucumber "outriggers" on the "spars" of each of the 5 canoes.

3. With kitchen shears, cut large, acute right triangles from the banana leaves. (These will be the sails.) Thread the longer rib "masts" through the longest side of the "sails." Continue until you have 5 "sails" and "masts" but do not attach them at this time; save for **Assembly.**

CARGO

$3/4$ pound of lobster meat, cooked and cut into $3/4$-inch chunks

$3/4$ pound of medium (31- to 40-count per pound) shrimp, peeled, deveined and cooked

$1/2$ cup of coconut cream *(see page 19)*

1 tablespoon of freshly squeezed lemon juice

$1/4$ teaspoon of paprika

$1/4$ teaspoon of cayenne

$1/2$ cup of seedless grapes

$1/4$ teaspoon of salt

1. In a large, non-reactive mixing bowl, combine all the ingredients. Toss and refrigerate until ready for use in Step 2, **Assembly.**

ASSEMBLY

the tray of Avocado Sea Foam

the 5 cucumber Outrigger Canoes

the 5 "mast" and "sail" assemblies

the Cargo

orchid or hibiscus blossoms for garnish

1. Set the **Avocado Sea Foam** tray on your working surface. Arrange the **Outrigger Canoes** as if they were sailing in formation across the foam. (Make sure they are all sailing in the same direction!)
2. Carefully spoon equal portions of the **Cargo** into each of the **Outrigger Canoes,** heaping it in the center to support the next addition of the "masts." Stick the "mast" with its "sail" through the center of the **Cargo.**
3. Garnish the tray with the blossoms and serve immediately as the centerpiece of an extravagant Oceanian buffet table.

TABOOS (TAPUS)

One day, over a decade past, the chief of tiny Ulithi atoll in the Western Carolines of Micronesia issued a draconian edict. For three weeks, no islander would be allowed to have anything to do with the sea. This created a severe hardship for the atoll dwellers: it meant an embargo on fishing, traveling, gathering seafood, cooking in seawater— even on personal ablutions. The crime that occasioned this punishment was that someone had anonymously killed and eaten a green turtle on the chief's island. To compound the felony, *only* chiefs were allowed to kill these harmless creatures; a

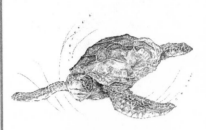

Green turtle

mandatory provision on this and many Pacific islands. Harsh and as broad as the pronouncement was, in bygone days, had the offender been found, he would have been immediately executed. By stern laws and taboos such as these, the most ancient order of reptiles that still exist, Testudines, was traditionally protected throughout Oceania.

Taboos and the relaxing thereof are the province of the chiefs and magicians. Sometimes they function as tribal laws. Many of them apply to women and the prohibitions of certain social conduct. Some taboos are issued for the preservation of fish and reptile

species. Other are meant as punishments on the village or certain members for misdemeanors or serious crimes. (The latter two are usually temporary. Those restricting women are permanent. So is the punishment applying to all upon transgression.)

Taboos are placed tribally on objects or animals reserved for special use. (They may be removed or rescinded in times of hardship or famine.) For instance, the women of the Fish Creek group (Australian aborigines) were forbidden to eat kangaroo meat. Since the men were only hunting kangaroos, the women eventually revolted against an almost exclusive diet of yams and the male-imposed taboo was hastily lifted!

KOVU VONU

Turtle Baked in Banana Leaves (FIJI)

Turtles provide some of the most highly prized meat for island feasts. While I do not advocate hunting that contributes to the extinction of any species of these incredible reptiles, on some of the Pacific Islands, the chiefly *tapu*, or preservation system, is enforced, backed by local, governmental regulation. These systems forbid the harvesting of turtles or their eggs until it is decided that their numbers have again become numerous and sustainable in local waters. This entails the raising of the young in protected water until they are old enough to withstand the depredations of their predators and successfully undertake their long, migratory sea journeys.

Because the focus of this preservation effort is not only to preserve an endangered species for posterity, but also to ensure that turtles may be taken for consumption in limited and controlled quantities, in this spirit and, considering the historic role of turtle in Pacific food, I include an authentic turtle recipe in this chapter.

Classically, this is an earth-pit oven recipe. Therefore, if you are fastidious about authenticity, please see page 129.

Serves 4

1–2 large banana leaves, softened *(see page 21)*, **central ribs two-thirds excised, or 18-inch × 14-inch rectangle of heavy-duty aluminum foil**

1 pound of turtle meat, cut into 1-inch cubes

1/2 pound of turtle fat, cubed

1 yellow onion, peeled and coarsely chopped

4 green onions, both white and green, thinly sliced into disks

2 medium tomatoes, coarsely chopped

2 cloves of garlic, smashed, peeled and minced

1 teaspoon of fresh gingerroot, peeled and minced

1 green chili pepper *(Serrano or Jalapeño)*, **minced**

a dash of White Wine Worcestershire sauce (optional)

1 teaspoon of smoke seasoning liquid

1/2 teaspoon of salt

1/4 teaspoon of freshly ground black pepper

1. Heat your oven to 300° Fahrenheit.
2. Arrange the banana leaves or foil on your counter top or large cutting board.
3. Place the turtle meat and its fat in the center of the banana leaf or foil.
4. Now, sprinkle over the top of the turtle meat the following: onion; green onions; tomatoes; garlic; ginger; chili pepper. Shake on the Worcestershire sauce and smoke seasoning liquid.
5. Season with the salt and pepper.
6. Carefully and tightly fold the banana leaves or foil over the mixture to form a neat package. (If you are using the leaves, tie the package securely with string. If using the foil, fold and crimp the edges to form a tight seal.)

7.   Place the packet in a large baking or roasting pan and add $1/4$ cup of water if you are using banana leaves, and tent them with aluminum foil. (If you are already using foil as a wrapper, you should not add the water.)

8.   Place the pan in your oven and cook it for about $1^1/_2$ hours.

9.   When the cooking is complete, remove the pan from the oven. Use cooking tongs to set the parcel on a large serving platter. Cut and remove the strings or partially unwrap the aluminum, peeling the top back to reveal the savory contents before serving. Present immediately.

Note: For substitutions, you may use chicken pieces (with skin) and any high-fat fish (see table, "A Selection of Popular Bony Fish in Oceania," on page 98) plus 1 tablespoon of canola oil.

SHRIMP IN A GARLIC, BANANA AND CHILI SAUCE

(GUAM)

This aromatic, robust sauce adds a new dimension to common shrimp. To enjoy the lusciousness of these crustaceans with garlic, banana and chili complement, you are invited, island fashion, to pluck them from the sauce by their tails and eat them with your fingers. (Of course, if digital dining offends your sensibilities, knives, forks and spoons are acceptable.)

Coconut Rice (see page 193) is the recommended accompaniment.

Serves 6

3 tablespoons of canola oil	$1/_2$ teaspoon of dried red pepper flakes
2 pounds of extra-large (16- to 20-count per pound) raw shrimp, shelled (with the tails left attached) and deveined	3 tablespoons of tomato paste
	$1/_2$ cup of water
	$1/_2$ cup of white vinegar
	$1/_3$ cup of sugar
1 medium onion, peeled and finely chopped	1 large banana, peeled and mashed
6 cloves of garlic, smashed, peeled and minced	2 green bell peppers, cored, seeded and sliced into slivers
$1/_2$-inch piece of fresh gingerroot, peeled and minced	$1/_2$ teaspoon of salt
	$1/_4$ teaspoon of freshly ground black pepper

1. Place a large, non-reactive frying pan over medium-high heat and pour in the oil. When a haze forms over the oil, carefully add all the shrimp. Stir, turn and fry them for less than a minute, or until they change color. Immediately remove the shrimp from the pan (with tongs) and set them aside for use in Step 5.
2. Reduce the heat to medium and stir in the onion. Stir-fry for about 2 minutes or until it is softened. Add the garlic and ginger and continue to sauté for about 1 minute.
3. Stir in the pepper flakes and tomato paste. Continue to cook, stirring, for about 2 minutes. Now add the water.
4. When the mixture returns to the simmer, add the vinegar and sugar, and stir to dissolve the sugar. Introduce the mashed banana, stir and reduce the heat to medium-low.
5. Add the bell pepper and let the mixture cook for about 1 minute, stirring. Season with the salt and pepper and return the shrimp to the sauce.
6. When the shrimp are just heated through, transfer the shrimp and sauce to a serving bowl and present immediately.

Note: This recipe could work very well with scallops as a substitute for shrimp.

KRAB KOKONAS WETEM SOS BLONG KOKONAS MO LAE

Coconut Crab in Coconut Cream and Garlic Sauce

(VANUATU)

One of the most memorable dishes I have ever experienced was in the restaurant of the Hotel Rossi in Port Vila overlooking the cerulean waters of Vila Harbor and Erakor Island (set like a verdant, upturned pudding basin in the middle of the bay). The dish was coconut crab.

Ten years before, while living on Guam, I became acquainted with the clanking monster crab the Chamorros call *ayuyu* (pronounced "a-juju"). I had speculated about the symmetry of coconut-eating crab simmered in coconut cream but I had never tried it.

Now I was eating this gastronomic poetry with an added Gallic touch—garlic and lots of it. Not only was the flavor and texture sensational—epicurean satori—

but it was one of the most gloriously messy, dig-in-up-to-your-wrists dishes I have enjoyed. (There was a large basin of water at my elbow, an outsized linen napkin tucked under my chin and a pile of additional napkins beside my place setting. I used them all and requested a fresh basin of water before I finished.) It was a Lucullan feast!

The chef was not able to give me the recipe because, by 4:00 p.m. when I was finally replete, he had already gone for a well-deserved break. However, with a grateful obeisance to the restaurant, here is my adaptation. You may substitute your favorite crab in place of the giant *Birgus latro*, but I guarantee you will never again accept any substitutions after you have experienced the original. (Unfortunately, this may require a trip to the South Pacific or Micronesia.)

Serves 1 (generously) or 2 (reluctantly)

1 4^1/$_2$-pound (or larger) coconut crab	2 cups of thick coconut milk (*see page 19*)
2 tablespoons of butter	1 heaped tablespoon of parsley, minced
6 cloves of garlic, smashed, peeled and finely chopped	4 green onions, both white and green, finely chopped
1 heaped tablespoon of flour	1 cup of whipping cream
1 cup of court bouillon or an equivalent volume of liquid from the crab boil in Step 2	2 tablespoons of coriander, chopped plus several sprigs reserved for garnish
1 teaspoon of sea salt	a soupçon of Ricard or Pernod
1 teaspoon of white pepper	

1. Almost fill a stockpot with water and bring it to a rolling boil over high heat. Introduce the coconut crab and cover. Reduce the heat to medium and cook the crab for about 5 minutes or until the shell turns scarlet.

2. When the crustacean is cooked, remove it from the water and set aside to drain and cool. After a few minutes, when it's cool enough to handle, crack the body shell and legs with a mallet and/or crab crackers. (Carefully and precisely crack the shell so the meat can be removed but not so vigorously as to dismember the creature.) Set aside for use in Step 6.

3. Set a large (large enough to accommodate the whole crab) saucepan over medium heat. Melt the butter and stir fry the garlic briefly, until it begins to change color. Add the flour and stir constantly to make a *roux*.

Coconut crab in coconut cream and garlic sauce

4.   Pour in the court bouillon, modulate the heat as necessary and stir frequently to create a smooth, thickened sauce. Season with the salt and pepper.

5.   Add **1 cup** of the coconut milk and stir in the parsley and green onions.

6.   While still on heat, deposit the crab in the sauce. Stir and turn the creature as necessary to thoroughly coat it with the sauce. Reduce the heat and let the mixture simmer for about 5 minutes.

7.   Pour in the remaining cup of coconut milk, stir and let the sauce return to a simmer.

8.   Add the chopped coriander and whipping cream. Stir and let the mixture heat through and thicken.

9.   Add the Ricard, stir a final time and remove the crab to a large heated serving bowl. Pour the sauce over the creature, garnish with the coriander sprigs and serve at once accompanied by crackers, mallet(s) and a generous supply of napkins.

Note: While authentic and traditional, the above method of serving may not be appropriate for a formal dinner party where evening finery is the sartorial imperative. When the linen is Irish and the porcelain is Spode, I recommend briefly rinsing the creature (after removing it from the sauce in Step 9), dismembering it and stacking the parts on a heated platter. Pour the sauce into separate serving bowls and decorate each place setting with finger bowls, crab forks and redundant supplies of your finest napery.

SWEET POTATO AND SHRIMP CAKES WITH TOMATO-ORANGE SAUCE

(NEW CALEDONIA)

This large island with a Mediterranean-type climate and a capital, Nouméa, with many of the amenities of a miniature Paris, is a contrast to the rest of tropical Melanesia.

Here is a crisp and satisfying version of fish cakes that has elements of *cuisine bourgeoise*. This is not surprising since the French colonialists were predominately middle class.

Serve this dish as a brunch buffet or at a lunch accompanied by a fresh, green salad.

Sweet Potato and Shrimp Cakes

Serves 4

4 cups of sweet potato, peeled, cooked and mashed

1/2 cup of small shrimp, peeled, cooked and minced

1 tablespoon of parsley, minced

1 teaspoon of Worcestershire sauce

1/4 teaspoon of cayenne

1/2 teaspoon of salt

1/4 teaspoon of freshly ground black pepper

1 egg, beaten

1 cup of thick coconut milk *(see page 19)*

2 tablespoons of dried, unsweetened coconut flakes

potato or all-purpose flour (as necessary)

1/2 cup of canola oil

1.   Place the potato, shrimp, onion, parsley and Worcestershire sauce into a large mixing bowl. Season with the cayenne, salt and pepper. Add the egg and coconut milk, and work lightly to a smooth batter. Sprinkle in the coconut flakes.

2.   Now, working with your hands and using as much flour as necessary, knead the mixture into a dough thick enough to mold. Separate and form the dough into small, flat cakes, each about 1/2-inch thick. Sift a dusting of additional flour over both sides of the cakes.

3.   Heat the oil, about 2 tablespoons at a time, in a large skillet over medium-high heat. Fry the cakes, three at a time, stirring and turning until they have a uniform, golden crust on both sides. Assemble the cooked cakes on a cookie sheet and hold in a low oven until all are fried.

4.   Serve hot or warm accompanied by the **Tomato-Orange Sauce.**

TOMATO-ORANGE SAUCE

1^1/$_2$ tablespoons of canola oil
1 medium onion, peeled and
     minced
1^1/$_2$ cups of tomatoes,
     blanched, peeled and
     coarsely chopped (canned
     tomatoes may be substituted)
1 cup of freshly squeezed
     orange juice

^{1}/$_2$ teaspoon of orange zest,
     grated
1 teaspoon of sugar
1 teaspoon of salt
1 tablespoon of basil leaves,
     chopped

1.   Place a medium, non-reactive saucepan over a medium-high setting, pour in the oil and let it come up to frying temperature.

2.   Sauté the onions, stirring, until they become translucent. Add the tomatoes, orange juice and zest, sugar, salt and basil. Stir and let the mixture come to a boil. Reduce the heat to low and simmer the mixture for about 25 minutes.

3.   Empty the contents of the pan into your blender and blend on a high setting to a smooth purée. After blending, return the sauce to the pan to reheat. (At this time, if the sauce is not suitably thick, you may increase the heat and accomplish a slight reduction.) Serve hot or warm with the **Sweet Potato and Shrimp Cakes.**

Chapter 6

The Finest Food on the Fin

Pacific Ocean Fish Offerings

*The aged king of Mangaia informed me that in those days
a fleet of, say two hundred canoes—carrying only one man
apiece—would assemble in front of the site of the present
village of Oneroa at the beginning of the fishing-season.
The little leaf-gods would be got ready against the
appointed night, which was indicated by the recurrence of
the phase of the moon favorable for catching certain kinds
of fish. It was for Namu to give the word, and then the
entire fleet of canoes would start off.*

William Wyatt Gill, 1894, *From Darkness to Light In Polynesia*

The Pacific Islanders are almost genetic fishermen, by culture, customs
and environment. The sea is essential to those who inhabit the low
coral islands, with sparse support for farming, and the virtually barren
atolls. In those habitats, from the smallest child crouching in a tiny pool on
the exposed reef to catch a minnow, to the weathered stalwarts who nego-
tiate their canoes down the perpendicular cliff faces of storm-born waves in
the hunt for bonito, everyone harvests the waters.

Hands, stones, sticks, spears, nets and lines are all used in Oceania and
the choice of fishing method depends on the habits of the particular species
being hunted. Sometimes the methods, while effective, can seem comical,
almost bizarre to Westerners.

Members of the Belonidae family, needlefish or gar, are favorite food
fish throughout the Pacific, with habits and appearance much like the
barracuda or pike. They are voracious carnivores who prefer the surface.
Highly excitable, they will jump out of the water at the slightest provoca-
tion. The Melanesians and the Yapese of Micronesia catch them by flying a
palm-leaf or breadfruit-leaf kite from a canoe. The kite's tail is a long, fine
line that trolls the surface of the water with a lure made from strong spi-
ders' webs. The needlefish snaps at the lure and entangles its long, slender
jaws in the webs.

The Tahitians traditionally built special rafts to hunt needlefish. These had a wooden wall built up along one side. When they located a school, they circled the rafts, wall sides on the perimeter. In the middle of the circle, men in a canoe would beat the water with long, white sticks. The frenzied needlefish would attempt to jump over the rafts to escape but would strike the outer walls and fall, stunned, onto the floor of the rafts. Now, they were easily gathered in baskets.

Traditional Oceanian fish hooks are both practical and *objet d'art*, worthy of becoming collectors' items. On the Pacific atolls, with little other suitable materials, hooks were—and still are—fashioned from large sea shells and turtle shells. The Tahitians traditionally carved mother-of-pearl into hooks for catching dolphin fish, bonito and albacore. In ancient times, it was the ultimate Tahitian insult to a slain enemy to make fish hooks from his bones. Dog bones were also used on many islands for the same purpose; wicked-looking larger wooden hooks for shark were often studded with dogs' teeth as barbs.

Although commercially manufactured lines and nets have largely supplanted those made by hand, the Pacific Islanders still craft some of their fishing cordage from natural fibers such as the yellow hibiscus (*Hibiscus tiliaceus*). The men of Oceania make the cord; sitting and twisting and rolling a trio of strands along one thigh. I have seen them produce line almost automatically, while deep in discussions of village affairs or fishing. (It reminded me of the way that women will knit, sew and crochet whilst gossiping to one another.)

The resultant cord is braided or twisted with other cords for thick ropes. Traditional Tahitian nets were worked of three-strand cord, knotted into mesh four inches square. The light wood of the same yellow hibiscus mentioned previously provided floats for the perimeter of the nets. Stones, about three inches in diameter, wrapped in matted fiber before being attached, were used as weights.

When night fishing, Micronesians jerk the lines in the water to create phosphorescence that attracts fish

Wood and mother-of-pearl shark hook, 10 1/2 inches long. Cook Islands. (From the author's collection.)

Hotu or utu (Barringtonia asiatica) fruits and flowers

to the bait. The Marshallese also fish at night for bonito and flying fish, using nets from their canoes and torches to lure the catch.

The Pacific fishermen are expert in the science of stunning fish. No, not with blunt instruments nor explosives. They have discovered the toxic or narcotic effects of several shrubs and trees, the various roots and seeds of which can immobilize fish. Used thus, these toxins are assimilated, diluted and/or have their chemistry changed so they are harmless to humans. The dopey catch is merely scooped up and carried home, cooked and eaten with impunity.

My favorite of these "fishermen's friends" is the *Barringtonia asiatica* tree. I have happily picked its large pink-and-white tassel flowers and marveled at its curious, four-sided, green fruits like Cubist pears. The islanders grate the kernels of these and sprinkle them in the reef waters at low tide to stun fish. The fruits also dry naturally into gourds and fishermen attach them to nets as floats. Because of this buoyancy, the fruits with their seeds float across vast stretches of water, which is why the

Barringtonia tree shades beaches from the Marshalls to Fiji and across to Tahiti.

On sunset evenings in Guam, I would walk from our house down to the lagoon and take photographs of the *y talajero,* the net fishermen. To watch them gracefully fling their round, weighted nets high in the air over the water to fall in a perfect circle over the trapped fish, is to witness an ancient skill that is gradually being lost.

Another Pacific fishing method—one of the noisiest and most enjoyable for both participant and observer—is fish circling. Called *tautai taora,* or stone fishing in the Society Islands and *alele* in the Marshalls, it is rarely performed nowadays except as a tourist spectacle; it requires the active participation of the entire community. Men in canoes beat the water with stones on lines or sticks and palm fronds to alarm and drive a school toward the beach where a semicircle of villagers with a line of nets or a chain of palm fronds traps the shoal into an ever-decreasing circle. Splashing, ducking, shouting and laughter mixed with taunts and jokes accompany the communal process; the noise aids in the herding until the fish are netted. The exercise is usually celebrated with a fish bake and feast.

Here are some notes on dressing many of the families of Pacific bony fish:

> **BARRACUDA**—Fillet, then cut the fillets, through the skin, into large pieces. Place the pieces skin-side down and, with surgical precision, use your knife to cut or slice the meat away from the skin.
>
> **BASS**—Skin before cooking. The scales will come away with the skin. Be careful with the sharp dorsal spines.
>
> **BONEFISH**—Lives up to its name. Gut before filleting and remove the backbone. Pacific cooks scrape the soft flesh away from the bones with a spoon. Use for quenelle and fish cakes.

CREVALLE—Same family as the jacks. Also known as trevally. Large fish are skinned and filleted. Small ones are cooked with skin and filleted afterwards, if desired.

GOATFISH—Often cooked whole, then filleted.

GROUPER—No intramuscular bones so they fillet easily. The skin is very tough so they must be skinned. The large, cartilaginous heads make excellent fish stock.

JACK—See crevalle. Yellow jack should have its small scales flaked off. Do not skin.

MILKFISH—Many small, fine bones. Filleting takes about 20 minutes. Treat like bonefish.

MULLET—Merely clean and scale.

NEEDLEFISH—Skin and cut into tubular sections like eel. (This will require cutting through the backbone at each section.)

PARROTFISH—Gut. Its large scales can be pulled off. Unnecessary to skin. If you do, skin and scales will come away together.

PORGY—Choose the larger fish. Scale, gut, remove head and fins. Score the fish then remove backbone after cooking. Most bones will pull away with the backbone.

SCAD—No need to scale.

SNAPPER—Generally scaled but cooked in their skins. Fillet if desired. Sharp dorsal spines. Try cooking a whole, small (2–3 pounds) snapper with the head, Chinese-style.

TUNA—Remove the skin before cooking. Dark meat near spine is strongly flavored. Remove if desired. Some tuna species should not be frozen because the meat becomes mushy when defrosted.

WAHOO—Treat like barracuda.

Following is a table of the more familiar Pacific bony fish that includes descriptions, cooking and preparation methods, and substitutions to be found in Western markets.

(Text continued on p. 105.)

A Selection of Popular Bony Fish in Oceania

NOMENCLATURE VERNACULAR NAME(S) Family Species native name(s)[1]	RANGE OF SIZE/WEIGHT[2]	COOKING/PREPARATION METHODS	APPEARANCE, FLAVOR, TEXTURE	SUBSTITUTIONS	MISCELLANEA
BARRACUDA Sphyraenidae **SHARPFIN** *Sphyraena novaehollandiae* **BLACKSPOT** *Sphyraena forsteri* H. *kaku* C. *alu* M. *manga*	24 in. approx.) 6–12 lb.	Fillet then cut through skin. Remove skin only for soups and stews. Fry, broil, bake or barbecue.	Soft flesh when raw separates along grain lines. Firm meat, distinctive flavor when cooked.	California barracuda (*Sphyraena argentea*)	Steer clear of the great barracuda (S. *barracuda*). It has been responsible for cases of ciguatera poisoning. Buy only the smaller fish of the species.
BARRAMUNDI Centropomidae *Lates calcarifer* P.M. *amma* A. *barramundi*	3–6 ft. (approx.)	First fillet and remove skin then fry, bake, poach or sauté.	Mild, white firm flesh.	Grouper, snapper	Has an identity crisis: spends time in both fresh and salt water and is a protandrous hermaphrodite. Most begin life as male, spawn for a season or two and invert to female. The adults are a fighting fish and fun to catch.

A Selection of Popular Bony Fish in Oceania—Cont'd.

NOMENCLATURE VERNACULAR NAME(S) Family Species native name(s)[1]	RANGE OF SIZE/WEIGHT[2]	COOKING/PREPARATION METHODS	APPEARANCE, FLAVOR, TEXTURE	SUBSTITUTIONS	MISCELLANEA
DOLPHIN FISH Coryphaenidae *Coryphaena hippurus* H. *mahi mahi* C. *botague*	5–6 ft., about 70 lb.	Purchase as fillets or steaks. Bake, fry, grill, barbecue, poach, smoke or use in chowder.	Firm, sweet, mild white flesh. Skin is tough.	Black cod, cod, halibut, pompano	Dolphin fish should not be confused with dolphins, which are mammals—small, streamlined whales.
FLYING FISH Exocoetidae *Cypselurus* spp. H. *malolo* C. *gaga*	8–16 in.	Bake, fry or poach.	Delicate flavor but bony.		Flying fish tailplane up to a take-off speed of 40 mph. They glide about 1 ft. above the surface for a 30-sec. flight, then repeat the process.
GOAT FISH Mullidae *Parupeneus bifasciatus* *Mulloidichthys* spp. H. *munu, moano, kumu, weke, weke 'ula*	12–24 in.	Fry, sauté, bake, grill.	White meat with high fat[3] content.	Mackerel or any other high-fat fish	So called because the two barbels below the mouth resemble a goat's beard. Family includes red mullets and surmullets.
GROUPER Serranidae *Epinephelus* spp. H. *hapu'upu'u* C. *gadau* M. *alean*	Between several inches to almost 10 ft. Up to 800 lb.	Smaller species can be steamed whole. Larger fish are filleted and fried.	Clear, white delicate flesh.	Snapper	Large family includes several hundred species. Sequential hermaphrodite. Some larger species may be ciguatoxic.

(Continued)

99

A Selection of Popular Bony Fish in Oceania—Cont'd.

NOMENCLATURE VERNACULAR NAME(S) Family Species native name(s)[1]	RANGE OF SIZE/WEIGHT[2]	COOKING/PREPARATION METHODS	APPEARANCE, FLAVOR, TEXTURE	SUBSTITUTIONS	MISCELLANEA
HAWAIIAN FLAG-TAIL or SILVER "PERCH" Kuhliidae *Kuhlia sandvicensis* H. *ahole*	9 in. (approx.)	Raw, dried, salted or in relish. Broil.	Silvery-gray skin fading to a white belly. Rich flavor esteemed by ancient Hawaiians.	Any small fish with high-fat content	Similar species found in Central Polynesia. Foreigners were sometimes called *aholehole* because of their pale skin.
JACK FISH (FAMILY) Carangidae RAINBOW RUNNER *Elagatis bipinnulata* H. *kamanu*	Up to 4 ft. and 33 lb. (max.)	Wrapped in ti leaves and baked in an *imu* or eaten raw. Bake, broil (skin before cooking).	Firm pink/white meat.	Cod, flounder, halibut	Available throughout the Pacific. Fished seasonally. Juveniles called *i'e* on Guam. (Family includes: pompanos, crevalles, runners.)
MARLIN or SAILFISH Istiophoridae H. *a'u* (all species) BLUE MARLIN *Makaira nigricans* SILVER MARLIN *Makaira indica*	Usually between 300–400 lb. but can exceed 1400 lb. and 11 ft.	Purchase as fillets or steaks. Broil, bake, barbecue, fry or smoke.	White, firm meat with good grain that behaves like beef steak.	Mako shark, swordfish	Can consume whole tuna or squid.

A Selection of Popular Bony Fish in Oceania—Cont'd.

NOMENCLATURE VERNACULAR NAME(S) Family *Species* *native name(s)*[1]	RANGE OF SIZE/WEIGHT[2]	COOKING/PREPARATION METHODS	APPEARANCE, FLAVOR, TEXTURE	SUBSTITUTIONS	MISCELLANEA
MULLET Mugilidae STRIPED MULLET *Mugil cephalus* H. *'ama 'ama* C. *laigwan*	Adults: 18–20 in.	Filleted and broiled in ti leaves. Stuff, bake, steam, fry, grill whole. Also use in casseroles and fish soups.	Marries well with strong flavorings, such as curries, because of the robust flavor of the flesh.	Any white-meat fish with a high fat content	Many popular species available throughout the Pacific. Ancient Hawaiians raised them in fish-ponds.
NEEDLE FISH or GAR Belonidae *Platybelone argala platyura* *Tylosurus crocodilus* *Ablennes hians* H. *'aha 'aha* C. *pulos* V.B. *longmaot*	For all species: 14–40 in.	Bake, steam, fry and sauce.	Firm, snow-white flesh with a delicate flavor. Tends to be dry after cooking.	Any white-meat fish with a low fat content	Fished throughout the Pacific. Particularly esteemed in Melanesia.
PARROT FISH Scaridae *Scarus* spp. H. *'uhu* C. *laggua*	Some species reach almost 4 ft. Most between 6–13 in. About 2–6 lb.	Wrapped in ti leaves and baked in an *imu*. Steam, fry, bake, braise. Eaten raw.	Pale pink meat, sweet and moist.	Wrasse, goat fish, red mullet	Numerous species Pacific-wide. Related to wrasses. Hawaiians relished the liver. Fish sometimes caught with octopus ink rubbed on hook.

(Continued)

A Selection of Popular Bony Fish in Oceania—Cont'd.

NOMENCLATURE VERNACULAR NAME(S) Family Species native name(s)[1]	RANGE OF SIZE/WEIGHT[2]	COOKING/PREPARATION METHODS	APPEARANCE, FLAVOR, TEXTURE	SUBSTITUTIONS	MISCELLANEA
RUDDER FISH Kyphosidae **HIGH-FIN RUDDER FISH** Kyphosus cinerascens H. *nenue* C. *guili*	Up to 14 in. About 2–5 lb.	Fry, bake, poach, broil. Use in chowders and soups. Eaten raw.	Mild, juicy white meat, but with the occasional pungent odor of entrails typical of herbivorous fishes.	Perch, snapper, porgy, flounder	Many species fished in Micronesia, Hawai'i, Tuamotus and the Great Barrier Reef. Highly esteemed by the ancient Hawaiian ali'i.
SCAD Carangidae **BIG-EYED SCAD** Selar crumenoph-thalmus H. *akule* C. *atulai*	12 oz.–2 lb.	Baked in ti-leaf bundles in an *imu*. Broil, bake, braise, steam. Eaten raw.	Similar to but stronger in flavor than mackerel scad (H. *'opelu*).	Any small mackerel	Fished at night with handlines, Feb. through Sept.
SNAPPER Lutjanidae Lutjanus spp. H. *'opakapaka*, *onaga, uku* C. *kaka'ka'* T. *to'au*	10–30 in.	Steam, fry, poach, bake, broil, dried. Eaten raw.	Mild, moist flesh; delicate flavor.	Flounder, sole, halibut, whiting	Red species sometimes used in ancient Polynesia as offerings. Throughout Oceania, certain larger species ciguatoxic. Choose only fish up to 4–5 lb. Skin all tuna before cooking.

A Selection of Popular Bony Fish in Oceania—Cont'd.

NOMENCLATURE VERNACULAR NAME(S) Family Species native name(s)[1]	RANGE OF SIZE/WEIGHT[2]	COOKING/PREPARATION METHODS	APPEARANCE, FLAVOR, TEXTURE	SUBSTITUTIONS	MISCELLANEA
TUNA Scombridae				For all tunas except the blue fin, substitute any of the large mackerel family	
ALBACORE (LONG FIN) *Thunnus alalunga* H. **'ahi palaha**	Up to 39 in., 40–80 lb.	Raw or baked, wrapped in ti leaves. Steaks can be broiled or poached.	Lightest meat of all tuna; white to pale pink. Mostly canned.		
YELLOW FIN (ALLISON) *Thunnus albacares* H. **'ahi**	Up to 8 ft. and 390+ lb. Up to 13 ft.	Sashimi. Marinate and barbecue, fry, poach, bake, broil. Also soups and stews.	Red soft flesh; firm and beige when cooked.		
BLUE FIN *Thunnus thynnus* H. **'ahi** J. **maguro**	and 1800 lb. (approx.)	Sashimi. Steaks can be barbecued or broiled.	Compact and heavy. Resembling beef.	Swordfish	
SKIP JACK (BONITO) *Katsuwonus pelamis* H. **aku** M. **lojabwill**	Up to 40 in. Between 3–40 lb.	Sashimi. Barbecue, fry, bake. Also used in soups and stews.	Red flesh, more flavorful than paler meat.		Do not freeze skipjack or little tunny because their flesh becomes mushy after defrosting.
LITTLE TUNNY (MACKEREL, BONITO) *Euthynnus affinis* H. **kawakawa**	Up to 30 in. Between 8–21 lb.	As above. But reduce the fat in cooking because the flesh is oily.	Flesh has more fat and richer flavor than skipjack.		

(Continued)

103

A Selection of Popular Bony Fish in Oceania—Cont'd.

NOMENCLATURE VERNACULAR NAME(S) Family Species native name(s)[1]	RANGE OF SIZE/WEIGHT[2]	COOKING/PREPARATION METHODS	APPEARANCE, FLAVOR, TEXTURE	SUBSTITUTIONS	MISCELLANEA
WAHOO or KING FISH Scombridae Acanthocybium solanderi H. ono	Up to 6 ft. Between 30–120 lb.	Do not over cook. Fry, bake, barbecue, grill, poach. Marinate first then serve with a sauce. May also be eaten raw.	Sweet and mild flesh.	Halibut, swordfish, haddock, cod	Surface-dwelling game fish that feeds on smaller fish and squid. Ono translates to "delicious."
WALU or OIL FISH Gempylidae Ruvettus pretiosus F. walu	Between 5–6 ft. About 100 lb.	Excellent smoked. Baked in taro leaves, stewed, curried. Marinated raw in lime juice for seafood salads.	White, flaky meat with extremely high fat content. Delicious, robust flavor.	Large mackerel, little tunny	Immensely popular in Fijian cuisine.

[1]H. = Hawaiian; C. = Chamorro; M. = Marshallese; P.M. = Papuan Motu; V.B. = Vanuatu Bislama; J. = Japanese; T. = Tahitian; F. = Fijian; A. = Australian
[2]Weights (oz. and lb.) are avoirdupois.
[3]Descriptive terms "high fat" or "oily" indicate concentrations of unsaturated fish oil (fatty acids). On balance, the current view is that a diet rich in fish oil tends to retard the development of heart disease.

KAMANO LOMI

Lomi Salmon (HAWAI'I)

From the historic (but unrecorded) occasion when a Hawaiian sailor off a whaler entered an eatery on the Pacific Northwest coast of America and tasted salmon, it was love at first bite. The first tasting could equally well have occurred in the islands, for salted salmon—similar to lox—was being shipped to Hawai'i as early as 1830. In whatever manner the acquaintance took place, the affection blossomed into a full-fledged love affair with the fish. Hawaiians undertook salmon-fishing trips to Klamath, Oregon. Hawai'i imported salted salmon in ever-increasing quantities.

Early on, salmon was christened *kamano* in the Hawaiian language. Moreover, it was elevated to feastly status, supplanting local fish in the traditional dish in which fish was massaged and mixed with onions and tomatoes. (Hawaiian for massage is *lomi,* thus the title of this traditional recipe.)

Salted salmon must first be soaked in several changes of fresh water for about 3 hours (similar to codfish). The traditional and natural partner to **Lomi Salmon** is *poi.*

Serves 10

1 pound of salted, boned salmon belly, skinned and soaked in several changes of fresh water for about 3 hours	1/2 teaspoon of white pepper
14 medium, firm tomatoes, blanched, skinned and finely chopped	1 bunch of green onions, both white and green, finely chopped, covered and refrigerated

1.   Drain the salmon, rinse it a final time and test for saltiness (the salinity should be evident but not dominating). Place the fish in a non-reactive mixing bowl and tear it into small pieces or shreds with your fingers, removing any stray bones, ligaments, pieces of skin, etc.
2.   Add the tomatoes and season with pepper. Thoroughly combine the mixture, cover and refrigerate.
3.   Fill a large, glass (punch?) bowl with cracked ice. Press a smaller glass serving bowl (large enough to accommodate the completed dish) into the ice. Place the bowl-inside-bowl arrangement in your freezer or refrigerator.

4.   Just before serving remove all the ingredients and the bowls from the refrigerator. Stir the green onions into the salmon mixture and transfer the **Lomi Salmon** to the chilled serving bowl on the ice. Serve immediately.

KARE JETAAR

Curried Snapper (MARSHALL ISLANDS)

Micronesia occupies a total area within the Pacific equivalent to the size of the continental United States, but the exposed square-mile-area of its islands are less than one-half of the total acreage of Rhode Island.

Obviously, much of its islanders' customs, crafts and cooking are focused on the sea. Not only are the Micronesians arguably the most skilled seafarers and navigators in Oceania, but they have built—and still do—some of the finest and fastest oceangoing outrigger canoes. Their navigational charts of atolls, currents and other maritime phenomena, fashioned from palm ribs and shells, are still made (if only for tourists). But it is fishing—the intimate knowledge and refinement of the art—that is their métier since, except on the taller islands, they are dependent on the sea's bounty for three-quarters of their food.

While the Micronesians intimately know their (sometimes) small specks of land, precarious and costly trophies from the ocean, their world is also a continuation of land to water: the lagoon and the sea beyond with its small, oft-visited but uninhabited atolls. They are familiar with those coral barriers to the waves, within which they remember instinctively where the best reef fish will be found. They also map the strong currents that guide the pelagic vagabonds; the giant, silvery oceanic pirates. The islanders know their seasons of traveling and wait patiently for them to come within reach of their lines and lures for that triumphant moment of capture.

To the people of the complex network of islands and sea, the whole cosmos is known: identifiable, ordered, understood and beloved.

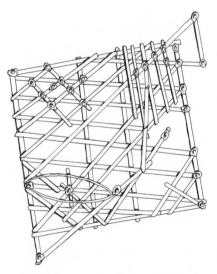

Carolinian navigational stick chart

The coral islands of the Marshalls lie at the extreme eastern end of Micronesia. They are low atolls, little more than bumps on the horizon, composed of white coral sand and coconut palm. They encompass one of the world's largest lagoons, Kwajalein, but the district capital is Majuro, far to the southeast. R. L. Stevenson is said to have called it "the pearl of the Pacific."

On Majuro, this dish is usually made with a local snapper they call *jetaar,* the native name for bluelined snapper (*Lutjanus kasmira*). We can substitute any snapper fillets that are currently available.

Serves 6

1/2 cup of flour
1/2 teaspoon of salt
2 tablespoons of curry powder
1/2 cup of thin coconut milk
    (*see page 19*)
6 snapper fillets (approximately
    6 ounces each)
6 tablespoons of canola oil
1 medium onion, peeled and
    finely chopped

2 cloves of garlic, smashed,
    peeled and minced
3/4 cup of water
1 cup of sweet potato, peeled
    and cut into 1/2-inch dice
1/2 cup of coconut cream (*see
    page 19*)
salt to taste

1. In a medium mixing bowl combine the flour, salt and **1 teaspoon** of curry powder. Pour the thin coconut milk into a shallow bowl.
2. Dip the snapper fillets first into the milk and then into the flour/curry powder mixture to coat them evenly. Shake off any surplus and arrange on a plate near your range top for use in the next step.
3. Heat **4 tablespoons** of the oil in a skillet over a medium-high setting and fry the fish until golden brown on both sides. Drain on a plate lined with paper towels.
4. Place a large, non-reactive saucepan over medium-high heat, pour in the remaining **2 tablespoons** oil and let it come up to frying temperature. Add the onion and stir-fry for about 1 minute. Continue with the garlic for about 30 more seconds.
5. Add the **remainder** of the curry powder, reduce heat to medium-low and continue stirring and frying for 1 more minute. Pour in the water and add the sweet potato. Increase the heat as necessary to bring the mixture to a boil. Immediately reduce the heat as necessary to maintain a simmer and let the mixture cook for about 5 minutes.
6. Introduce the fish fillets from Step 3 into the sweet potato/curry sauce. After the fillets come up to temperature (less than 1 minute), add the coconut cream. Salt to taste and let the liquid return to a simmer.
7. Transfer to a serving bowl or plate and accompany with plain rice. Serve immediately.

PEARL DIVER'S MARINATED SHARK STEAKS

(TUAMOTUS)

Apart from providing utterly beautiful examples of perfectly-formed atolls, the Tuamotuan archipelago in French Polynesia has several claims to fame. Its north-easternmost island, Pukapuka (a tiny dollop of coral, 100 miles from its nearest neighbor), was the first land within the Pacific Ocean that the exhausted discoverer, Ferdinand Magellan, sighted. Fortunately for his half-starved sailors there were turtles to kill and fresh water to drink. (Refreshed and replenished, they then headed northwest across the ocean, ending up in Guam, where they killed more than turtles.)

The Tuamotus are a center of the Pacific pearling industry, producing superb black gems that are merely pieces of sand surrounded by calcium carbonate. (There are, of course, many other varieties besides black.)

The commercial pearling enterprise began serendipitously. In the first decade of the 19th century, whilst looking for a source of pigs for the lucrative Polynesian salt-pork trade, Captain John Buyers and (Supercargo) John Turnbull (of the

Magellan's ship Victoria (Adapted from an old print.)

108

Margaret) landed on Makemo atoll. In the course of bargaining for porkers, they noticed a warrior wearing a necklace of pearl oyster shells. At a neighboring island, they bartered a mirror for a collar of pearls. Subsequently, Buyers founded the first pearling company in the Pacific.

In the early days, the islanders dove to depths of up to 100 feet, exhibiting extraordinary lung capacity with the only diving aid available—goggles.

An early account of the perils of pearl diving follows (*Encyclopaedia Britannica or, a Dictionary of Arts and Sciences,* etc., M,DCC,LXXI, by a Society of Gentlemen in Scotland):

> At whatever depths the divers are, the light is so great that they easily see whatever passes in the sea: and to their great consternation sometimes perceive monstrous fishes, from which all their address in mudding the waters, *etc.* will not always save them, but they unhappily become their prey: and of all the dangers of the fishery, this is one of the greatest and most usual.

There is an element of classic reversal and retribution in the title and content of this Tuamotuan recipe; a possible subhead: "Man Bites Shark!"

Serves 6

1¹/2 pounds of shark steak, ¹/2-inch thick (approximately), **cut into 6 equal portions**	1 teaspoon of ginger juice (optional)
¹/2 cup of thick coconut milk (*see page 19*)	1 small onion, peeled and minced
¹/2 cup of mayonnaise	1¹/2 tablespoons of soy sauce
¹/4 cup of freshly squeezed lemon juice	¹/2 teaspoon of freshly ground black pepper
	2 tablespoons of butter
	1 teaspoon of canola oil

1.   Place the shark steaks in a large, shallow dish. Combine all the remaining ingredients **except** the fat (butter and canola oil) in a small, non-reactive mixing bowl. Mix and combine all the ingredients and pour it over the fish. Cover, refrigerate and let the shark marinate for about 3 hours.
2.   Drain the fish from the marinade and pat dry with paper towels. Reserve the liquid for the next step. Heat the fats in a large frying pan over a medium-high setting. When the oils are up to temperature, carefully deposit the fish into the pan. Fry the fillets, about 3 minutes on a side. Drain the excess oil over the frying pan with a spatula and collect the fish on an ovenproof serving dish. Keep the dish warm in your oven at its lowest setting.
3.   Return the marinade to the frying pan over medium-low. (If the consistency appears too thick, dilute it with about 1 tablespoon of water.) Heat the marinade

for about 2 minutes, or until it is warmed through. (Modulate the heat as necessary to prevent boiling.)

4.   Pour the heated marinade back over the shark steaks and serve immediately.

Note: Another firm-fleshed white fish, such as swordfish or marlin, may be substituted.

MAHI MAHI KAENA

Dolphin Fish with Mountain Apples and Japanese Horseradish Cream (HAWAI'I)

Originally, these pelagic nomads were not particularly prized by the Hawaiians, being difficult to catch—their velocity in the water required lines and reels rather than nets. It was only when tourism came to the Islands in the '50s that *haoles* discovered and popularized *mahi mahi*. Today, unfortunately, almost none is caught fresh in island waters; most of the vast harvest is supplied, already frozen, by Taiwanese or Japanese fishing boats.

Mahi mahi

However, regarding fishing territories, an old Hawaiian legend explains the role the gods played in determining the areas of the sea in which fishermen would find their catch. It tells of the man, Maikoha, who was driven into exile for some misdemeanor. (In mythology, even the most inconsequential oversight could offend any of the many tribal rules and taboos.) Maikoha's four sisters dutifully followed him from home to fates apportioned to them by the gods. Each was changed into a fishing area or fish pond and to each sister came the fish allocated to that area. The third of Maikoha's sisters married a chief, named Kaena, from the Wai'anae Mountains in northeast O'ahu and the gods changed her into the fishing grounds off Kaena Point in the Kaua'i Channel. These waters were then ordained to be a haunt of the *mahi mahi*.

This dish contrasts the texture of the fish with the crispness of the local mountain apple or Malay apple. These little (3-inch long), scarlet fruit, called *'ohi'a 'ai*, were introduced to the islands by the early Hawaiians (please see Glossary, page 257).

The piquancy of Japanese horseradish, *wasabi*, is a tribute to the culinary ethnic patchwork in the Hawaiian Islands. Contrary to popular notion, *wasabi* (*Wasabia japonica*) and horseradish (*Armoracia lapathifolia*) are distant relations since they share the same mustard family, *Cruciferae*.

Serves 6

1/2 teaspoon of Japanese horseradish *(wasabi)*

2 teaspoons of freshly squeezed lemon juice

1 cup of whipping cream, chilled

1/4 teaspoon of salt

24 mountain apples

1 cup of cold water, acidulated with 1 teaspoon of lemon juice

2 1/2 pounds of *mahi mahi* steak, 3/4-inch thick (approximately) cut into 6 equal portions

2 tablespoons of peanut oil

freshly ground black pepper

freshly ground sea salt

sprigs of watercress to garnish

1. Preheat your oven to 200° Fahrenheit and place a large, ovenproof dish or platter inside.
2. Mix the Japanese horseradish with the lemon juice to an even consistency and set aside for use in the next step.
3. Whip the cream in a chilled bowl until the liquid stiffens and forms soft peaks. Blend and fold in the horseradish/lemon mixture and add the salt. Cover the bowl and set aside for use in Step 9.
4. Quarter lengthwise and remove the core from **18** of the mountain apples. Slice the cored quarters into paper-matchstick-sized slivers. Deposit the slivers in the acidulated water. Set aside the apple water bath and the **6** remaining apples.
5. Pat the fish steaks with paper towels to remove any excess moisture. Place a large, heavy frying pan over a medium-high setting and add the peanut oil. Heat the oil until a haze forms over the top and, with a spatula, introduce the fillets. Fry for about 2 minutes, moving each occasionally, until the bottoms begin to darken. Rotate and continue frying the other sides of the fillets for another

2 minutes. While frying, dust the sides of the fish with grindings of pepper and sea salt. When the fillets are externally crisp but moist and tender internally, remove each with the spatula, draining over the frying pan, and place on the dish in the oven.

6. To the frying pan, while still on heat, add the **6** remaining, whole apples from Step 4. Stir and fry briefly until the skins just begin to blister. Remove the pan and its contents from heat and set aside for use in Step 8.

7. Carefully drain the apple slivers from Step 4 in a colander. Divide the drained slivers into six equal bundles on your serving plates.

8. From the oven, deposit a cooked fish fillet on each pile of apple slivers. Place a fried apple alongside each serving.

9. Top each of the fish steaks with a generous dollop of the horseradish cream and insert a sprig of watercress. Serve immediately.

Note: Although it is satisfying to prepare a recipe with all the original ingredients, it is not always possible. In that instance, if *mahi mahi* is unavailable in your local market, try halibut, or other firm-fleshed white fish. Slivers of the Japanese pear apple or even crisp cooking apples may take the place of the *'ohi'a 'ai*. White horseradish can supplant *wasabi*, although both cans of the powdered version and tubes of the Japanese horseradish paste are usually available in Oriental markets and/or the special food sections of major supermarkets.

SEARED BARRAMUNDI FILLETS WITH A MACADAMIA AND BUNYA BUNYA NUT CRUST ON QUANDONG PURÉE

(QUEENSLAND)

Most Australian bush ingredients are unique to the continent of "Oz" and, although we can cook their recipes with substitutions, they do lose that Aussie charm. Fortunately, many Australian foods may now be ordered by mail (please see page 285).

The barramundi lurks only in the waters of Northern Australia and Papua New Guinea, but grouper and snapper can take its place. (For more information, please see table, "A Selection of Popular Bony Fish in Oceania," on page 98.)

Although indigenous to Queensland, macadamias are now as close as your supermarket shelf—unfortunately, bunya bunya nuts are not. As a substitute for the latter, I suggest you try chestnuts, treated in the same manner. Dried quan-

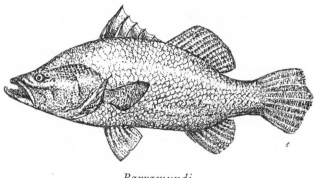

Barramundi

dongs may be mail-ordered but, if you cannot wait to experiment with this recipe, use young, dried peaches or apricots.

Serves 4

1½ cups of dried, pitted quandongs
1½ cups of water
½ cup of sugar
the juice of 1 lemon
¼ teaspoon of salt
4 7-ounce (approximately) barramundi fillets, skinned
salt and freshly ground black pepper to taste
1 egg white, beaten

6 bunya nut kernels, boiled for 30 minutes, shelled and finely chopped
⅓ cup of macadamia nuts, crushed
3 cloves of garlic, smashed, peeled and minced
½ cup (1 stick) of unsalted butter, softened
3 tablespoons of olive oil
4 sprigs of basil to garnish

1. Place a medium, non-reactive saucepan over medium-high heat and add the quandongs, water, sugar, lemon juice and salt and bring the mixture to a boil. Immediately reduce heat to maintain a simmer and cook the fruit for about 5 minutes. Transfer the mixture to a medium-sized glass or plastic mixing bowl, cover with plastic wrap and let the mixture stand, at room temperature, to macerate for about 24 hours.
2. Place the marinated fruit and its liquid in a blender and blend on a high setting to a smooth even purée. Set aside for use in Step 6.
3. Pat the fish fillets dry with paper towels and season both sides with the salt and pepper. Paint the top of each of the fillets with the egg white.
4. Combine the bunya nuts, macadamias and garlic in a small mixing bowl. Mash the butter into the solid ingredients with a fork and season with additional salt and freshly-ground black pepper. Spread the seasoned nut/butter over the

surfaces of each of the fillets to a depth of about $1/4$ inch and set aside for use in the next step.

5.   Preheat your broiler to the highest setting. Then heat the olive oil in a large frying pan over a high setting. When the oil comes up to frying temperature and a haze forms over the top, carefully place in the coated fillets and fry each for about 30 seconds or until the bottom is crisp.

6.   Transfer the fillets with a spatula to a baking sheet. (The butter on top of the fish will have melted and drained into the frying fat but the chopped nuts will have been captured by the coagulated egg white.) Place the baking sheet under your broiler and let the fish cook for less than 30 seconds to just brown and crisp the fillets.

7.   Remove the fillets and transfer them to 4 (warmed) serving plates. Pool the quandong purée around the fillets and garnish each serving with a sprig of basil. Serve immediately.

Note: To shell bunya nuts: After cooking, hold the hot nut with a towel. Use a sharp knife to slit the shell from end-to-end. Rotate the nut about 180° and make a second, longitudinal incision. Force the knife through the cooked shell at the second incision and separate it into two halves. The cooked kernel can then be removed, leaving behind both the red skin and shell.

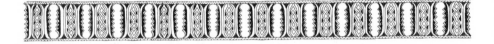

ALICE'S FISH STEW
(PAPUA NEW GUINEA)

Alice has a soft, gentle voice, large brown eyes and skin the color of burnt caramel. She works as a housekeeper in one of the major hotels in Port Moresby. She loves to eat. She loves to cook.

"I'm getting too fat," she says. "I have to cut down on my eating." But Alice is a zaftig Melanesian foodie. She enjoys talking about food. She tells me, "When I cook for my family, I cook with many vegetables and meat and fish. I cook simple. Put in tomatoes, onions and . . ." She fumbles for the word in English. "Capsicums," she says triumphantly. "You know, hot ones!"

Alice does her marketing on her days off, taking along her *bilum* (a colorful, finely-woven fiber bag with long plaited handles which many Melanesian women suspend from their foreheads, letting it hang down their backs; it keeps their hands free and is the Papuan version of the universal string bag). "I'll get you one," she says with a wide smile exposing a toothpaste commercial for white, perfectly-formed teeth. (As it transpired, Alice was required to work an extra shift so she introduced me to Doreen, a younger Melanesian waitress who took me to buy my own *bilum*. That's another story.)

Here is Alice's stew, as she described it.

Serves 6

1 pound of fish trimmings (heads, bones, tails, etc.)	1 medium carrot, peeled and coarsely chopped
2 quarts of water	$1/2$ teaspoon of salt
1 bay leaf	$1/2$ teaspoon of freshly ground black pepper
1 teaspoon of salt	
2 tablespoons of peanut oil	$1^1/2$ pounds of shark fillets, sliced into 1–2-inch long pieces
1 large onion, peeled and coarsely chopped	
2 stalks of celery (plus leaves), coarsely chopped	6 winged beans, washed and sliced into 6 sections of almost equal length
4 medium tomatoes, coarsely chopped	$1^1/2$ tablespoons of tapioca flour
2 green chili peppers *(Serrano* or *Jalapeño)*, minced	$1/2$ cup of thick coconut milk *(see page 19)*
1 large taro corm (approximately $3/4$-pound), peeled, cut into 1-inch cubes and covered with cold water	2 tablespoons of parsley, minced

1. Place the fish trimmings in a large saucepan over high heat. Pour in the water, add the bay leaf and salt, and bring to a full boil. Reduce the heat to medium and cook for about 45 minutes, or until the stock has reduced by nearly one-half. Strain the stock through a sieve or colander, discarding the solids, and reserve for use in Step 3.
2. Heat the oil in a large, non-reactive saucepan over a medium-high setting. Add the onions, stir and fry for about 1 minute. Drop in the celery, continue stirring and frying for about 2 more minutes.
3. Add the tomatoes and chilies and continue to cook, stirring, until the tomatoes soften and begin to disintegrate. Drain and add the taro and carrot. Pour in the fish stock from above. Let the mixture come to a boil, reduce the heat and let simmer for about 10 minutes.

4. Season with the salt and pepper. Deposit the shark pieces and let them simmer for about 2 minutes. Add the winged beans and continue simmering for a further 2 minutes.

5. Remove about 3 tablespoons of the stew liquid and, in a small bowl, combine it with the tapioca flour to form a smooth sauce. Spoon the thickener back into the stew. Stir the mixture until it begins to thicken.

6. Add the coconut milk and parsley. Let the mixture heat through but not come to a boil.

7. Transfer the completed stew to a serving bowl and present immediately.

Note: You may substitute any firm, white bony fish, such as cod, halibut or swordfish, for the shark.

LAULAUS

Leaf-Wrapped Fish and Pork Bundles (HAWAI'I)

These savory bundles or packets of fish and meat may take the place of *kalua* pig at a Hawaiian feast or *poi* supper. *Laulaus* have the same concept as the Samoan or Fijian *palusami* although they contain no coconut milk. In Hawai'i, they are wrapped first in young taro leaves and then in ti leaves. We can substitute spinach leaves and aluminum foil for the double wrapping. *Laulaus* are traditionally filled with a mixture of Boston pork butt, beef chuck, salted salmon and salted butterfish (black cod). For our new-style *Laulaus,* we use only pork for the meat and substitute fresh salmon or strips of lox for the salted salmon and mackerel fillets for the butterfish.

Ideally, you need a two-tiered steamer to accomplish the steaming in one episode. The alternatives are (a) to repeat the steaming session with a single-tiered steamer and, effectively, double the time or (b) use two steamers simultaneously.

Serves 10

5 bundles of fresh spinach, thoroughly washed and stems removed	1/2 pound of king mackerel, skinned, boned and cut into 1-inch chunks (or 1/2 pound of shark steaks, cut into 1-inch chunks)
4 pounds of lean pork loin, cut into 1/2-inch cubes	1 medium onion, peeled and minced
1 pound of fresh salmon, skinned, boned and cut into 1-inch chunks, or 1 pound of lox, cut into 3/4-inch wide strips	a few drops of smoke seasoning liquid
	salt to taste
	freshly ground black pepper to taste

1.   Place the steamer trays alongside your working surface for easy access. Fill your steamer to the customary depth with cold water, cover, increase the heat so that the water reaches a boil coincidental with your completing the preparation of all the **Laulaus.**

2.   Prepare 10 rectangles of heavy-duty aluminum foil (12 × 18 inches each). Have some kitchen twine handy.

3.   Lay out a foil rectangle. Place the spinach leaves in the center of the foil radiating out from the center in a multi-pointed star shape. Continue to create the leaf mat, using about 10 leaves per mat, until you have covered the surface with a circle the circumference of a dinner plate.

4.   Place alternating chunks of pork, salmon and mackerel in the center of the leaves. Top with a heaped tablespoons of onion and a drop of smoke seasoning. (Each *Laulau* should contain a total of between 7 and 8 ounces of meat and fish.) Season with the salt and pepper.

5.   Neatly fold the spinach leaves around the meat and fish mixture to form a compact package. Tie each with the twine, as you would a gift, with a bow knot for easy unwrapping.

6.   Fold the foil over the package, beginning with the longer ends and following with the shorter sides to form a tightly sealed packet. Stack the packet in the steamer tray.

7.   Continue until all the **Laulaus** are prepared and stacked in the steamer trays. Confirm your steamer is up to temperature, a rolling boil. Using oven mitts, stack the trays on the steamer and cover it. (If you are using a bamboo steamer, you may help seal the top with a weight.) Steam the entire assembly for about 30 minutes, replenishing the water from time to time.

8.   Remove the steamer from heat. Disassemble the steamer and set the trays aside to cool for about 15 minutes. Unwrap the foil, using caution to avoid any escaping steam that may be trapped in the packet. Untie the string from each, place them all on a serving dish and present at once.

Note: Other non-traditional *Laulaus* may be made alternatively from beef, tongue or turkey. Of course, fish remains as an essential element.

BUI DAMU VAKALOLO

Red Snapper with a Spicy Tomato and Coconut Sauce (FIJI)

I really think one must explore the food markets of a country to fully appreciate the scope of the local cuisine. Of course, that's a wonderful excuse to while away the hours just walking up aisles between counters or strolling around floor displays of vegetables, fruits and fish set out on mats in the open air. When I traveled in the Pacific, the first day after arrival was usually spent investigating the farmers' market—and so it was in Suva, the capital of Fiji. It's a handsome, covered bazaar where the finest of the native harvest is on display. (Unlike our carefully trimmed and cosseted vegetables, in Melanesia, most produce is left on the stem, attesting

to its freshness.) In the municipal market of Suva, taro rested in regimented bundles, 8 to 10 large globes in each. Tied around the top of the stems with white strings, they looked rather like Indian clubs. Close to the market, fish was laid out in neat rows on reed mats along the cement banks of Nubukalou Creek in the city's center.

Hungry at lunchtime and satisfied with my tour, I treated myself to a baked fish similar to this recipe in presentation.

Accompany this snapper with cooked taro and, perhaps, the **Three-Bean Sauté** (see page 187), and you have a complete meal with an inspired balance and contrast of colors, flavors and textures.

SPICY TOMATO AND COCONUT SAUCE

Serves 4

2 tablespoons of canola oil
1 medium onion, peeled and
    finely chopped
2 cloves of garlic, smashed,
    peeled and minced
1 teaspoon of fresh gingerroot,
    peeled and minced
4 medium tomatoes, blanched,
    peeled and coarsely
    chopped
1 heaped tablespoon of tomato
    paste
1/4 cup of Rhine or other
    fruity, white wine

2 tablespoons of water
1/4 teaspoon of dried red
    pepper flakes
a dash of Tabasco sauce
1 teaspoon of sugar
1 bay leaf, torn into pieces
8 basil leaves, chopped
a pinch of nutmeg
1/2 teaspoon of salt
1/4 teaspoon of freshly ground
    black pepper
1/2 cup of coconut cream
    (see page 19)

1.   Heat the oil in a medium, non-reactive saucepan and sauté the onion over medium-high heat, stirring, for about 3 minutes. Add the garlic and ginger, continue stirring and frying for about another minute.
2.   Add the tomatoes and cook for an additional 2 minutes. When the tomatoes begin to disintegrate, add the tomato paste, wine, water, pepper flakes, Tabasco, sugar, bay leaf, basil and nutmeg. Sprinkle with salt and pepper, stir, cover and let the mixture come to a boil. Immediately reduce heat to low and simmer the sauce for about 20 minutes.
3.   Uncover, turn off the heat and transfer the sauce to your blender. Quickly purée the sauce on a high setting for about a minute. Return the purée to the pan on the range top. Stir in the coconut cream and let it sit until Step 4, **Baked Snapper.**

BAKED SNAPPER

2 tablespoons of unsalted
   butter
4 red snapper fillets (about 8
   ounces each)

$1/4$ teaspoon of salt
$1/4$ teaspoon of white pepper
$1/2$ cup of Rhine or other
   fruity, white wine

1. Preheat your oven to 350° Fahrenheit.
2. Grease a large baking dish with small portions or wipings of the butter.
Evenly arrange the fillets in the dish and season with the salt and pepper. Pour in
the wine.
3. Dot or spread the remaining butter over the top of the fish. Bake in your
oven for about 15 minutes, or until the fish is just tender and the flesh firm.
4. Reheat the **Spicy Tomato and Coconut Sauce** on a low setting.
5. Arrange the serving plates and pour equal-sized pools of the sauce on each.
Place a cooked fillet in the center of each pool and serve immediately.

MELANESIA

*Papua New Guinea (and its islands), Solomon Islands, Vanuatu (New Hebrides),
New Caledonia, Fiji, etc.*

Melanesia: 202,886 square miles of green land set in tropical seas. Fragmented
volcanic archipelagoes bulwarked behind barrier reefs; giant portions of terra
not-so-firma studded with mountains, stabilized by plateaus, split by wide rivers and
shaken by earthquakes. All of it is clothed in jungles, scrub, grasslands, rain forests
and more jungles.

These are lands of dark, secretive tribes; semi-naked peoples whose superstitions
and spells hold them fast in a web of ancient magic; lands of ink-black figures who
merge into forest shadows; lands of peoples with skins drenched in coconut oil to the
rich hues of mahogany-colored satin.

Melanesia is mosquitoes and crocodiles, skull cemeteries and yam gazebos, shark
men and cults; where the Melanesian smiles a thin, black smile. But Melanesia is also
marsupials and brilliant-plumaged birds, azurite-blue lagoons, cocoa-brown swamps,
feet-stamping dances, face-painting, giant flower blossoms and haunting, polytonal
music.

These are the islands of fire walkers, *kava* drinkers and land divers (the
inspiration for today's bungee jumpers). These are the islanders with one foot in the
past of constant warfare and cannibalism, and the other in the present of warm
hospitality, wide betel-stained grins, Quonset-hut modernization and hopes for a
better future.

(Continued.)

There are few towns and cities in Melanesia. Villages are sprinkled throughout the islands, primarily on the coasts. (The exceptions are on the large islands where crop raising in the highlands and water trade on the rivers has spread the population inland.) Some settlements are mere hamlets with a scattering of earthen-floored, thatched huts. In sodden, malarial-ridden areas with year-round rainfall, villagers construct houses raised on stilts. Often fishing villages are built on platforms atop pilings, connected by rickety walkways; an entire community over the shallow waters of a bay or lagoon.

At Walter Bay on the outskirts of Port Moresby, near Koki Market, there is a former fishermen's village, now on stilts over the water. They dismantled their canoes and used them for core wood for the village. The reality is not picturesque. It is a huddle of tin and wooden-roofed shacks on emaciated legs crowned by a bristle of television antennae. The inhabitants are now fat and unhealthy from inactivity. They watch television commercials about food and buy most of their comestibles canned or packaged from the store. They ignore the wealth of fresh food at Koki Market. The media proclaims a better life in which they believe and to which they aspire.

However, far away from the dislocating sprawl of urban life, island cultures continue much as they have for centuries. Although some of the young (mostly males) have been drawn by the magnet of employment in the population centers, the rule of the chiefs and cohesiveness of village life still holds. The centers of *kastom* survive within the intricately-carved and ornately decorated chiefs' houses, the mens' communal dormitories and village clubhouses. The rituals of *kava* or *yagona* ceremonies remain at the core of traditions and beliefs; linking the old with the new. They connect the ancestral spirits with those living and mollify fears of the future.

That is village life. Its essence is simplicity. But it is also complicated by time-consuming taboos, ceremonies and rituals that define and circumscribe daily life. These mark signal human events and behavior: birth; puberty; marriage; hunting, gathering and cultivation of food; *kava* drinking; warfare; death, particularly death. This fascination or preoccupation is especially pronounced among those tribes who have had little contact with Westerners and, therefore, whose beliefs and customs have remained intact.

The core of the catechism of ancestor cults is the belief that the dead can only survive in immortality if their memory is perpetuated by the living. Some tribes consider the head the source of supernatural power, therefore the skulls of ancestors or even enemies are preserved; at the same time conferring additional power on the living. Other groups even wrap and mummify entire bodies of the dead, generally the remains of significant chiefs. Some tribes wear grotesque and purposefully exaggerated masks, or hoods of plaited grass, which represent the spirits of the departed. The living man, wearing the mask, temporarily becomes the ancestor, acquiring his supernatural attributes.

The practice of gift giving, or the exchange of wealth between villages and tribes and its reciprocation, is a fundamental tenet in Melanesia and the thread of social fabric. The formal presentation of highly-esteemed possessions such as pigs, yams and *kava,* demands a ceremony and celebration. That, of course, infers a feast; dancing, singing and music, which are the highlights of life in Melanesia.

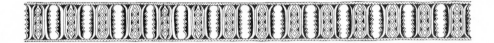

MAKIRA YAM AND SAVORY FISH PUDDING

(SOLOMON ISLANDS)

While on Guadalcanal, I met this distinguished, expatriate gentleman who told me that his cook (from the neighboring island of Makira, southeast of Guadalcanal) prepared delicious vegetable "puddings" for him, which he never tired of eating. I soon learnt that these puddings were a major division of Melanesian cooking, particularly featured at feasts (the Fijian *vakalolos* are an example).

The outer dough wrapping is made from any of the following, grated, or cooked and mashed: taro, sweet potato, cassava, sago or yams; occasionally from a mixture of two or three of the starches. The fillings may be grated coconut, shell-fish, meat, onions and chili peppers, etc. Plain puddings are merely made from the starch, coconut milk and, sometimes, grated coconut.

Melanesian puddings are traditionally wrapped in banana leaves before being baked in the earth-pit oven or *mumu* (see page 127). This recipe features yam for the dough casing and a filling of white fish. We can, of course, substitute foil for the wrapping and bake it in our domestic ovens.

Serves 4 to 6

2 medium-sized (about 2 pounds) **cooked yams**

1 teaspoon of salt

1 teaspoon of freshly ground black pepper

2 tablespoons of tapioca flour or cornstarch

1/2–3/4 cup of thick coconut milk *(see page 19)*

1/2 pound of firm white fish fillets, steamed or boiled briefly until just firm

1/2 cup of spinach, finely chopped (frozen spinach may be substituted)

1/2 small onion, peeled and finely chopped

2–3 dashes of Tabasco sauce (optional)

2 tablespoons of parsley, minced

1 teaspoon (approximately) of vegetable oil

1.   Preheat your oven to medium, about 300° Fahrenheit.

2.   Place the yam in a medium mixing bowl. Mash the yam as you would a baking potato and sprinkle in the pepper. Add a tablespoon or two of coconut milk and continue mashing and stirring to make a stiff dough.

3.   Place the cooked fish in another non-reactive, medium mixing bowl and separate it into flakes with a fork. Stir in the spinach and onion, and pour in the remainder of the coconut milk. Add the Tabasco and stir in the parsley. Set aside for use in Step 6.

4.   Using a small (about 2-quart), ovenproof mixing bowl as a form, line it with kitchen foil, leaving a generous margin, enough to be folded over and cover the top. Using the vegetable oil and your fingers, smooth the foil to conform to the inside of the bowl, at the same time greasing it.

5.   Divide the yam dough into 2 portions, an approximate ratio of two-thirds to one-third. With your hands, quickly form the larger dough portion into a ball and place at the center of the foil in the bowl. Work and pat the dough with enough pressure to force the dough to evenly cover the interior of the bowl and protrude in about a 1-inch collar above the rim.

6.   Spoon in the fish mixture from Step 3. Gently place and press the dough collar inward and over the surface of the filling. Form the remaining one-third dough portion in the form of a thick disk with the approximate diameter of the bowl. Place the disk on top of the contents in the bowl, compressing the dough edges around the perimeter of the pudding, to completely seal the mixture.

7.   Draw up the foil margins and bring them to the center, crimping and folding them as necessary to further seal the pudding. Transfer the bowl to your oven and bake for about 1 hour, until the yam casing has formed a firm, but uneven, crust.

8.   After removing from the oven, let the pudding cool and set up for about 10 minutes. Peel back the foil from the upper surface. Invert the bowl over a serving dish. Remove the bowl and carefully peel the foil from the pudding. Serve at once.

Note: You may wish to accompany this dish with a citrus-based sauce such as the **Tomato-Orange Sauce** (see page 91) or the **Pepper-Lime Sauce** (see page 125).

HAANGI TUNA HEKE

Broiled and Baked Wrapped Eel (NEW ZEALAND)

Although the Maori traditionally consumed their eels with little or no adornment, I encountered the following recipe in Rotorua. I think it has more character than the usual Spartan offerings while retaining the primitive charm.

For aesthetics and convenience, I recommend that eel fillets be purchased from your fish merchant already skinned. In New Zealand, eels are usually sold whole (with the skin and head removed) and are wrapped in flax leaves, *harakeke*, for baking in the *haangi* (see page 127).

Serves 4 to 6

2 tablespoons of butter, melted
2 pounds of eel fillets, cut into
    4-inch-long pieces
1 teaspoon of dried thyme
1/2 teaspoon of salt
1/2 teaspoon of freshly ground
    black pepper
4–6 large collard or cabbage
    leaves, washed, drained
    and softened *(see page 21),*
    stems removed

1/2 large onion, peeled and
    finely chopped
1/2 teaspoon of dried sage
2 tablespoons of parsley, finely
    chopped
a few drops of smoke season-
    ing liquid
1/4 cup of white wine

1.   Preheat your broiler and at the same time, if possible, your oven to 350° Fahrenheit.

2.   Lay the eel pieces in an even, single layer in a large, disposable aluminum tray. Brush the meat with butter and season with thyme, salt and pepper.

3.   Broil the fillets for a few minutes. Open the broiler and both rotate the fillets and brush them with additional butter. Broil for an additional 1 or 2 minutes. The meat should be just browned on all sides.

4.   When cooked, remove the eel from the broiler and adjust your oven temperature (if necessary) to 350° Fahrenheit.

5.   Lay out 4-6 rectangles (approximately 12 inches × 10 inches) of aluminum foil. Place a softened collard leaf in the center of each rectangle. Divide the eel fillets and apportion equal amounts to each leaf. Scatter the onion, sage and parsley over all the eel fillets. Sprinkle a few drops of smoke seasoning on each followed by a soupçon of wine.

6. Fold the leaves around the contents of each to form a firm packet. Follow by bending the foil around each and crimping to seal them.

7. Bake the foil packages in your oven for abut 20 minutes.

8. When the cooking is complete, remove the packages from the oven and let them stand for a few minutes to cool. Carefully remove all the foil and transfer the leaf packets to a warmed serving dish and present at once.

Note: When serving as a main dish or entrée, accompany the eel with cooked and buttered sweet potatoes (*kumara*) and a green salad.

BARRAMUNDI FILLETS
IN A PEPPER-LIME SAUCE
(PAPUA NEW GUINEA)

We may not be able to sample this delectable fish unless we are in the Southwest Pacific or Northern Australia but it is definitely worthwhile pestering your local fishmonger or importer for barramundi. Perhaps, with sufficient demand, we shall find barramundi in our neighborhood fish cases. Until that time, grouper or sea bass are honorable substitutes.

The order of preparation for this recipe is significant because of the disparity in cooking times between the **Pepper-Lime Sauce** and the **Fish Fillets.** If the order is reversed, e.g., the sauce is made last, it will not be required to hold the sauce but there is the distinct probability that the fish will be overcooked.

PEPPER-LIME SAUCE

Serves 4

1 tablespoon of mixed (color) peppercorns (black, white, pink, green), **smashed and cracked**	1/4 teaspoon of salt
	1 cup of whipping cream
	1/2 teaspoon of lime zest, grated
2 cups of fish stock or clam juice	1 stick (4 ounces) of unsalted butter, cut into eighths
1/4 cup of freshly squeezed lime juice	

1.   Place a small skillet over a high setting and roast all the peppercorns for less than a minute, or until they begin to release their aroma. Remove the pepper-corns to a small bowl and set aside for use in Step 5.

2.   Pour the fish stock into a small saucepan and place it over medium-high heat. Let the stock reach a boil and continue cooking until it is reduced by about one-half. Add the lime juice and salt. When the liquid returns to the boil, let it continue until it is, again, reduced by one-half.

3.   Assemble a double boiler (with the requisite volume of water in the bottom) and place it over a medium-low setting.

4.   From Step 2, while still on heat, stir the cream and lime zest into the sauce. Continue the reduction until only two-thirds of the volume remains, stirring occasionally. Drop in the butter pieces and whisk the mixture to a smooth, creamy sauce.

5.   Stir in the peppercorns from Step 1. Transfer the sauce to the top of the double boiler and modulate the heat to produce the lowest water simmer. Stir occasionally and let the sauce remain on heat until the **Fish Fillets** are prepared.

FISH FILLETS

1 teaspoon of sea salt
1-inch piece of fresh ginger-
    root, peeled and grated
4 7-ounce (approximately) bar-
    ramundi fillets

1 tablespoon of butter
2 tablespoons of peanut oil

1.   In a small bowl, thoroughly mix the salt and ginger to a coarse paste. Rub the paste over all the surfaces of the fish.

2.   Heat the butter and peanut oil in a large frying pan over medium-high heat. When a haze forms over the fat, carefully introduce the fish fillets. Fry them for about 1 minute per side, or until they begin to turn golden and the flesh is firm.

3.   Drain the fish and place a fillet on each diner's plate. Spoon enough of the **Pepper-Lime Sauce** over each of the fillets to create a small pool for each. Serve immediately accompanied by the **Three-Bean Sauté** *(see page 187)*.

Chapter 7

Intromission

The Earth-pit Oven

*Tradition rules each step of the way; the ovens are dug in
the right kind of soil, the right kind of wood is chosen, the
heat regulated by its judicious application, the right stones
are heated in the flame-filled oven.*

Olaf Ruhen, 1978, *The Tongans*

Before we approach the cooking of meats island-style (in the following
chapter), it will be helpful to examine the cooking method/apparatus
both central and common to all cooking in the Pacific Islands—the earth-
pit oven. It is the technological equivalent of Esperanto but of more sig-
nificance to pan-Pacific culture than either the *tandoor* (oven) to India or
the barbecue to the Americas. It is the sine qua non of an island feast or
celebratory meal.

From New Guinea in Melanesia to Kusaie (Kosrae) and Pohnpei
(Ponape) in the Caroline Islands of Micronesia, from Tahiti in French
Polynesia across to New Zealand and Arnhem Land in northern Australia,
the earth-pit oven was—and still is—the historic method of cooking
throughout Oceania. The only slight change—sometimes paronyms or
cognates—in the labels between regions and languages reflects its univer-
sality: *imu, umu, um, haangi, mumu, ahima'a.*

Waikiki—A Lu'au

The evening breeze rustles the palms and the flags on the terraces of the
beachfront hotels as the sun sets on one of the most photographed tropical islands in the Pacific—Oahu. The last of the outrigger canoes is dragged
up on to the sand after its load of tourists has disembarked; now the dinner cruise boats nose out, lights twinkling, over toward Diamond Head.
Hard-core surfers take a final ride in, then tuck their boards underarm and
trudge up the beach.

The rosy light of the afterglow intensifies the stuccoed hue of The Pink Palace—as the stately Royal Hawaiian Hotel is affectionately known—and the Mai Tai drinkers around the Garden Bar pluck the orchids and pineapple spears from the glass buckets and slide the last drops down. (Enough diminutive oriental paper parasols are stacked behind the counter to make Chinese coolie hats for all the sparrows along Kalakaua Avenue.) Beyond the low wall of privilege that separates the cocktail guests from the beach, jostling package tourists head for their economy cement hostelries, two blocks from the ocean. In their wake, an old man moves slowly, passing a metal detector in sweeps across the trampled sand. The pickings are lean.

At one of the nearby hotels, a bronzed figure stands silhouetted against the evening sky. He raises a conch shell to his lips. The mournful, eerie sound reverberates against the masonry towers. A clot of people forms in front of the herald—like ancient Hawaiians, they obey the summons of the conch shell. As they gather, a platform is set up on a terrace; covered in green outdoor carpeting and then swagged with garlands of plastic flowers. The evening breeze tugs at the cotton drapery concealing the legs of the structure. Microphones and amplifiers are positioned on the platform as the crowd files obediently around the long tables and sits in passive expectancy. The flaming torches are lighted and smudges of smoke dissipate against the sky's afterglow.

Musicians test the equipment, hastily switching down an earsplitting squeal of feedback, then an announcer, in an island shirt and long, white trousers, takes up a microphone and warms up the crowd. "A–LowHA!" he calls. "A–LowHA!" they dutifully respond. He commands them again: "A–LooOW-HA!" Now the crowd responds with increasing fervor.

"You all got dinna tickets? You hungry? You ready to *luʻau*? We got one fine fellah *kalua* peeg fo you! You gonna have one *gooood* time!" The assembly applauds. The emcee smiles broadly, flashing his perfect, white teeth. Some matrons in the audience think he would make a nice friend for their daughters on the mainland. Others have more personal thoughts. The musicians swing into a hackneyed "Blue Hawaii," with a steel guitar lead. The announcer steps down and walks over to the bar where he teases one of the sarong-clad cocktail waitresses. Now his conversation is without accent or dialect; no trace of the island pidgin. (He lives in a little wooden house over in Pearl City with his wife and two daughters. The daughters are enrolled in Punahou School. He reflects that this job, along with a few gigs doing TV commercials, has allowed him the opportunity of considering private schools for his offspring.) Leaning his back against the service bar, he surveys the dinner crowd. Four waiters of Filipino extraction, masquerading as native Hawaiians in flower-printed loin cloths and wreaths of genuine hibiscus, are uncovering a huge, whole pig. Its crisp brown skin glistens in the light of the flaming torches. Several hours earlier, a few curious onlookers had watched the workers line the *imu* pit oven with hot stones and leaves before the large porker was lowered in and covered.

Now the conch blower, bare except for a loin cloth or *lava-lava*, takes up a long knife and brandishes it over his head as the crowd applauds. He ceremoniously slices several pieces of pork; no more. (Aside from the centerpiece *kalua* pig, the entire *lu'au* has actually been prepared in the kitchens of the hotel.) The waiters now file out bearing laden trays of pork and roasted taro.

But the spectacle—a cliché of lighted torches against the darkening sky, the electronic wail of plaintive guitars, mingled smells of suntan oil, plumeria and *pikaki* perfumes, and roast pork—somehow becomes transformed. The evening wind peels back layers of memory to the tradition and beauty underlying the tourist glitz—and the magic returns.

Even in Honolulu—arguably one of the most densely populated and westernized cities in Oceania—beyond the tourist canyons of Waikiki and away from the traffic of the downtown area, in streets lined with little single-storey houses with backyards overgrown with papayas, dusty banana fronds and lines of flapping washing, there are rectangular pits in the far corners of those yards, outlined by scorched or blackened grass. These are the real *imus*. As the backyard, black iron barbecue is to most of mainland America, so the *imu* is to the Hawaiians—the center of family gatherings and festive occasions—the heart of the *lu'au*.

Traditional Construction

Throughout the Pacific, the basic construction of the oven and the method of cooking is simplicity itself. A pit is dug in the earth or sand and lined with heated stones, which are then covered with a thick layer of leaves. This thermal lining is then packed with the various foods to be cooked. Another layer of leaves tucks them in, then more leaves, grass mats or plant fibers are piled on top, at or above ground level, to help seal in the heat. The food cooks slowly by a combination of steaming and baking. All the juices, aromas and flavors are sealed in, together with the bonus of many of the valuable nutrients.

In some areas, such as tribal New Guinea, the fires stones are heated in a separate, above-ground pyre—a rectangular platform of stacked wood—before being transferred to the pit. This does have one advantage: it keeps the ashes away from the food. In many other cultures, the fire is set in the pit itself. Tribes who live near rivers choose the rounded, compact river stones. Islanders without those amenities use lumps of coral; even termites' nests. In the older coral islands of Micronesia, pieces of limestone are utilized for heating, whereas those who live on isolated atolls are reduced to picking out pieces of coral that, naturally, lie around in abundance. Those islanders who have the luxury of choice in fire stones agree on certain principles of selection: the stones should not be too hard; otherwise they will split in the heat and, sometimes, explode, with disastrous consequences. Likewise, the stones should not be too soft or they will disintegrate and crumble into the food—gritty food is most disagreeable, even to the most stoic of islanders. The dictum prevails: the density—or, better yet, the specific gravity—of stones for earth ovens is paramount.

After the stones are heated, the ashes have to be removed. This necessitates removing the stones and disposing of the powder and ash of burnt wood. Tongs of bent wood or bamboo are used to displace the hot stones.

When it comes to the size and shape of the earth-oven pits, there are numerous variations, according to the demands of the shapes and kinds of food to be cooked. Also, depending on the density of the earth or sand, the pits can range from several feet in depth to mere indentations. In the latter case, the layers of food, vegetation and coverings form a large mound above ground.

Small, circular pits of about three feet in diameter and one foot in depth are dug for the cooking of vegetables. These domestic pits are usually scooped out by women. In Tahiti, historically, the digging of a giant pit for breadfruit was a communal affair. In the same fashion, communal earth ovens are still used for the cooking of meat, which is not eaten on the spot in the barbecue style, but carried off to the individual huts—similar to the manner in which European women used to take their bread dough to the village *boulangerie* to be properly baked. The communal oven continues to be used for leaf-wrapped foods. Different styles of wrapping or of tying twined leaf ribs into knots identify the packets of each household.

In days gone by, men also dug large pits for the cooking of pigs and dogs. These pits were prepared for special feasts by the men of the tribe at the chief's behest. A large feast could feature hundreds of pigs and, predictably, there would be several ovens.

Earth oven (Lovo). Food "to go"— parked in downtown Suva, Fiji

. . . *And if You Don't Live in Tonga*

Let's move from the evolution of the earth oven to the possibility of replicating it in the West.

In the near future, restaurants specializing in "South Seas" cuisines may choose to install raised, brick-walled, Oceanian-style ovens as an adjunct to their kitchens, perhaps with one long side wall of heat-proof glass exposed to the interior of the restaurant. (This could allow diners to view the cooking of their own—as well as others'—meals, similar to the use of *tandoors* in Indian restaurants.) Indeed, many luxury hotels in the Pacific and New Zealand have permanent earth ovens where the guests gather round to watch the unwrapping of the *umu* pig and other earth-oven items. This cooking showmanship excites the diners' appetites, increases their anticipation, includes the customer as participant and frequently results in larger returns for the establishment.

Earth-oven cooking is also feasible at home. If your living space includes a yard, you possess the absolute location for an earth oven. However, certain sensible precautions should be observed. Not too many years past, a group of expatriate Samoans, holding a backyard cookout in Newport Beach, California, were visited by the beach city's finest. It

131

seemed neighbors of the newly-arrived islanders complained about not only the noisy slaughtering of a piglet without benefit of an *abattoir* and requisite licensure, but, certainly, creating a large open fire with the accompanying smoke for the recently-dug pit oven.

However, with planning, you can create your own "island bake" and remain a law-abiding citizen. Even if the slaughter of live animals did not violate reams of local ordinances, I doubt most of us would be eager to participate in this endeavor. For those seeking extravagant authenticity, a fully-dressed porker may be ordered from most competent butchers. A large open fire is not necessary; neither to heat the stones nor in the pit for cooking. You can preheat the stones in a charcoal or gas-fueled barbecue; several will be required depending on the amount and volume of stones.

First, to the pit. Check your local building supply, hardware store and/or nursery for some of the following:

- 30–40 small, dense stones or fire bricks (halved or quartered)
- 4 pounds of whole cabbage leaves or an equivalent weight of banana leaves, divided into one-third portions
- 2–3 cartons of large (long), heavy-duty aluminum foil
- 1 lawn (30+ gallon) trash bag, filled with fresh grass clippings (optional)
- 3–4 woven rush mats (beach mats) or sacking
- 4 or 5 large rocks or whole bricks to anchor the mats

Choose a secluded corner on your property and mark out a circle of not less than one yard. (You can easily accomplish this with a stake, a measured piece of string and a gardening spade.) If your plans include a *lu'au* or "island bake" for more than ten people, the pit's diameter should measure at least four feet. Encourage any energetic teenagers to do the digging, to a center depth of about two to three feet. The sides of the pit should slope like a basin. If you plan to bake a whole *kalua* pig (see page 140), you will need a greater depth in the soil, about three to four feet. (When large pieces of meat are cooked, vegetables are normally excluded. To cook both meat and vegetables at the same time, the meat must be cut into small strips.) You will also need to supply additional large, heavy-weight, garden trash bags for the excavated soil.

After the pit is dug, line it with the aluminum foil, allowing for about an 8-inch foil margin to extend beyond the edge of the pit. Cover the foil with a layer of the first one-third of the leaves. (Banana or ti leaves are best, if they are obtainable, but cabbage or collard leaves can substitute. All other large, non-toxic leaves are acceptable; do not use rhubarb.) Let the leaves also extend into a collar over the foil. You should still have the remaining two-thirds of the leaves reserved for two more layers, following.

Now, place your barbecues near the pit and put the fire stones over the heat sources and light them. While the stones are heating, prepare the food to go into the oven and place it on trays, conveniently close to the pit. Check that you have enough leaves remaining, grass clippings, mats and rocks at hand.

Heat the stones to a temperature where a drop of water on one will sizzle and instantly evaporate. Now transfer two-thirds of the stones to the pit, using stout barbecue or fireplace tongs, and place them, side-by-side, in a single layer. (Protect your hands from the heat and accidents with a pair of heavy garden gloves.)

Cover the stones with the second one-third layer of leaves, poking extra leaves into the gaps between the stones. Now pack the food (both wrapped and exposed) into the pit, with the items that take the most heat at the bottom next to the stones. (See "Earth-Pit Oven Food Placement" diagram at the top of the next page.) Set a few more stones around the food and a few on top. Cover the food and stones with the remainder of the leaves and then fold the collar of leaves and foil inward over the pit, thus helping to seal the heat. Dump the optional grass clippings over the top and spread them evenly. Cover this arrangement with the rush mats and anchor everything down with the rocks or bricks, so there is no displacement if an island tradewind should arrive uninvited.

A 3-foot-diameter pit should be left alone for between $1^1/2$ to 2 hours, for the contents to cook properly. (Additional time will be required for such food items as major pork cuts or whole chickens.) Now is a convenient time to break out the cocktails, uncover the hot tub, set up the lawn croquet and/or serve some *pupus*. These devices may postpone your guests' eagerness to consume the food prematurely. ("No swine before its time.")

After you have sufficiently impressed your friends, with your overwhelming knowledge of earth ovens and, therefore, chosen the correct moment, unpack your oven and serve the *lu'au*. Set the stones on a metal tray or trash can lid to cool off. You may fill in the pit with the reserved earth, or, after the party, place a *secure* wood cover over it until your next *lu'au*.

The previous explanation may be interesting and inspirational, but scarcely relevant to an apartment dweller. You could find it difficult to dig

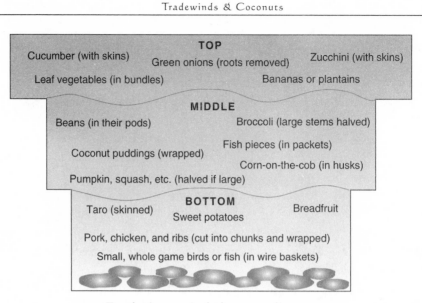

Earth-pit oven food placement diagram

through your floor to the apartment below, and constructing an *imu* in your shower might be awkward. Don't despair. If you have a terrace or a wide balcony that you use for entertaining, the bottom half of a clean oil drum can be transformed into an above-ground *imu*. A more elegant substitute would be one of the larger Japanese ceramic fire pots (preferably over 3 feet in diameter), since they have been fired to withstand the thermal shock. You will still need a large barbecue to heat the stones or bricks, but you can congratulate yourself on avoiding the labor of digging a pit.

So, you have no terrace, and your balcony is only 2 feet wide. All is not lost. Your own oven can be used to cook a magnificent facsimile of *kalua* pork (see page 140). Merely wrap individual portions of meat in aluminum foil lined with cabbage or spinach leaves before baking.

At serving time, cover your table with woven rush mats. If necessary, enlist the help of friends or florists to locate as much fern leaves and other greenery as you can scrounge (particularly banana leaves, if available), and lavishly decorate your table and room with exotic plants. Pile fresh tropical fruit into a centerpiece of munificence and scatter flowers between the fruit and around the served dishes. Perhaps even invest in giant clam shells to be used as serving bowls, and display as many baskets or wood trays and platters as you can muster. Invite your guests to come in flowered island attire, concoct a devastating tropical punch and turn on the Alfred Apaka music. *'Aloha!*

Chapter 8

The Commonplace

Familiar Meats of Oceania

I ate when I got hungry a very good sort of meal, consist-
ing usually of a tiny piglet cooked in native fashion,
swathed in succulent leaves and laid between hot stones
till ready for eating . . .

Charles Warren Stoddart, 1899, *South-Sea Idyls*

The pig insists on pride of place as the meat animal of Oceania. In a time shrouded in the mists of antiquity—20,000 to 30,000 years ago—men, women and children struggled southward through the humid jungles of Southeast Asia, capturing wild pigs and eventually "domesticat-ing" those they did not immediately consume. Their descendants, together with the food animals, crossed narrow straits of water finally arriving on the vast island we call New Guinea.

Their semi-wild boars could (and would, judging from early accounts of their disposition) have taken on our modern giant porkers, three times their size, and prevailed. They were wiry and lean, aggressive and hairy. They frequently poked their long snouts into the air to sniff for food or an enemy.

Those were the pigs, probably seasick and squealing, that were crammed in woven housing on the narrow, pitching decks of the long oceangoing canoes of the ancient pioneers and settlers of the Pacific. Their vessels must have resembled Noah's ark in that a collection of animals, primarily dogs and chickens, were also penned onboard with the pigs as breeding cargo. The sound of the consistent pounding of waves splashing against the hulls was undoubtedly obliterated by the barking, crowing, squealing and clucking of the shanghaied livestock.

It was a grand and necessary experiment: most of the islands in the Pacific had no meat animals, unless you counted bats and lizards (see the Glossary pages 279–280).

Over time, the settlers formed tribes and codified their societies. The role of the pig evolved with them. Beyond mere sustenance, the animals provided the centerpiece for feasts and ceremonies. They became prized

Pacific pig

possessions representing personal wealth. In a natural extension of their valuation, pigs were the principal articles of barter and exchange between tribes. Also, predictable anthropomorphizing occurred as they became significant objects destined for religious sacrifices and offerings to the gods.

In Melanesia a form of intertribal diplomacy involved ritual exchanges of pigs. Several thousand could be slaughtered for one occasion of the meeting of chiefs. Virtual stockades of spitted porkers, ready for roasting, were a testament to tribal pride and status. Pigs were considered a bride price. They became on-the-hoof currency for bribes and fines. Paradoxically, pigs could become much-loved family pets, pampered and adored while they lived and mourned when they expired.

The ancient Polynesians also raised pigs for religious sacrifice. When a new stone *marae* (temple) was dedicated at a ceremony for the faithful, the priests first invoked the gods to take up temporary residence. Prior taboos upon the people were recalled and slaughtered pigs were offered to the deities in return for the pardon of previous transgressions.

Teuira Henry of Tahiti described it:

Hear, O God, our petition for a pig without blemish.
A pig of appeasement to liberate sinful man,
A pig for great crimes,
A pig for family discords . . .
A pig for idle words,
A pig for lack of respect for the gods . . .

The ruins of the ancient stone temples of pagan times

Some of the offerings remained at the high altar in the *marae* to be consumed later by the priests; the majority of the hog meat was *indulged* at a great feast—a virtual orgy of pork followed by singing, dancing and coupling. Christian missionaries finally all but obliterated the old religions and their traditions. Today, the ancient stone temples of pagan times lie in crumbled ruins, chained in vines.

Pork still takes pride of place among the meats of Oceania. When cooked in an earth-pit oven, it undergoes a sublime transference of flavors and aromas, exchanged under sealed conditions with heat and time. The leaf wrappings lend their subtle imprint of taste. Smoke permeates in a benediction. When coconut and other foods are combined with the pork, flavors slowly combine to become a memorable taste experience in the closed environment. The wrapped dishes do not betray a hint of their bouquet until the food is unveiled.

Of course, there are additional cooking methods for pork in the Pacific. The lure of crackled pork skin, crisped over a bright fire is fundamental. Roasting whole pigs on spits over open flames provides that sizzle and snap as the melting fat drips down, the seductive aroma rises, the skin glistens and browns: literally, meat for the gods.

A Running Fowl

Chickens provide the more commonplace—but by no means common—meat in the Pacific. Poultry seem to be everywhere in the islands, running free range, which also means underfoot. (I don't know what muddled neural signals impel them to swerve at the last second and dash in your path, but I took a tumble over a jungle fowl on a dirt track in the Solomons. The chicken uttered a loud squawk and escaped from our entanglement like a flustered feather duster, shedding down in its wake. It was not ordained to have our collision hasten its demise and expire in my shadow, but would undoubtedly meet its fate at the hands of a native and fulfill its destiny in an island pot or a shroud of leaves in an earth oven.)

The Pacific chickens' pedigree can be traced back to the jungle fowls of Malaysia and they cruised to the islands in cabins adjacent to the pigs. In those early days, if they were to be stewed, a large gourd or wooden bowl would be filled with water and brought to a boil by the addition of heated stones. The chicken, in pieces, was then introduced. If a whole chicken was to be cooked, then a preheated stone was placed inside the carcass, ensuring a uniform cooked temperature throughout the bird.

The Hawaiians also ate the Hawaiian goose and wild duck, in addition to numerous other land and sea birds. Unfortunately, they consumed many species into extinction.

Bull-o'-ma-cow

Beef is not a traditional meat in Oceania because cattle were introduced by European missionaries and settlers.

When one of the first western entrepreneurs brought cattle to Fiji, the island folklore has it that the natives asked what the alien, large, male four-legged animal was named. Misunderstanding the question, the would-be rancher replied, "Oh, that's the bull-o'-ma-cow." Story has it that this is why beef is called *bulumakau* in Fijian. Comfortable mythology and an entertaining anecdote but, the truth is that the word was already in use in pidgin before the advent of commercial cattle ranching: the first cattle in Fiji were one or two milk cows. No bull.

Currently, beef cattle are raised in Fiji and the Solomon Islands, but some of the largest herds in the South Pacific are in New Caledonia and Vanuatu. On the island of Éfaté in the latter republic, pastures for cattle grazing are surrounded by "living fences" of yellow hibiscus, as well as triple strands of barbed wire. The main perimeter road runs through a large, government-owned cattle range and you can see Charolais cattle on one side, Brahman on the other. Because foreign ownership of cattle ranches in Vanuatu is permitted, on Espiritu Santo (merely "Santo" to the locals) the largest cattle station is Australian owned, the second largest Japanese. Both export beef primarily to Japan. However, there is ample beef for local consumption and thus many island methods of preparation.

(I certainly don't mean to dismiss the plenitude of prime beef forthcoming from the Parker Ranch on the Big Island of Hawai'i but their reputation of excellence in husbandry is solid and their produce more visible.)

The following recipes for the above-mentioned meats are a selection of fundamental, traditional dishes, as well as modern, updated recipes. (The instructions on cooking a whole pig in splendor are primarily for chefs and caterers with vision and an appreciation of the ethnic cuisines of Oceania.)

IMU KALUA PA'A PUA'A

Whole Pig Cooked in an Earth Oven

(HAWAI'I)

The following recipe is ambitious by any measure but it showcases the central dish of Oceanian cooking. Intended for institutional preparation (chefs in restaurants, hotels, clubs, etc.) or a community pig bake, it was specially tested for me on Oahu by a talented chef who regularly prepares **Imu Kalua** for a major hotel in Waikiki.

First, ordering the pig: You can calculate the weight of the pig you require by allowing one pound of live pig, on the hoof (sorry, trotter), per person. After dressing (slaughtering, bleeding and gutting) and cooking, that "pound" will have been reduced to a normal serving portion of 6 to 8 ounces. If a porker weighs 200+ pounds then, after dressing, his carcass will weigh in at about 170 pounds. With the shrinkage occasioned by moisture loss during baking, he will probably tip the scales at about 110 pounds, ready to eat. (That's still a lot of *kalua* pig dinners.)

When ordering a dressed pig, specify that the hair be removed. Otherwise you will be presented with a messy process.

So, we'll begin with a 170-pound, dressed porker. (For further information about the *imu*, please see Chapter 7.)

Following is a checklist of required implements/appliances/utensils to accomplish the cooking:

- enough fire stones or bricks to line the bottom of the earth oven (the stones should be smooth, round, dimpled and very dark)
- 1 roll of commercial, heavy-duty aluminum foil (18 inches × 200 feet), most used to line the pit but some reserved for use in Step 11
- 1 sheet of chicken wire, longer and wider than the dressed pig
- woven rush mats or burlap sacks sufficient to cover the top of the oven with about a 1-foot margin overlap
- 1 heavy, polyurethane ground sheet
- 2 large, plastic bags (33 gal.) of shredded banana stalks (or other edible plant stalks), or 2 large bags of grass clippings, well dampened and separated into thirds
- 6 or more large metal trays or roasting pans

Yield: 110 pounds (approximately) after cooking
Serves 180 to 200

1 170-pound pig (after dressing), hair removed	5 pounds of rock salt, sea salt, Hawaiian salt, or 1–2 gallons of soy sauce

1. Heat the fire stones until they are red hot.

2. Make incisions between 6 and 18 inches in length through the skin and into the flesh of the porker in the thicker and more dense meat sections: shoulders, back, hams. (This scoring allows the heat to penetrate better and cook the meat evenly, and provides an exit for the fat to drain.)

3. Rub the pig (*pua'a*) completely and thoroughly (inside and outside, as well as the incisions) with the salt or soy sauce.

4. Lay out the chicken wire. Force and bend the edges to create a tray with a 4-inch vertical rim. Line the wire tray with overlapping layers of the aluminum foil, shiny side uppermost.

5. Verify the order of the materials for lining the pit: (a) aluminum foil; (b) one-third of the banana stalks, leaves or other herbage; (c) fire stones.

6. Now cover the fire stones with the second one-third of the dampened herbage, layering it more thickly where the heat may be concentrated.

7. Hoist the pig onto the lined wire tray. Lower the tray into the fire pit on top of the previous layer of herbage.

8. Cover the pig with the final one-third layer of herbage. Layer the rush mats or burlap sacks over the top.

9. Cover the entire exposure with the ground sheet and seal the margins with sand or dirt, heaped into berms about 4 inches tall. Leave a small section of the ground sheet unsecured. Underneath this portion of the covering you will place the nozzle of a hose to let water trickle on the hot stones from time to time to augment the steam, if necessary. This will, obviously, create steam under slight pressure to aid in the cooking (roasting).

10. The pig (presuming 170 pounds, dressed) will take between 5 and 6 hours to cook from the time the earth oven is sealed. (The pressure from the steam in the oven will inflate the ground sheet if it is securely sealed. When the sheet collapses from lack of steam pressure, the pig should be properly cooked, because most of its internal moisture will have been released and dissipated.)

11. When the cooking is complete, uncover the pit, spreading the ground sheet beside the pit. Cover the sheet with the mats or sacks as you remove them. Layer the remaining foil on top of the mats or sacks, preparing for the reception of the wire tray with the pig in the following step.

12. Carefully shovel and sweep out the herbage off the pig and out of the pit. Using heavy-duty garden gloves, lift the tray with the pig out of the earth oven and place it on the foil. Clean and remove any remaining leaf fragments from the pig.

13. Decapitate the porker and reserve the head for the centerpiece. At the same time, remove the bones, separate the pig into large sections, detach the skin, trim off the fat and discard the bones, skin and fat, or save those elements from which you plan to make a stock.

14. Shred the remaining lean meat and spread it on the metal trays to cool. Sprinkle each portion lightly with salt and serve immediately.

Note: The meat must be refrigerated if it is not to be served at once. You may reheat it in an oven. Present it with a rich gravy made from a stock of the bones and trimmings. Obviously, cover the pan or tray of meat before placing it in the oven to prevent further dehydration.

KALUA *PORK IN YOUR OVEN*

(HAWAI'I)

Here is a version of **Kalua** Pork specifically styled to be baked in your domestic oven. Although scaled to manageable proportions, it nevertheless approximates the authentic traditional Hawaiian style of cooking pig for feasts in an *imu*.

I have cooked **Kalua** Pork on many occasions for many and diverse guests. They have unanimously remarked on the succulent flavor and delicate texture.

Leaf vegetables and foil substitute for the island wrappings of banana and ti leaves, and the dash of smoke seasoning recreates the robust flavor of the earth-oven pig.

Serves 6

4–5 pounds of boneless pork butt, fat scored into diamonds

1 teaspoon of 'alae or sea salt

2 tablespoons of soy sauce

1 teaspoon of smoke seasoning liquid

1 teaspoon of Worcestershire sauce

2 cloves of garlic, smashed, peeled and minced

1 teaspoon of peeled and freshly grated gingerroot

1 teaspoon of canola oil

6 large collard leaves, washed, drained and softened (*see page 21*), stems removed

1 bunch of spinach leaves, washed, drained and softened (*see page 21*), stems removed

1. Place the pork butt in a large (gallon size), resealable plastic bag. Add the salt, soy sauce, smoke seasoning, Worcestershire sauce, garlic and ginger. Seal the bag and massage the marinade into the pork. Set aside to marinate for at least 1 hour at room temperature.

2. Preheat your oven to 325° Fahrenheit.

3. Place a large (about 8 inches longer than the pork) rectangle of heavy-duty aluminum foil on your counter or cutting board. Spread the oil on the surface of the foil with your hands. Cover the oiled surface with the collard leaves, leaving a 2–3 inch margin on all sides. Layer the spinach leaves over the collard leaves, overlapping as necessary to stay within the borders.

4. Remove the pork from the marinade and place it near the edge, but within the leaf bed. Bend the edges of the foil on all sides to form a tray. Pour the remaining marinade over the pork. Now, carefully and tightly fold the leaves over the pork. Fold up and crimp-seal the foil to form a compact package.

5. Place the package in a roasting pan and bake for 3 hours. When cooked, remove the pork from the oven and carefully unwrap the packet. (The meat should be fork-tender, almost falling apart.) Use a pair of spatulas to gently transfer the leaf-wrapped pork to a serving dish. Serve **Kalua Pork** hot or warm.

POAKA TIO PAI

Maori Pork Chops Stuffed with Oysters

(NEW ZEALAND)

New Zealand's oysters are justly famous and are certainly beloved of the Maori. In New Zealand, this dish is often made with the Auckland rock oyster (*tio* in Maori), which is smaller and sweeter than the Stewart Island oyster. In the West we have a number of oyster species that we can successfully substitute.

Serves 6

6 large loin pork chops (1$^{1}/_{2}$
   inches thick, minimum)
14 oysters, shelled and minced
   (the liquor reserved for the
   gravy in Step 6 or clam juice
   may be substituted)
2 tablespoons of breadcrumbs
$^{1}/_{2}$ teaspoon of salt
$^{1}/_{4}$ teaspoon of freshly ground
   black pepper
a pinch of cayenne

1 tablespoon of canola oil
2$^{1}/_{2}$ tablespoons of butter
$^{1}/_{2}$ cup of unsweetened apple
   juice
2 apples, cored and sliced
1$^{1}/_{2}$ tablespoons of all-purpose
   flour
$^{1}/_{2}$ cup of dry sherry
2 teaspoons of freshly
   squeezed lemon juice
sprigs of watercress for garnish

1.   Preheat your oven to 350° Fahrenheit.
2.   Make deep incisions in the edge of the chops to create pockets. Set aside for use in the next step.
3.   In a small mixing bowl, thoroughly combine the minced oysters, bread-crumbs, salt, pepper and cayenne. Force equal portions of the stuffing mixture in the pockets of the chops and secure them with toothpicks.
4.   Place a large frying pan over high heat and add the canola and $^{1}/_{2}$ **table-spoon** of butter. When the fat comes up to temperature or a haze forms over the oil, fry the stuffed chops until they are browned on both sides. (Remove the pan from heat but let it remain on your range top.) Transfer the chops to an oven-proof baking dish, pour in the apple juice and bake in your oven for about 45 minutes.
5.   While the chops are baking, put the **remaining** butter in the frying pan and place it over medium heat. Add the apple slices and sauté them until they are light gold. Again remove the pan from heat but let it remain on the range top. With a slotted spoon, transfer the apples to a small, ovenproof dish. (Place the dish in the oven with the pork during the last several minutes of their cooking to keep the apples hot and use in Step 7.)
6.   Return the frying pan to a medium-low heat and add the flour, stirring to make a paste or *roux* with the residual fat. Draw off any excess cooking juices from the pork chops with a bulb baster and, together with the oyster liquor and sherry, pour into the frying pan. Stir and cook, reducing as necessary, to produce a smooth, thick sauce. Add the lemon juice, stir and remove from heat.
7.   Transfer the pork chops to a serving dish and remove the toothpicks. Surround the chops with the sautéed apples and pour the sauce over the assembly. Garnish with the watercress sprigs and serve immediately.

Note: Serve these succulent pork chops accompanied by creamed sweet potatoes and either a green-leaf vegetable or squash.

VUAKA KEI NA URA TAVUTEKE

Pan-Fried Fillets of Pork and Shrimp with Asparagus,
Broccoli and *Vudi* in Orange Sauce (FIJI)

This dish was part of a dinner I enjoyed just prior to a *meke*, an evening of local song and dance, at the Suva Travelodge. I was so taken with the extraordinary combination of ingredients, colors and flavors that I have attempted to recreate the original as closely as possible.

Vudi is Fijian for banana or plantain. The pork was originally served with what the Fijians call *duruka*, or flower stalk of local, wild sugar cane. I have substituted broccoli because of its similar texture and color. Thus, this showpiece remains intact. Ah! I almost forgot. The **Vuaka** was presented on a plate lined with a circle of banana leaf.

ORANGE SAUCE

Serves 6

2 cups of freshly squeezed
   orange juice

1/2 teaspoon of orange zest,
   grated

2 tablespoons of bitter orange
   marmalade, rinds minced

1/2 teaspoon of garlic, smashed,
   peeled and minced

1/2 teaspoon of fresh gingerroot, peeled and grated

1 teaspoon of basil leaves,
   minced

1/4 teaspoon of salt

1/4 teaspoon of freshly ground
   black pepper

1 teaspoon of dried mustard

1/4 teaspoon of ground
   cardamom

1 tablespoon of cornstarch,
   mixed with 2 tablespoons
   of warm water

2 tablespoons of unsalted
   butter

1. Place all the ingredients except the last two in a medium, non-reactive saucepan and bring the mixture to a slow boil over medium heat. Reduce heat and simmer for about 15 minutes, or until the sauce is reduced by one-quarter.

2. Stir the cornstarch and water into a smooth cream and spoon it into the sauce. Continue to stir, on heat, until the sauce thickens and becomes silky.

145

3. Remove the saucepan from heat and gradually introduce the butter until it is dissolved and incorporated in the sauce. Hold the sauce in the top of a double boiler or by placing its saucepan in a larger pan of simmering water. (Plan for use in Step 1, **Assembly.**)

PORK, SHRIMP AND VEGETABLES

4 tablespoons of butter
2 tablespoons of canola oil
3 large, ripe plantains, peeled
    and sliced lengthwise on
    the diagonal into 1/4-**inch**
    thick spears
2 pounds of pork tenderloin,
    sliced into fillets 3/4-**inch**
    thick and each pounded
    briefly to slightly flatten
12 spears of asparagus (each
    about 5 inches in length)

6 large broccoli flowerets
1 pound of extra-large (16–20
    count per pound) **raw**
    shrimp, shelled and
    deveined
1 whole orange, sliced into
    1/4-**inch thick disks, seeds**
    removed
18 (approximately) **basil leaves**
    to garnish

1. Turn on your oven to its lowest setting.
2. Place **1 tablespoon** of the butter and **2 teaspoons** of canola oil in a large frying pan. Set the pan over medium-high heat and let the oil come up to frying temperature.
3. Sauté the plantain slices, turning as necessary (about 2–3 minutes per side) until all are dark golden. Reduce heat to low and cook for a further 30 seconds. Transfer the plantains to a heatproof plate or platter lined with paper towels. Hold them in your oven for use in Step 3, **Assembly.**
4. Add another **1**1/2 **tablespoons** of butter and **1 tablespoon** of the canola oil to the same frying pan and increase heat to medium-high. Sauté the pork fillets, about 6 at a time (do not crowd the pan), for about 2 minutes per side, seasoning with the salt and pepper. With each episode, drain the meat over the pan and transfer the fillets to another heatproof dish. Continue until all the pork has been cooked and is being held in the oven for Step 2, **Assembly.**
5. Wash the frying pan and replace it on your range top.
6. Fill the base of a steamer with the requisite amount of water and bring it to a boil over medium-high heat. Place the asparagus and broccoli in the steamer tray. Assemble and cover the steamer. Steam the vegetables for about 6 minutes, or until both are just tender. Turn the heat off under the steamer but let the vegetables remain on hold in their tray until Step 3, **Assembly.**

7.   Place the remaining butter and oil in the frying pan from Step 5. Bring the fat up to frying temperature over medium-high heat. Add the shrimp and sauté, stirring, until they change color to pink. Remove them with a slotted spoon and set aside for use in Step 2, **Assembly.**

ASSEMBLY

1.   Set out 6 dinner plates. Pool equal portions of the **Orange Sauce** from the double boiler on each plate.
2.   Arrange 3–4 pork fillets from Step 4, **Pork, Shrimp and Vegetables** along one side or edge of each plate. Deposit about 3 cooked shrimp from Step 7 next to the pork.
3.   On the remaining surface of each plate, arrange equal portions of plantains from Step 3, the asparagus spears from Step 6, the broccoli flowerets from Step 6.
4.   Garnish the perimeter of each plate with the orange slices and decorate with the basil leaves. Serve immediately.

PORK, APPLE AND KUMARA CASSEROLE

(NEW ZEALAND)

Kumara (Maori for sweet potato) was probably brought to New Zealand from Eastern Polynesia during the large immigration in the 7th or 8th centuries and flourished in the sandy soils of the North Island. Later, when the Maori settled in the Rotorua thermal area, they brought their tubers with them.

I first came to Rotorua in November, in the middle of a seasonal storm. Rain pelted down and the sulfurous fumes from the vents hung in the air like a miasma. The view from my bedroom window overlooking Lake Rotorua was worthy of description by Dante Alighieri. Lowering black-steel clouds obliterated the hills and Mokoia Island in mid-lake. The water itself was a curious hue of metallic beige and ascending clouds and puffs of cream-colored steam stood out against the murky sky. It was ten o'clock in the morning.

Later, the weather cleared slowly and defining hills, cradling the lake, became slowly apparent. Splashing through the puddles, I walked to the large and glorious Edwardian architectural relic, the Bath House Museum. Built to allow the early tourists to "take the waters," it is restored to its original beauty, gabled, half-timbered and with a steep scarlet roof. There I absorbed much of the pictorial history of the Maori in the Rotorua–Taupo area.

Ravenously hungry by the shag-end of lunchtime, I chose the satisfying **Pork, Apple and *Kumara* Casserole**. The *kumara* balanced the pork and the apple complemented both. It was an appropriate dish for a rainy day.

Serves 4 to 6

1 teaspoon of canola oil	1 teaspoon of salt
8 loin pork chops, trimmed of excess fat	1/4 teaspoon of freshly ground black pepper
1 teaspoon of dried mustard dissolved in sufficient water to make a thick cream	2 cups of tomato juice
	2 large cooking apples, peeled, cored and thinly sliced
2 large onions, peeled and thinly sliced into slivers	1/4 cup of freshly squeezed lemon juice
2 tablespoons of parsley, minced	2 tablespoons of sugar
1/8 teaspoon each of sage, rosemary and marjoram	2 large sweet potatoes, peeled, sliced crosswise and soaked in cold water

1. Preheat your oven to 375° Fahrenheit.
2. Place a large frying pan over medium-high heat and add the oil. When the oil comes up to frying temperature, carefully deposit the pork chops, several at a time, and quickly dry-fry (practically) until brown on both sides. Continue until all the chops are cooked and set aside for use in the next step. Trace a smear of the mustard cream on each chop.
3. Place **one-half** of the onions in the bottom of a large casserole with a lid. Layer the pork on top of the onion. Combine the **remaining** onion with the parsley, dried herbs, salt and pepper in a small mixing bowl, then pour it over the chop mixture. Add the tomato juice, cover and bake for about 20 minutes.
4. Meanwhile, place the apples, lemon juice and sugar in a small, non-reactive saucepan and set it over medium-low heat. Adjust the heat to maintain a simmer, cover and cook for about 15 minutes, or until the apples are just softened. Remove from heat and set aside for use in the next step.
5. After the casserole is precooked, remove it from the oven, uncover and pour the apple mixture over the contents of the casserole. Drain the sweet potato slices and layer them over the top.
6. Return the casserole to the oven and bake for between 45 minutes and 1 hour, or until the sweet potato slices are browned on top. Serve at once.

Note: You may like to vary this casserole by substituting pork sausages and/or thick slices of ham for the pork chops. (The sausages should be browned before adding to the casserole in Step 2.)

LU PULU

Leaf-Wrapped Chicken and Fish (TONGA)

The only kingdom (a constitutional monarchy) remaining in Polynesia, these are the islands that Captain James Cook named "the Friendly Isles" because of the generous hospitality offered to visitors. Historically though, the Tongans were aggressive warriors and engaged in a series of bloody wars with neighboring Fiji.

Tongan feasts are legendary: tables groaning with dishes of chicken, fish, vegetables and pork. (Regarding the last, at one recent monarchial coronation, a whole roast pig was provided for each of the thousands of guests.)

This leaf-wrapped parcel, cooked in an earth-pit oven, is a cousin to the Fijian *palusami* (see page 182). Although we are unused to the combination of chicken and fish together, the two blend remarkably well. The visual and aromatic surprise when opening the package is a gift to both the palate and the "inner man."

Lu Pulu has become a favorite in our family to the point where those who had never sampled Oceanian dishes not only adored this recipe but promptly prepared it when they next entertained.

(For the absolutely authentic preparation of this recipe in an earth-pit oven, please see Chapter 7).

Serves 2 to 4

1 banana leaf, washed, drained and softened *(see page 21)*, or a 20-inch length of heavy-duty aluminum foil

6 collard leaves, washed, drained and softened *(see page 21)*, stems removed

14 large spinach leaves, washed, drained and softened *(see page 21)*, stems removed

1 cup (approximately 8 ounces) of shark or other firm whitefish fillets, cut into 1/2-inch-long pieces

1 cup (approximately 8 ounces) of chicken breast meat, cut into 1/2-inch-long pieces

1/2 medium yellow onion, peeled and coarsely chopped

1 medium tomato, coarsely chopped

1/4 teaspoon of salt

1/4 teaspoon of freshly ground black pepper

a dash of White Wine Worcestershire sauce (optional)

1/4 cup of thick coconut milk or coconut cream *(see page 19)*

2 tablespoons of dried, unsweetened coconut flakes

3–foot length of kitchen twine (optional)

149

1. Preheat your oven to 350° Fahrenheit.
2. In a 16-inch reusable foil pan, spread out the banana leaf or the aluminum foil and arrange thereupon overlapping layers of collard and then spinach leaves, leaving a 1–2-inch margin on all sides.
3. Place the fish and then the chicken pieces, followed by the onion and tomato in a mound in the center of the leaves. Season with the salt and pepper. (Sprinkle with the optional Worcestershire sauce.)
4. Carefully pour the coconut milk over the mixed meats. (If using aluminum foil, bend all four sides to help prevent any overruns.)
5. Now gently mold the banana leaf or foil over the filling, encasing and wrapping it into a sealed parcel. (Make sure all the loose corners or edges are tucked in.)
6. Tie the parcel securely with twine. (Islanders use the full ribs of the banana leaf as cordage.)
7. Place the packet into a greased oven dish and bake it for about 1 hour.
8. After the cooking time has expired, place the packet on its serving dish and let it cool for several minutes before unwrapping and serving.

MICRONESIA

Mariana Islands [Guam, Saipan, Tinian, Rota, etc.], Caroline Islands [Belau (Palau) and Yap, Chuuk (Truk), Pohnpei (Ponape) and Kusaie (Kosrae), etc.], Marshall Islands (Kwajalein, Majuro, etc.), Nauru, Kiribati (Gilberts)

The islands of Micronesia lie scattered across the Pacific like the reflection of stars in the sky. Micronesia is 3,000,000 square miles of ocean north of the Equator containing some 2,200 islands, many of which you could fly over at 35,000 feet on a fleecy-clouded day and not even see. (Historically, for that matter, and for the preservation of the islanders' continued tranquillity, the early Europeans in the Pacific managed to sail past many without even suspecting their existence.) This is not surprising since Micronesia's aggregate of land mass is only 919 square miles. Guam, as the largest island in that entire quadrant of Oceania, is a mere 30 miles in length by nine miles wide, with a total surface area of only 212 square miles.

Micronesia's four main—but scattered—groups of islands are divided into the Marianas, the Carolines (East and West), the Marshalls and the Gilberts. (Nauru is a sovereign island-nation unto itself.) Simple as this looks in an atlas, some 20 different languages are spoken through the area. This reflects a diversity in cultures and customs and, because Micronesia contains both "high," fertile islands (the peaks of a volcanic, sub-oceanic mountain range extending from Japan to Papua New Guinea) and "low" islands, or typical sand-swept Pacific atolls (a lone coconut palm on a swelling of sand), island lifestyles are very different from one archipelago to the next.

Much more than statistics, Micronesia is full of superlatives. It is home to the world's greatest ocean depth, the Mariana Trench (trough or deep). It is 1835 miles long and borders the east (extending to south) side of the Mariana Islands where the ocean reaches a depth of 7 miles.

(Continued.)

Micronesia boasts some of the world's largest atolls. Kwajalein atoll in the Marshalls has 97 tiny islands ringing its 900-square-mile lagoon (often called the world's largest aquatic target, since it is the splashdown area for U.S. ICBMs, test-fired from Vandenberg Air Force Base in California). Next largest is also in Micronesia, Truk lagoon in the Carolines: 822 square miles of a gigantic, sunken, volcanic crater, enclosed by 140 miles of coral reef (the graveyard for some 60 World War II Japanese ships and, obviously, a haven for wreck divers).

Micronesia is lost civilizations. Nan Madol on Pohnpei was a royal and governmental enclave of 92 man-built islets, edged in hewn basalt and bisected by canals and waterways. Like an island Pompeii, it contained mansions for royalty, houses for priests, temples, tombs, bathing pools and fish ponds, and was populated continuously for about 300 years until the 18th century.

Consider the venerable Chamorro civilization in the Marianas, which was begun about 1500 BC. The ancient Chamorros quarried massive limestone pillars with integral rounded caps, called *latte* stones. They were used to support the houses of the nobility and the men's halls. That long-lived and cohesive society lasted until their genocide at the hands of the Spanish during the 150 years subsequent to the islands' discovery by Ferdinand Magellan.

Micronesia is also Yap; four main islands within a coral reef (there are about 134 tiny outer islands), originally formed by gigantic upheavals of the Asian continental shelf. Yap's currency was, to say the least, the most static and stable in the world. It consisted of circular stones, called *rai,* with a central hole. (They still exist, primarily as a sign of individual wealth.) Some *rai* are massive, often measuring up to twelve feet in diameter and as much as five tons in weight. Even more extraordinary is that the stones were quarried in ancient times on an island hundreds of miles away, Belau, and brought to Yap on barges at a substantial cost in lives to the Yapese crewmen because of frequent storms.

In the population centers of Micronesia, supermarkets and stores are stocked (well, almost stocked) with imported canned and frozen fish, meats and vegetables. These conveniences have obviated the frequent requirement to provide daily sustenance by fishing, breeding and growing. But, yes, even in the most urbanized areas, the men still go fishing, primarily for sport; however, often to stretch their household budgets and/or provide supplementary income.

On outer islands and small atolls, although there are food stores, supplies are infrequent. Water is carefully husbanded to grow breadfruit, taro, pandanus, as well as primary leaf vegetables, and coconuts in the thin topsoil. Of course, chickens and pigs are bred and raised. However, it is the fish, including crustaceans and mollusks, that provide much of the food.

The waves of colonialism that have washed the shores of Micronesia have deposited a flotsam of food and cooking techniques. The Spanish legacy of cakes and bread still remains. There is an unmistakable and hearty Filipino influence in the food of the Marianas. (This influence began when the islands were under Spanish domination and the seat of the colonial government was in Manila. The link has been strengthened by the continuing influx of Filipinos to the islands through the years to the point where *pancit* is a household word on Guam.) Rice is no longer grown as it was under Japanese occupation but is widely eaten. Imported *sashimi* and its more elegant cousin, *sushi,* is served at almost every cocktail party.

MERIZO CHICKEN TINOLA

(GUAM)

One highway circumnavigates almost the entire periphery of Guam. (The exception to general access is the northern end of the island, occupied by Andersen Air Force Base and a naval communications unit.) The end-up-where-you-started theory is comforting to visiting motorists so long as the temptation to take small side roads—usually unpaved—is resisted.

In the vicinity of the more densely populated areas of the capital, Agana, Tamuning and the tourist center at Tumon Bay (with an amazing concentration of high-rise tourist hotels rivaling Waikiki for glitz), the road is multi-laned, well-surfaced and even boasts the Guamanian version of morning and evening rush hours. However, as you drive east over the high, moor-like central plateau and then turn southward, both the scenery and the highway change dramatically. The coastline becomes rugged. The road narrows to the equivalent of a driveway; descending and bending around small, sharp escarpments. Potholes test your shock absorbers and springs. Jungled vegetation casts pools of shadows, and dried pods and branches of the ubiquitous *tangantangan* (*Leucaena* species) shrubs swipe at the car windows.

Traffic thins and, except for the occasional bus filled with Japanese tourists ("Circular Route—See Authentic Chamorro Villages and Visit Native Life"), the only moving violations are the perpetually-over-the-speed-limit Guam Bombs. This is the affectionate sobriquet given to local vehicles whose sheet metal has been transformed to tattered and rusted metal lace by the salt air and whose engines continue to function in spite of sounding like there is a hostile military engagement under the hood.

Gaps in the rocky hills suddenly reveal lone houses, chickens pecking at their skirts and the requisite pickup truck parked in the front yard like a guard dog. A swooping curve downward and thick ranks of palm trunks part to reveal semi-hidden beaches, jagged rocks of coral, trickling freshwater streams and the pounding blue Pacific. The route levels and passes by palisades of palms sheltering deserted sand beaches and a sea that is suddenly calm. You are entering the realm of the southern villages. Protected by deep bays and lagoons, cradled by rolling hills at their backs, the string of sleepy houses and whitewashed churches belong to another time. Talofofo, Inarajan, Merizo, Umatac—their names evoke a litany of Chamorro history.

But visit on a fiesta weekend and Rip Van Winkle has awoken. The road is lined with parked vehicles. Laughter and music come from every house, and marvelous aromas of roasted pork, chicken, garlic and fish compete with the scent of flowers. It is a block party on steroids. Everyone visits but nobody arrives empty-handed. Cases of beer and soft drinks are lugged along the road. Women cradle large, disposable aluminum baking dishes filled with home cooking to donate to the various feasts. One such dish is this **Chicken Tinola.**

Serves 4 to 6

1 tablespoon of canola oil

1 large yellow onion, peeled
 and sliced into slivers

3 cloves of garlic, smashed,
 peeled and finely chopped

1 whole chicken, skinned and
 cut into serving parts
 (legs, thighs, breast halved,
 etc.)

5 tablespoons of soy sauce

1/2 teaspoon of freshly ground
 black pepper

1 bay leaf

1 tablespoon of rice flour, dissolved in 5 cups of warm
 water

1 medium, green (unripe)
 papaya, peeled, seeded and
 cut into medium-sized
 pieces (approximately
 1 inch square) or an equivalent amount of chayote

1/4 cup of chili pepper leaves
 (see Note)

1.   Place a large, non-reactive saucepan over medium-high heat. Pour in the oil and let it come up to temperature. Quickly stir and fry the onion slices until they are translucent. Add the garlic and continue stirring and frying for less than a minute.

2.   Carefully add the chicken parts to the frying oil. Turn and stir the pieces to uniformly cook the meat.

3.   When the meat whitens and becomes opaque, season with the soy sauce, black pepper and bay.

4.   Pour in the rice starch water and modulate the heat to bring the mixture to a rolling boil.

5.   Now reduce the heat to low, cover the pan and simmer until the chicken is almost completely cooked, approximately 40–45 minutes.

6.   Uncover the pan, increase the heat slightly and stir in the papaya or chayote. Cook for a further 5 minutes.

7.   Remove from heat and stir in the chili pepper leaves just before transferring the **Tinola** to a serving bowl. Accompany the chicken with cooked rice and *Finadene* (see page 226).

Note: Pepper plants may be conveniently grown at home from the seeds of packets of whole, dried chili peppers (usually available in Asian or specialty markets). Place the pots in a sunny location (terrace, balcony, windowsill, etc.). Once the seeds have sprouted, the plants need little attention, save watering, grow quickly, and are hardy and prolific. You may substitute 1 small green pepper, seeded, cored and sliced into matchstick-sized strips, adding it with the papaya in Step 6.

CHILI-GARLIC CHICKEN
WITH MANGOES

(FIJI)

There is a small restaurant in Suva on a back street (Carnarvon) with an improbably long name, Old Mill Cottage Café Restaurant. Located behind the government ministries, its setting is a red-roofed bungalow with a wide front verandah, protected by green wooden railings and shaded by red-and-green-striped awnings. A local haunt, it serves unpretentious but delicious Fijian dishes and curries at lunchtime to a packed crowd of government employees, local politicos and businessmen, seated on benches around red Formica-topped tables. I lunched at the Old Mill several times and, on one occasion, I selected this **Chili-Garlic Chicken,** which I balanced with *Palusami* (see page 182) and plain rice.

Serves 6 to 8

3–4 pounds of chicken parts
(legs, thighs, breast halved,
etc.), **skinned**
**8 cloves of garlic, smashed,
peeled and chopped**
1 teaspoon of salt
3 tablespoons of peanut oil
**2 medium onions, peeled and
finely chopped**
**1 tablespoon of fresh ginger-
root, peeled and minced**
3 red chili peppers (*Serrano* or
Jalepeño)**, minced or 1 teaspoon of dried red chili
flakes**

1 teaspoon of paprika
**1/4 teaspoon of freshly ground
black pepper**
**2 large tomatoes, blanched,
peeled and coarsely
chopped**
1 tablespoon of soy sauce
1 teaspoon of sugar
**2 medium, ripe mangoes,
peeled and the flesh thinly
sliced**

1.   Place the chicken parts in a large mixing bowl. Pound the garlic and salt to a paste in a mortar and rub it to thoroughly coat the chicken pieces. Tightly cover the bowl and let the chicken macerate at room temperature for at least 2 hours.
2.   Place a large wok over a medium-high setting and pour in the oil. When a haze begins to form over the oil, carefully insert the chicken parts from above and stir-fry until the outside of all the parts is uniformly golden. Add the onions and ginger and reduce heat to medium-low. Continue frying and stirring until the onions are translucent.

3.   Add the chili peppers, black pepper and tomatoes. Stir, then cover and simmer for about 25 minutes, or until the chicken is tender. (If you are not satisfied with the volume or consistency of the sauce, you may consider uncovering the wok during all or part of the simmering process.)

4.   Pour in the soy sauce and sugar. Stir until the sugar is just dissolved and transfer the mixture to a large serving bowl. Line the dish with the mango slices and serve at once accompanied by rice.

TAKIA NI TOA PAINAVIU
Chicken in Pineapple Canoes (TAHITI)

Papeete has had a face-lift and, although modernization is as inevitable in the Pacific as it is anywhere, it still comes as a shock. The capital has lost much of its ramshackle and picturesque charm; great if you live there but not so accommodating for camera-clicking tourists. You need to get out into the countryside to recapture the Tahiti of old and the unhurried, French-Polynesian way of life. Go down to the central market on Rue 22 Septembre and, close by, you will find "le truck" depot. These are the ubiquitous little buses that are the public transportation system of Tahiti. The fares are very reasonable but watch your head. You cannot stand upright inside, and a neck-jolting collision with the roof by a gangling tourist causes much mirth among the locals.

Take the southwestern arm of the route around Tahiti Nua—the larger of the two geographic segments of the figure eight that forms the island. Ride, with frequent stops to dispatch passengers, past the site of Paul Gauguin's wooden hut (since disappeared) at Km 12, and on through Punaauia then Paea. Here you can see a few of the remaining Tahitian *fares,* bamboo-walled and pandanus-thatched. Other homes are more modern; painted rainbow colors and with corrugated tin roofs. Barnyard fowl peck within the small compounds that are surrounded by mixtures of bushes, fences, rocks and posts. In the rural areas, you are never far from someone's chickens.

Chicken is as important to the Polynesian diet today as it was when they packed the scrawny, long-legged birds into their canoes and made landfall in what is now Tahiti. William Ellis wrote of the Tahitian chicken in 1831:

> The most useful bird, however, is the common domestic fowl, called moa by the natives. These were found among the island by their discoverers, and appear to have

155

been there as long as the people. They are of the same kind as those reared in England; the bodies are smaller, and the legs longer, but this may perhaps have arisen from their not being confined, and seldom fed by the people. Those that are tame usually live upon what they find in the garden, or the fragments of breadfruit, &c. left after the native meal. During the day they seldom wander far from their owner's dwelling, and at night, either take shelter under the same roof, or roost on the boughs of the trees by which it is overshadowed.

The chickens you now see are descended from European stock; brought to the islands to upgrade the local variety. Today, there are productive poultry farms on Tahiti, some quite close to Papeete, and these farms provide the local *poulet*.

Pineapples, however, are among the more recent introductions to the Society Islands and are widely cultivated on Moorea, Tahiti's closest island neighbor.

For this recipe, you will need two medium-sized, ripe pineapples. To check their state of ripeness before you buy, hold the fruit with its crown away from you and press your fingers at the central base. The resistance should duplicate itself when you apply the same pressure against your own wrist.

To make pineapple boats, cut off the green crown; then use a sharp knife to halve each lengthwise. With a paring knife, slice sections deep into the halved fruit both horizontally and vertically to create a checkered board appearance with about $1/2$-inch wide by 1-inch long sections, leaving a $1/2$-inch margin of pineapple meat inside the skin.

Now, using a grapefruit knife, cut out the flesh to form a uniform cavity. Cut the pineapple sections into equal chunks and remove any hard pieces of core. Wrap the pineapple sections in paper towels and refrigerate. Turn the pineapple shells onto paper towels and let them drain, upside down, until ready to serve.

Serves 8

the shells and flesh from 2 medium-large pineapples
3 tablespoons of unsalted butter
1 small onion, finely chopped
4 boned chicken breasts, skin removed, cut into medium (approximately $1 1/2$-inch long) pieces
3 heaped tablespoons of all-purpose flour
$3/4$ cup of chicken stock
1 cup of thick coconut milk (*see page 19*),

3 tablespoons of light rum
3 tablespoons of coconut cream (*see page 19*)
$1/4$ cup of slivered almonds
$1/2$ teaspoon of salt
$1/4$ teaspoon of white pepper
2 tablespoons of minced parsley
4 wooden satay skewers
2 6-inch squares of banana leaf or paper, each cut in half diagonally

1.   Turn your oven on to its lowest setting, about 200° Fahrenheit. Place the drained pineapple halves on a large heatproof platter or tray and place them inside the oven.

2.   Remove the pineapple sections from the refrigerator and let them drain on additional paper towels.

3.   Place a large, heavy frying pan or wok over medium-high heat and melt the butter. When the butter stops foaming, stir-fry the onion until it is softened and translucent. Add the chicken pieces and continue to stir and fry. Sauté the mixture, stirring and turning, until the chicken is white and firm.

4.   Sprinkle in the flour and stir until the sauce is thickened and the chicken is coated. Now pour in the chicken stock and continue stirring. Add the thick **coconut milk** and stir until the sauce is silky.

5.   Add the pineapple chunks from Step 2. Sprinkle in the rum. Stir in the **coconut cream** and the almonds. Season with salt and pepper. Continue to stir for about 2 more minutes, then remove the pan from heat.

6.   Take the platter from the oven and invert the shells. Spoon equal portions of the chicken/coconut/pineapple mixture from Step 5 into shells. Sprinkle the surface of each with the parsley.

7.   Thread a *satay* stick through each triangular piece of banana leaf or paper to form a sail; starting from the middle of one of the shorter sides and ending up through the top at one of the acute points. Insert the sail/mast into the center of each pineapple boat. Bring to the table at once.

POULET AVEC DES LIMETTES

Chicken with Limes (MOOREA)

Moorea works its magic from the first encounter. Mine was from the deck of the Tahiti–Moorea ferry. I wrote in my journal:

> The wide lagoon was milky turquoise. The sun turned the nearest mountainsides the brilliant light green of young lettuce. Where the clouds sat over the peaks, they cast dark green shadows. A ruffle of palms fringed the lagoon and the coast road. Except for a few dockside buildings, little habitation was visible. Rickety buses and trucks were lined up at the jetty. As we climbed into ours, a square powerful man hefted large, blocky pieces of what looked like audio equipment. A passenger struggled onto the bus with two long rolls of carpeting and a bicycle

wheel. They were good-naturedly passed over everyone's heads amid much laughter and banter.

The first kilometer or so of the round-island road (traveling clockwise) was pot holed and patched, and the antique bus rattled so badly I though it would fly apart. Just as a sleek Mercedes passed us in the opposite direction and I began to wonder why anyone would subject an expensive car to such a beating, the road surface smoothed out.

There were little villages tucked into pockets of flat land between the mountain ramparts; houses both thatched-traditional and cement-block modern, painted Gauguin hues of orange, rose, blue and yellow. There were gardens bursting with flowers, flowering trees, chickens and dogs dashing along dusty lanes. Rounding a sharp, mountain-defined corner we dived abruptly into pouring rain and just as smartly emerged from it further on where the clouded slopes ended.

The bus stopped everywhere. The passenger with the rolls of carpet and bicycle wheel staggered off at the first village. We passed a riding stable and a man, who had been coughing consumptively, dismounted. We reached my stop and the driver called out "Hibiscus." I was relieved because I had no idea where it was. There was a spacious, velvet-grassed enclosure by the sea, sprinkled with *ares* (thatched huts). Hibiscus hedges and crotons drew curtains of privacy around them. At the edge of the beach was a gigantic rubber tree, some 50 feet across. Interwoven within it were two pandanus buttresses and several coconut palms. The peaceful lagoon spread in front and, behind me, the verdant hills thick with foliage, rose steeply against the sky.

This was where I discovered *Poulet avec des Limettes.*

Serves 6 to 8

2¹/₂ **pounds** (approximately) **of chicken parts** (legs, thighs, breast halved, etc.), **skinned**	**2 tablespoons of butter**
the juice of 8 limes	**1 cup of chicken stock** (canned chicken broth may be substituted)
the zest of 1 lime, finely grated	**1 teaspoon of sugar**

$2^1/_2$ **pounds** (approximately) **of chicken parts** (legs, thighs, breast halved, etc.), **skinned**
the juice of 8 limes
the zest of 1 lime, finely grated
$^1/_2$ **teaspoon of salt**
$^1/_4$ **teaspoon of white pepper**
1 large sprig of fresh thyme or
  $^1/_2$ **teaspoon of dried**
  thyme
4 tablespoons of peanut oil

2 tablespoons of butter
1 cup of chicken stock (canned chicken broth may be substituted)
1 teaspoon of sugar
1$^1/_2$ **tablespoons of cornstarch, dissolved in 2 tablespoons of warm water**
$^1/_2$ **cup of whipping cream**
1 lime, thinly sliced into disks

1. Place the chicken parts in a large (1 gallon), resealable plastic bag. Add only **one-half** the lime juice, all the lime zest, salt, pepper and thyme. Seal

the bag, massage it briefly, and marinate for 2 hours, turning the bag occasionally.

2.   After marinating, drain the chicken and pat dry with paper towels. Reserve the marinade and set both the meat and the liquid aside for use in the next step.

3.   Place a large, non-reactive saucepan over medium-high heat, add the oil and butter and let the fat come up to frying temperature. Then carefully deposit the chicken parts. Brown the chicken on all sides, turning frequently. Pour in the marinade and chicken stock. Let the liquid come to a boil. Reduce the heat to low and simmer the chicken for 10–15 minutes. (While simmering, turn your oven to its lowest setting and place a large, ovenproof serving dish inside.)

4.   Drain the chicken over the saucepan and accumulate the parts on the dish in the oven. Adjust the heat as necessary to maintain a full boil and reduce the sauce to approximately 1 cup. After the reduction, modulate the heat to maintain a simmer and add the **remainder** of the lime juice and the sugar. Stir the cornstarch/water into the sauce and whisk until it thickens.

5.   Take the pan off heat and stir in the cream. Remove the chicken from the oven and pour the sauce over it. Garnish with the lime slices and serve immediately.

CORNED-BEEF PALUSAMI

(FIJI AND SAMOA)

I ate this traditional dish several times in Suva, Fiji. The first occasion was in the dining room of the old Grand Pacific Hotel, prior to remodeling. It was then still a first cousin to the Raffles Hotel in Singapore and the Oriental in Bangkok, in architecture and atmosphere, if no longer in class. A white Edwardian structure with the interior, two-storey balconied hall of an ocean liner, it was down-at-the heels like an aging dowager: fresh paint to mask a withered complexion but with dignity shining through. Ghosts of ambassadors, royalty and colonial civil servants walked in its corridors and danced in its halls.

W. Somerset Maugham had remarked in 1916, two years after the hotel was built, that it was ". . . cool and empty. . . . The food is very bad, but the rooms are pleasant, fresh and cool." Sir Noel Coward, visiting Suva, was shown the hotel by the magistrate. The barman was asleep at the bar. Coward stuck his aristocratic and pointed nose in the air and epigrammatized, "Pacific? Undoubtedly. Hotel? Perhaps. Grand? Never."

Perhaps in its new incarnation it will be "grand." I found my room spacious and cool. The food was excellent. But the dowager was almost deserted.

Arriving late in the evening, I sought the dining room. Only one table was occupied. I wanted to separate myself with my thoughts and food.

By the time my *Palusami* arrived, I was the lone diner. A five-piece group of Polynesian musicians, dressed in red and white flowered Hawaiian shirts, were playing—primarily for their own enjoyment—respected favorites on slack-key guitar and ukuleles. One of the hotel "boys" was sitting in with them. A tall, dark Fijian in a blue floral shirt and dark-blue traditional man's skirt, he livened the rhythm with his gusto, slapping his thighs and legs with paradiddles. He was vastly enjoying himself. I applauded enthusiastically to help compensate for the fact that I was their sole audience. The musicians grinned broadly; played to and for me.

The main dish was set before me, shrouded in leaves; the white plate almost invisible against the starched, long white tablecloth. A glass of wine was placed reverently on my right. I unfolded my carefully fanned, starched napkin and tasted the *Palusami*. It was aromatic, moist and appetizing. The moon swung up over Suva Bay. The palms were black silhouettes outside the tall windows. I ate. The band played on. It was a splendid welcome to a Fiji of 60 years past, frozen in time in the 1990s.

Serves 6

2 cups brisket or canned corned beef

1 cup of coconut cream *(see page 19)*

6 collard leaves, washed, drained and softened *(see page 21)*, stems removed

16 spinach leaves, washed, drained and stems removed

1 cup of sweet potato, peeled, cut into $1/2$-inch cubes and cooked

3 medium tomatoes, sliced

1 medium onion, peeled, sliced and the slices separated into rings

3 green onions, both white and green, finely chopped

2 green chili peppers *(Serrano* or *Jalapeño)*, sliced into $1/4$-inch disks

6 drops (approximately) of Worcestershire sauce

3 drops (approximately) of smoke seasoning liquid

$1/2$ teaspoon of freshly ground black pepper

1. Preheat your oven to 350° Fahrenheit.

2. Combine the corned beef with about **one-half** of the coconut cream (reserve the remainder for use in Step 6).

3. Spread a 24-inch length (× 18-inches wide) of heavy-duty aluminum foil over a disposable foil baking pan (18 × 12 × 2 inches). Press the foil to conform to the interior of the foil pan. Layer the foil with the softened leaves, using the largest first and overlapping as necessary to form a firm base that extends beyond the edge of the foil pan.

4. Mound the corned-beef/coconut cream mixture from Step 2 in the center of the leaves. (The rim of the foil pan will retain the liquid but you may want to also fold or crimp the edges of the foil inward.)

5. Next, layer the sweet potato and about 3/4 of the tomato slices over the corned beef (reserving 1/4 of the tomatoes for use in Step 10). Continue layering with the onion rings and 3/4 of the green onions (again, reserving about 1/4 of the green onions for use in Step 10). Arrange the chili pepper disks over the top of the assembly.

6. Slowly—so as not to create a tidal wave—pour in the remaining cup of coconut cream over the top and season with the Worcestershire sauce and the smoke seasoning. Add the pepper to taste.

7. Fold the leaves over the mixture, beginning with the inner leaves and, continuing toward the outer, fold and press the mixture until it forms a tightly-packed envelope. Fasten the parcel with toothpicks.

8. Bring the foil, as firmly as possible, over the leaf package and crimp the edges to form a tight seal.

9. Deposit the foil-wrapped *Palusami* onto a large cookie sheet or heatproof baking pan. Bake for 1 hour.

10. After the cooking time has expired, remove the cookie sheet with the package from the oven and let it sit for about 10 minutes, or until it is cool enough to handle. Partially unwrap the foil and carefully spread the edges of the leaves open to reveal the filling. Decorate the top of the filling with overlapping slices of the tomato and sprinkle it with the remaining green onions (both reserved from Step 5).

11. Place the pan back in the oven, while on temperature, for about 5 minutes, or until the tomato slices have wilted and some of the liquid from the mixture has evaporated. Transfer to a serving platter and present hot, warm or at room temperature.

Note: For a variation on this *Palusami,* use commercial corned-beef brisket. More elegant substitutions can be shrimp or bony fish.

LAPLAP

Baked Beef and Coconut Milk in a Starch Paste,
Wrapped in Leaves (VANUATU)

These oven-steamed, leaf-wrapped bundles of taro, cassava, yam, sweet potato and/or plantain paste around a variety of fillings are a feast staple in the archipelago of Vanuatu (New Hebrides). I have eaten them on many occasions and they equate with home cooking; filling and rib-sticking delicious.

Before preparing authentic *Laplap,* you must first locate ethnic (Asian, African or Central American) markets in your area that might carry the requisite root vegetables. (Ethnic markets also stock dried banana leaves.)

Beef is the primary filling for this leaf-wrapped dish, since Vanuatu raises some of the largest and most prized beef cattle herds in the South Pacific. (Incidentally, pork, chicken, fish and even flying fox, can also be wrapped and cooked for this recipe.)

Laplap is one of those useful dishes that you can put in a slow oven for a lengthy bake and, in the meantime, prepare the rest of the meal.

Serves 6 to 8

8 small taro corms or 2 large corms

1 6-inch length of cassava root

1 6-inch length of yam

1 1/2 pounds of beef round, trimmed of fat and cut into 1-inch cubes

6 green onions, both white and green, coarsely chopped

3 cloves of garlic, smashed, peeled and chopped

1 green chili pepper *(Serrano* or *Jalapeño),* seeded and chopped

1/2 teaspoon of salt

1/4 teaspoon of freshly ground black pepper

1/4 teaspoon of ground coriander

a pinch of ground cinnamon (optional)

several drops of smoke seasoning liquid

1/2 cup of thick coconut milk *(see page 19)*

rice or tapioca flour (optional)

6 large collard leaves, washed, drained and softened *(see page 21),* stems removed

20 spinach leaves, washed, drained and softened, stems removed

1. Fill a large mixing bowl with water and deposit the contents of your ice tray therein. Peel the taro corms, cassava and yams, placing each in the iced water as you proceed. Let the root vegetables soak while you continue with the next step.

2. Place the beef in a medium, non-reactive mixing bowl and add the garlic and chili pepper. Season with the salt, pepper, coriander, cinnamon and smoke seasoning liquid. Stir to thoroughly combine and coat the beef. Set aside for use in Step 6.

3. Preheat your oven to 300° Fahrenheit. Place the coconut milk in a medium mixing bowl for use in the next step.

4. In sequence, drain, pat dry and grate each of the root vegetables. (You may accomplish this manually with the finest section of a hand grater or by using the grating attachment on a food processor. At the end of each grating episode, deposit the vegetable in the coconut milk. Try and work quickly so the vegetables will not discolor by exposure to the air.) When the grating is complete, stir the vegetable/coconut milk mixture thoroughly. The mixture should have a paste-like consistency. (If it appears too liquid, you may add rice flour, 1 tablespoon at a time, stirring, to achieve a cohesive paste.)

5. Spread a 30-inch length of heavy-duty aluminum foil on your counter top or large cutting board. Alternate the collard and spinach leaves on the foil to form a leaf bed with approximately a 2-inch margin. Now spread the root-vegetable paste from the step above over the leaf bed, again leaving a 2–3 inch margin on all sides.

6. Spoon the beef mixture from Step 2 in a mound on the paste. Roll the leaves and paste neatly and tightly around the beef. Tuck in the loose ends and secure with toothpicks.

7. Bend and fold the foil around the packet, and crimp the edges to tightly seal.

8. Place the *Laplap* packet into a large baking dish and bake in your oven for about 3 hours.

9. When cooked, remove the dish from the oven and the foil packet from the dish. Let it cool for about 15 minutes and carefully remove the foil. Transfer the leaf packet to a serving dish and present at once.

FAI 'ULU PISUPO

Stuffed Breadfruit (SAMOA)

I was on a pilgrimage. I had taken Falealili Street from the waterfront of Apia, Western Samoa, all the way up the hill toward Mount Vaea, the engine of my ancient taxi straining at the incline. Like most visitors to Western Samoa, I wanted

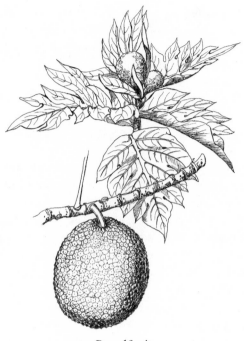

Breadfruit

to see Vailima, the house that Robert Louis Stevenson, the beloved *tusitala,* or writer of tales, had built for himself.

Vailima is now the official residence of the chief of chiefs, head of state, and the public is generally denied admission by the sentries guarding the roadside gate. It transpired that my taxi driver knew the sentry. We also learned that the chief was away so were waved through. From the gate to the house there is a long tree-lined avenue. Teak trees arch overhead and RLS himself directed their planting. There is a splendor to the house, and isolated grandeur. Perhaps it is the architectural balance of the two-storey colonial building with its overhanging eaves and wooden balconies (an entire wing has been added since Stevenson's time). Perhaps it is the undeniable majesty of its setting: the wooded craggy crest of Mount Vaea behind and to one side, guarding Stevenson's grave; rolling green lawns dropping away in front and down the mountain; the isolation and quiet, being removed from the din of Apia and the sea beyond.

On the way up, I was too preoccupied with thoughts of Stevenson to intimately notice my surroundings. Now, on the way down, I observed the unbroken tarmac. (Possibly in the best condition of all roads in Apia and wasn't it originally *Alo Loto Alofa,* the Way of Loving Hearts, dug and built by Samoan chiefs in gratitude to Stevenson?) I looked out the taxi window at the large mansions in their own compounds; none as large as Stevenson's. Hibiscus hedges protected their privacy but I could see along the driveways to gardens. Most had their own multi-pillared *fales* or meeting and guest reception structures. Many had imposing breadfruit trees as well.

Two days later, I sampled this breadfruit dish. I wonder, did the *tusitala* also eat it (perhaps with fish instead of corned beef) when he descended the mountain to dine with the chiefs?

Serves 6

1 large mature but firm bread- fruit, washed and dried	1 tomato, chopped
1 tablespoon of safflower oil	2 cups of corned beef

1 medium onion, peeled and
    finely chopped
	2 tablespoons of parsley,
	    minced

1 green bell pepper, cored,
    seeded and the flesh
    coarsely chopped
	1 teaspoon of salt
	$1/2$ teaspoon of freshly ground
	    black pepper
	1 egg, beaten

1. Preheat your oven to 350° Fahrenheit.
2. Pierce the skin of the breadfruit all over with a fork, place it in a baking pan and cook for about $1^1/2$ hours, or until it is soft to the touch. (During the baking, continue with Step 3.) When cooked, remove the fruit from the oven to set aside and cool, and for use in Step 5. Increase the heat in the oven to a temperature of 400° Fahrenheit.
3. While the breadfruit is cooking, heat the oil in a large frying pan over medium heat and stir and fry the onion and pepper until the onion is golden and the pepper limp.
4. Add the tomato, continue stirring and frying for 1 more minute. Stir in the corned beef to help it separate and season with the parsley, salt and pepper. Continue stirring on heat for 1 final minute. Remove the pan from heat and set aside for use in Step 6.
5. Cut a thick slice from the top of the breadfruit much as you would remove the top of a soft-boiled egg. (Save the top for use in Step 7.) Scoop out most of the fruit pulp from the interior leaving a $3/4$-inch-thick shell inside the skin. Remove and discard the seeds from the excavated pulp. Coarsely chop the remaining pulp.
6. In a non-reactive mixing bowl, combine **one-half** the pulp (reserving the remainder under refrigeration for use in fritters, soups, etc.) with the stuffing from Step 4. Stir in the egg and thoroughly mix the stuffing.
7. Loosely pack the stuffing back into the breadfruit. Replace the top and wrap the assembly in aluminum foil. Bake for an additional 30–40 minutes.

8. When cooked, remove the wrapped fruit from the oven and let it set to cool for several minutes. Unwrap the foil, slice the breadfruit into wedges or sections. Serve hot or warm.

Note: This recipe can also be made with cooked pork, ham, chicken or fish (based) stuffing. If the dish is to be served at a common, non-festive, meal occasion, you may accompany it with a meat gravy or cheese sauce.

TOURNEDOS POMARE

(TAHITI)

Pomare celebrates the line of Tahitian monarchs who took over from the prior Teva dynasty of chiefs at the time of European discoveries in Polynesia. Pomare I, previously only a local chief, seized ascendancy by force of European arms, supplied to him in return for large quantities of pigs for the salt-pork trade with Australia. His descendants (including Queen Pomare Vahini IV, the most illustrious and long-reigning sovereign) ruled Tahiti until 1880 when the last monarch, Pomare V, donated the islands to the French.

These succulent steaks from the smaller end of the beef fillet, garnished with breadfruit and topped with a papaya/mango sauce, are named after Tahiti's historic royal family.

Serves 6

6 beef tenderloin fillets, $3^{1}/_{2}$–4 ounces each, cut 1-inch thick	6 shallots, peeled and minced
4 tablespoons of olive oil	1 large clove of garlic, smashed, peeled and minced
$1/_{2}$ teaspoon of freshly ground black pepper	4 tablespoons of dry white wine
$1/_{4}$ teaspoon of salt	$1/_{2}$ teaspoon of Dijon mustard
1 small breadfruit	a small pinch of ground cinnamon
$1/_{3}$ cup of papaya, peeled, seeded and chopped	3 tablespoons of coconut cream *(see page 19)*
$1/_{3}$ cup of mango flesh, chopped	6 sprigs of parsley for garnish
$1/_{2}$ cup of all-purpose flour	6 thin slices of ripe mango flesh
2 tablespoons of canola oil	

166

1. Preheat your oven to 400° Fahrenheit.

2. Place the beef fillets in a medium, non-reactive mixing bowl. Pour in **2 tablespoons** of the olive oil. Season with the pepper and salt. Turn the steaks to evenly coat and cover with the oil and spices. Cover with plastic wrap and refrigerate to marinate for at least $1^1/_4$ hours or until use in Step 7.

3. Place the breadfruit in a small baking or casserole dish stem-end up. Fill the dish with water to a depth of 1 inch. Bake the breadfruit in its water for just under 1 hour.

4. Remove the breadfruit and its pan, and turn your oven to its lowest setting. Remove the breadfruit from its water to set aside and cool. When cool enough to handle, halve the fruit lengthwise and pull out the core. (You may tightly wrap and refrigerate the unused half for use in another recipe.) Peel the other half and slice it crosswise $1/_2$-inch thick 12 slices minimum). Set aside for use in Step 6.

5. Place the papaya and mango in your blender and blend on a high setting to a uniform purée. Set aside for use in Step 9.

6. Place the flour in a paper bag and add the breadfruit slices. Shake the bag vigorously until they are evenly coated. Heat the canola oil in a large frying pan over medium-high heat. When the oil reaches a frying temperature, remove the breadfruit slices, shaking off the excess flour, and fry, several at a time until they are golden (turning once or twice). Accumulate the fried breadfruit on a large, ovenproof plate in your oven. Continue until all the slices are coated and fried, and collected on the plate in your oven for use in Step 10.

7. Remove the steaks from the refrigerator and pat each with paper towels to absorb excess oil. Place the remaining **2 tablespoons** of olive oil in a frying pan over high heat. When a haze forms over the oil, pan-fry the steaks, about 90 seconds on the first side and 30 seconds on the reverse. Reduce the heat to medium and continue cooking the steaks for a further 2 minutes per side. Collect the fried steaks on the same plate with the breadfruit in the oven to keep them warm for use in Step 10.

8. In the same frying pan, while still on medium heat, sauté the shallots and garlic, stirring constantly, for about 1 minute. Deglaze the pan with the white wine and reduce heat to low.

9. Add the papaya/mango purée, stirring, and cook for a further 1–2 minutes or until the mixture is heated through. Season with the mustard and cinnamon. Rapidly stir in the coconut cream to thoroughly combine all the ingredients and immediately turn off the heat to prevent further cooking. (Do not allow the mixture to boil.)

10. Set out 6 dinner plates and place two slices of the fried breadfruit on each plate, the flat sides facing each other to create the outline of a donut. Place a steak in the center of each breadfruit circle. Pour the papaya/mango purée over the top of each steak allowing the sauce to pool slightly on the plates. Garnish each plate with a parsley sprig and place a mango slice on top of every steak. Serve immediately.

TINAKTAK

Braised Beef in Lemon Juice with Vegetables and Coconut Milk

(GUAM)

Tinaktak is a very popular and traditional dish, prepared on many other islands in Micronesia besides Guam. Typical of the tropical cooks' treatment where they combine assortments of vegetables in light but vibrant blends of flavors, it bears the Oceanian signature of gravy enriched by coconut milk. Its Chamorro name is delightfully onomato*poetic* (I prefer the rhythmic allusion of the secondary spelling), since it imitates the beat of a cleaver chopping and pounding the beef.

Serves 4 to 6

1 tablespoon of canola oil
1 small onion, peeled and
    finely chopped
3 cloves of garlic, smashed,
    peeled and minced
$1^{1}/_{2}$ pounds of flank steak or
    beef round, pounded with
    a meat mallet and finely
    chopped
2 tablespoons of lemon juice
1 teaspoon of salt
$1/_{4}$ teaspoon of freshly ground
    black pepper

4 small, Oriental eggplants,
    stemmed and sliced into
    sticks the size of French
    fries
$1/_{2}$ cup of green beans, sliced
    on the diagonal into
    $1^{1}/_{2}$-inch-long pieces
1 red bell pepper, cored,
    seeded and cut into
    $1/_{2}$-inch dice
1 cup of thick coconut milk
    (*see page 19*)

1. Heat the oil in a large, non-reactive saucepan over a medium setting. Carefully drop in the onion pieces, stir and fry for a few seconds until they are translucent. Add the garlic and continue stirring and frying for about 1 more minute.
2. While still on heat, deposit the meat into the frying mixture. Continue to cook and stir until the meat is browned on all sides.
3. Pour in the lemon juice, season with salt and pepper, cover the pan and, reducing the heat to low, let the meat mixture simmer for about 20 minutes.

4.   When the first stage of simmering is complete, uncover the pan and add the eggplants and green beans. Re-cover the pan, while still on heat, and simmer for a further 5 minutes.

5.   Uncover the pan for the final time and stir in the red pepper. Pour in the coconut milk. Modulate the heat so the *Tinaktak* mixture is just below the boil and let it cook for about 3 more minutes, stirring occasionally.

6.   Correct the seasoning, then transfer the mixture to a serving bowl and present at once.

Note: The traditional accompaniment for *Tinaktak* is plain, cooked rice. *Tinaktak* may also be made with pork or chicken, adjusting the cooking time accordingly. Pumpkin tips or spinach leaves can be used as a variation instead of eggplant.

KANGAROO STEAKS WITH DAVIDSON PLUM AND PORT SAUCE

(NEW SOUTH WALES)

Davidson plum *(Davidsonia pruriens)* is a large, very sour, deep-red-to-blue-black fruit that, with the addition of sufficient sugar, makes flavorful jams, jellies and sauces. Because of their acidity, the plums are also used as a vinegar substitute in salad dressings. As game, the flavor of 'roo meat benefits from this rich, fruity sauce of plums and port.

Serves 6

6 Davidson plums, washed, halved and seeded	1/2 teaspoon of salt or to taste
2 cups of water	1/4 teaspoon of freshly ground black pepper
1/2 cup of sugar	1/2 cup of Australian port
6 5-ounce (approximately) kangaroo fillets	1/2 cup of freshly squeezed orange juice
1/2 cup of red Burgundy	1 tablespoon of orange zest, grated
1 small onion, peeled and chopped	salt and pepper to taste
2 cloves of garlic, smashed, peeled and chopped	2 tablespoons of butter
1/2 teaspoon of dried thyme	3 tablespoons of olive oil
a pinch of ground cinnamon	6 sprigs of watercress
	6 thin orange slices

1.   Place a medium, non-reactive saucepan over medium-high heat and add the plums, water and sugar. Bring the mixture to a boil and reduce heat to maintain a simmer. Cook for about 30 minutes or until the plums are soft. Remove from heat and set aside for use in Step 6.

2.   Place the kangaroo steaks in a large (1-gallon) resealable plastic bag and add the Burgundy, onion, garlic, thyme and cinnamon. Seal the bag and shake and massage it to evenly distribute the ingredients. Marinate the steaks for 4–6 hours.

3.   After marinating, remove the steaks and pat them dry with paper towels. (Reserve the marinade for use in the next step.) Season the steaks with the salt and pepper and set aside for use in Step 6.

4.   Return the saucepan with the plums to a medium-high heat and add the marinade from above. Pour in the port and orange juice, and bring the mixture to a full boil. Modulate the heat to maintain a boil and reduce the mixture by about one-half. Add the orange zest and correct the seasoning with salt and pepper, if desired.

5.   Pour the contents of the saucepan into your blender and blend on a high setting to produce a smooth sauce. Wash the saucepan and return it to a medium-low heat. Pour the sauce back into the saucepan and adjust the heat to maintain a simmer. While the sauce is simmering, prepare the steaks.

6.   Place a large, heavy skillet over medium-high heat and pour in the butter and olive oil. Let the fat come up to frying temperature when a haze appears over the oil. Carefully introduce the kangaroo steaks and cook them about 4 minutes on one side. Turn the steaks and fry them on the reverse side for about 3 minutes, or until they brown.

7.   Place the cooked steaks on individual serving plates. Pour the simmering sauce over each of the steaks (enough sauce to form a small pool). Garnish each plate with the watercress and orange slices and serve immediately.

EMU SATAY WITH
A CITRUS-HONEY GLAZE

(CANBERRA)

The first impression I got from the emu I encountered in semi-captivity within an animal park in Australia was hostility. A wire fence separated us, and I was glad for

Emu

the barrier. The animal stalked over to me, fixed me with a beady eye (they do not stereoscopically *see*), opened its powerful beak and exhaled forcibly and rather foully in my face. It then commenced to strut back and forth on its large, three-toed feet, like a drill sergeant reprimanding a recruit. I promptly abandoned any attempts at encouraging friendship.

A few days later, at a chic bush-food restaurant in Canberra, I retaliated. I ordered emu *satay* with a citrus-honey glaze. The saddle meat of an emu resembles lean steak and the *satay* tasted somewhat of beef. However, the chef had presented the meat in chunks on the skewer like kebab instead of in the thin strips of the conventional *satay*. (I suspect this particular emu had placed first in the 1600-mile race around the Great Australian Bight region between Perth and Adelaide.) The meat was well exercised, in a word—tough.

My variation (below) first marinates the meat—to start the long tenderizing process—and then slices it before grilling.

2 cups of water
1/4 cup of cider vinegar
1/4 cup of olive oil
1 medium onion, peeled and
    chopped
3 whole cloves
1/2 stick of cinnamon
3 tablespoons of sugar
1/2 teaspoon of salt

1 bay leaf, torn into pieces
2 pounds of emu saddle
1 cup of honey
1/4 cup of soy sauce
1/2 cup of freshly squeezed
    lemon juice
1/2 cup of freshly squeezed
    lime juice
1 teaspoon of salt

1. Combine the first 9 ingredients (up to but not including the emu meat) together in a medium, non-reactive mixing bowl. Stir until the sugar is dissolved and set aside for use in the next step.

2. Place the emu meat in a large (1-gallon) resealable plastic bag. Pour in the marinade from above, seal and let the meat marinate in your refrigerator for about 24 hours, turning and massaging the bag occasionally.

3. When the marinating is complete, remove the meat from the marinade, drain it well and pat it dry with paper towels. Encase the meat in plastic wrap and place it in your freezer for 15–30 minutes, or until it becomes very firm but not frozen.

4. Begin soaking the contents of a packet (50–80, approximately) of *satay* sticks (7 inches long, approximately) in cold water. Immerse the sticks for no more than 10 minutes and set aside for use in Step 8.

5. Remove the meat from the freezer, place it on your cutting board and slice into ribbon-like strips approximately 1-inch wide × 6-inches long × 1/4-inch thick.

6. Preheat your broiler or barbecue.

7. In a small, non-reactive mixing bowl, stir together the honey, soy sauce, lemon and lime juices and salt until the ingredients are thoroughly mixed and the salt has dissolved and set aside for use in the next step.

8. Thread the emu strips on the *satay* sticks lengthwise in wavy formations, about 2 or 3 to a stick. Place the threaded sticks on a large dish or platter with the sharpened tips pointed toward the center. Brush or pour the citrus glaze over the meat. (Reserve the excess glaze for use in the next step.)

9. Broil or barbecue the *satay*, turning and brushing with the reserved glaze, until they are brown and glistening.

10. Arrange the cooked emu *satay* on a platter and pour any remaining glaze over them. Serve at once.

"PIDGIN" PIE

(VANUATU)

By now, from other passages in this book, you may have experienced some of that charming, bastardized—but practical—language of Melanesia, called "pidgin." It changes from island to island. Indeed, in Vanuatu it has been codified and given the imprimatur of being their official language, Bislama. Even with local variations, it requires little application for English speakers to become comfortable with the changes in morphemes that constitute a different inflection or morphology; relax, parse each sentence and then pronounce it aloud. With a little practice you will feel the patois and begin to understand the meaning—perhaps enough to try this **"Pidgin" Pie!**

(My thanks to the Vanuatu Red Cross Society for this recipe.)

Takem three boys, sixis cartriss, one feller muskit and one large piece bush wetem plenty pidgin long hem. Boy i holem musket i really good blong time two fala boy i finem pidgin. Time twofala i finem pidgin, boy i holem musket i shootum out grass belong three fala pidgin, another boy i takem out gut and chuckem hem long puss cat.

Time all i ready belong cookum, you cutem algether pidgin long four piece, rubem all piece long flour and putum long grease i boil. Time all piece pidgin i brown good, takem out long grease and putum one bigfala onion where you cutem small small long grease and wait long hem i brown olsem pidgin.

Time olgeta i brown good, putum more onion long pidgin long one casserole dish.

Makem goodfala gravy where i brown good wetem plenty salit mo pepper, and capsitem long pidgin more onion long dish. Putum two cup red wine long dish wetem pidgin and cookum slow slow long oven blong two hour more three hour. Time olgeter he cook good, makem gravy i strong good wetem one bigfala spoon flour.

Time olgeter i ready makem pastry. Putum andap long dish where pidgin stap long hem. Blong finishim, cookum back again blong 10 minutes or 15 minutes.

PIGEON POT PIE WITH COCONUT BISCUIT TOPPING

(VANUATU)

Here is a recipe for a "pigeon" pie that does not call for *"three boys, sixis cartriss, one feller muskit"*!

PIGEONS AND VEGETABLES

Serves 4

3 tablespoons of unsalted butter

2 large onions, peeled and finely chopped

2 pigeons, table dressed (as for other small game birds)

1 cup of red wine

3 cups of beef stock or canned beef broth

1 teaspoon of salt

1 bay leaf

a generous pinch of mixed herbs (thyme, rosemary, sage, etc.)

1 cup of water

2 medium carrots, peeled and diced

1 large potato, peeled and cut into 1/2-inch dice

1. Set a large, non-reactive saucepan over medium-high heat. Melt the butter and sauté **one-half** of the onions, stirring for about 1 minute. Add the pigeons, modulate the heat as necessary, and brown the birds evenly on all sides.
2. Pour in the wine and let the mixture come to a boil. Add the beef stock, season with the salt, bay leaf and mixed herbs. Bring the liquid back to a boil, cover, reduce the heat to medium-low and simmer for about 1 1/2 hours, or until the flesh of the birds is just tender. (Continue with the remaining steps.)
3. Pour the water in a medium saucepan and place it over high heat. Add the remaining onion, the carrots and potato. Let the mixture come to boil and cook for several minutes, or until all the vegetables are tender. Drain and set aside for use in Step 7.
4. Preheat your oven to 375° Fahrenheit.
5. While waiting for the pigeons to cook, continue with the **Coconut Biscuit Topping** and return when it's complete.
6. Drain and remove the pigeons to a cutting board. (Leave the liquid on the range top, increase the heat and reduce it to about 1 cup.) When cool enough

to handle, remove all the bones from the birds and cut the meat into small, 1-inch-long, pieces.

7.   Combine the vegetables from Step 3 with the pigeon meat in a large, oven-proof casserole. Pour the reduced pigeon-cooking liquid from above over the mixture. Top with the biscuits from Step 2, **Coconut Biscuit Topping.**

8.   Place the pie in your oven and bake for about 20 minutes, or until the biscuit topping is light brown.

COCONUT BISCUIT TOPPING

2 cups of all-purpose flour, sifted

$2^1/2$ teaspoons of baking powder

$1/2$ teaspoon of salt

1 tablespoon of dried, unsweetened coconut flakes

2 tablespoons of vegetable shortening

$3/4$ cup of coconut milk *(see page 19)*

1.   In a large mixing bowl, thoroughly combine all the dry ingredients. Using a fork, mix and cut the shortening into the flour until the consistency resembles fine bread crumbs. Make a well and pour in the coconut milk. Vigorously stir to produce a thick, uniform dough.

2.   Roll the dough to a thickness of about $1/4$ inch. With a glass or cookie cutter, cut the dough into disks about $1^1/2$–2-inches in diameter. Set aside for use in Step 7, **Pigeons and Vegetables.** (Return to Step 6, above.)

Chapter 9

From Jungle Gardens and Farmers' Markets

Island Vegetables and Grains in Main and Side Dishes

When the market opens before 3 A.M.— . . . sleepy heads give way to fresh-gathered bread-fruits and nets of fragrant oranges; bananas are swung up within tempting reach of everybody; all sorts of natives come in from the four quarters of the Papeetean globe with back-loads of miscellaneous viands, a mat under one arm, and a flaming torch in hand . . . boys sit demurely over their meagre array of temptations in the shape of six tomatoes, three eggs, a dozen or so of guavas, and one cucumber.

Charles Warren Stoddard, 1899, *South-Sea Idyls*

Renovated in 1986 from its previous picturesque, but somewhat dilapidated, existence, the new two-storey Marché Papeete is now one of the most splendid markets in the South Pacific. Named *Mapuru Paraita*, after the area donated for its construction (one square block), its elegant but eclectic architecture, which includes white-painted iron columns and trellises, glass panels and brick-tiled floors, is reminiscent of a cross between the Palm House at Kew Gardens in London and a Victorian railway station. However, it blends very well amid the charming remnants of old Papeete that stand alongside more modern buildings.

Aesthetics aside, what about the produce? It is a feast for the senses. Giant, striped watermelons abut piles of small, brilliant green limes. The more somber hues of taro and cassava roots contrast with ranks of scarlet tomatoes. Bundles of greens spill from cartons and baskets. Onions, sweet potatoes, carrots, avocados, beans, star fruit, coconuts, yams, mangoes, cabbage, *mape* (Polynesian chestnuts), celery, breadfruit, ginger-roots, pineapples, green-skinned oranges—they are all here in profusion and abundance. Native Tahitians sell the classic Polynesian vegetables, fruits and fish; Chinese-Tahitians purvey the other vegetables.

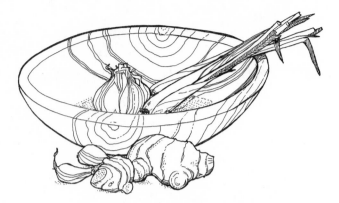

To add to the air of festivity, red and blue paper garlands loop wildly (and lopsidedly) from the pillars above the stalls. Brightly-colored table umbrellas shelter those sellers who sit amidst their wares outside the entrances to the market. Many of the stall holders wear straw hats wreathed in flowers. Others wind garlands of blossoms around their hair.

After five AM, when the market opens, the wide aisles gradually fill with shoppers; making inquiries, bargaining and surreptitiously squeezing or tapping the produce to check for ripeness. The perimeter streets act as an unofficial depot for the multicolored Tahitian buses, called *"le truk."* The buses disgorge loads of market goers. Cars and taxis now begin to clog the one-way thoroughfares. Morning comes alive and it's all here: smiles; flowers; yipping taxi horns; soft Polynesian voices; the fragrance of freshly-baked bread and continental coffee. The *marché* is at once controlled chaos and retail fiesta. It's Papeete at its most vivid and compelling.

Garden Plots

In many archipelagoes away from the sprawl of French Polynesian urban life, the cohesiveness and predictability of country life continue to be dominated by farming and husbandry. Outside the villages of Melanesia, areas of scrub have been cleared (they may have lain fallow for 15 or more years since last cultivated). Some old wood trees still remain: mango, citrus, coconut. Taro has been planted near stream beds. Just above, the slopes sprout with rows of eggplant, cucumbers and carrots. Higher up, sweet potatoes and yams flourish. Other plots support cassava interspersed with pineapple plants. (Mixed plots often feature patches of cassava, chili bushes, pineapples, eggplants and a straggle of papayas.) On the hillsides, dry taro and *kava* vines compete with banana plants. Scattered coconut palms and papaya plants balance the contours. It may appear haphazard and indiscriminate but the villagers are intimately familiar with the topography and the personality of the soil; moisture, drainage and shade. This land represents an investment in hard-won knowledge and sweat, and the yield, of course, is life.

These plots and gardens are scattered around the village; some as much as a half-hour's walking distance. One man may work two distant plots, spending up to 24 hours a week on each. Most of the produce supports the individual (and extended) family; surplus is sold at the nearest market. For the villagers, the time devoted to agricultural chores is alternated between time spent on ritual ceremonies and odd jobs they pick up to supplement their income, including handicrafts and boat building. (This pattern of life applies, not only to Melanesians, but also to most islanders in Oceania.)

The Best of the Fresh

It took me a while to understand why Oceanian food *tastes* so good: the ingredients are unassuming, the cooking styles are basic. The seasonings are not complex, yet every mouthful can be an enjoyable experience, featuring a full spectrum of natural flavors and textures. The answer is simple: the foods of the Pacific Islands are hand picked, organically grown or straight from the water. The air is fresh, the water is pure, the soil is uncontaminated. Tomatoes grown in village garden plots may not be as cosmetically appealing as those I used to purchase at the Central Market in downtown Los Angeles but their stems are a healthy green and their flavor incomparable. Pacific limes may be smaller than those in our supermarkets but the aroma of their zest and the zip of their juice is unmatched. Root vegetables carry the taste of good earth. Island greens are fresh, crisp, fragrant, pungent and delicious. And for those fortunate few who have enjoyed the luxury of slaking their thirst with the juice from a freshly-cracked coconut straight from the palm, well. . . .

How can you attempt to match this quality in your produce? Shop at farmers' markets; make friends with the sellers and purveyors. Grow your own: even the smallest patch of earth, when cosseted, can achieve remarkable results. You have no spare land? Then resort to container gardening.

During many years spent in Japan, on a little cement pad in front of our house (designed to park another car), during the fierce, hot, typhoon-threatened summers, I managed to raise quantities of lemon grass, Italian tomatoes, zucchini, citrus, cilantro, basil, English mint, marjoram, parsley, ginger, chives and sage. When typhoons loomed I shifted to overdrive, dragging the pots in under the shelter of the front porch. In the winters with single-digit temperatures (Celsius), the lemon grass, cilantro, mint, parsley and chives flourished inside the sunny window of my office even when the balcony outside was covered with snow. I even tried to sprout a coconut but it was obstinate . . . ah well.

Persevere. The rewards of good, fresh food are inestimable; to the psyche, in the kitchen, on the table.

VEGETABLE AND PEANUT STEW
(PAPUA NEW GUINEA)

Although peanuts were introduced to Papua New Guinea only (comparatively) recently, they are now cultivated and consumed in quantity, overtaking many indigenous nuts with their popularity due to their flavor and ease of preparation. Locally-ground peanut butter is commercially produced in Morobe Province. (Morobe is a port city almost due north of Port Moresby on the Huon Gulf.)

After my father spent the better part of 2 years in East Africa as engineer-in-charge of the British government's ill-conceived "groundnut" scheme, my mother adapted the African custom of adding ground peanuts to soups and stews. Upon their return to England from Tanganyika (now the Republic of Tanzania), I learned to relish the thick, rich and creamy gravies produced through the addition of ground peanuts or peanut butter. Therefore, it was with pleasure and instant recognition that I ate this vegetarian stew-like dish in Port Moresby. It is both simple and satisfying, and can be accompanied either by rice or a crusty French bread.

Serves 4 to 6

2 tablespoons of peanut oil

2 large onions, peeled and finely chopped

3 cloves of garlic, smashed, peeled and minced

3 large tomatoes, blanched, peeled and chopped

1 bay leaf

a pinch each of ground thyme and marjoram

2 cups of taro, peeled and cut into 1-inch cubes

2 cups of sweet potatoes, peeled and cut into 1-inch cubes

2¹/₂ cups of water

1 teaspoon of salt

¹/₂ teaspoon of freshly ground black pepper

6 long beans, cut into 2-inch lengths, or an equivalent amount of green beans, halved crosswise

4 heaped tablespoons of unsalted peanut butter

¹/₂ cup of thick coconut milk (*see page 19*)

1 cup of spinach leaves, washed, drained and coarsely chopped

1.   Place a large, non-reactive saucepan over medium-high heat. Add the oil and, when it comes up to temperature, fry the onions for several minutes, or until they become translucent.

2.   Add the garlic, continue stirring and frying for about 30 more seconds. Carefully place the tomatoes into the frying mixture, stir and continue cooking until they soften and begin to disintegrate. Season with the bay leaf and ground herbs. Add the taro and sweet potatoes and stir to evenly mix all the ingredients. Pour in the water, cover and let the mixture come to a boil. Reduce heat and simmer for about 15 minutes.

3.   Uncover, season with salt and pepper, add the beans, stir and let them simmer for about 4 minutes.

4.   Remove approximately 1 cup of the simmering liquid to a heatproof container. Blend the peanut butter into the liquid to form a smooth sauce and return it to the saucepan.

5.   Stir in the coconut milk and spinach. Modulate the heat until the mixture almost reaches a boil and continue cooking for about 1 more minute.

6.   Remove the saucepan from heat and transfer the contents to a warm serving bowl. Present at once.

Note: For those who wish to augment this stew with meat, add 1 pound of skinned chicken parts (legs, thighs, breast halves, etc.) after the onions have fried in Step 1. Reduce the volume of taro and sweet potato to 1 cup each and replace the water with an equal volume of chicken stock.

PALUSAMI

Baked Coconut, Onions and Chili Peppers Wrapped in Taro Leaves

(SAMOA)

This basic recipe is repeated—with different local names—throughout many island groups in the Central Pacific, including Fiji. The coconut cream filling (*Miti* or *niu*, see page 227) is traditionally wrapped in young taro leaves to form the little, individual packets. These are then further wrapped in banana leaves and tied with slender leaf ribs or string before being placed in the top layer of an earth oven. When cooked at home, they can either be placed in the hot ashes of an open fire or barbecue or, in a domestic kitchen, baked in your oven or cooked in a steamer.

We can substitute locally available leaves for the inner wrapping, such as collard, Swiss chard, beet, spinach, etc. (Please see **Chapter 1** for more detailed instructions on leaf wrappings and their preparation.)

Serves 6

6 large collard leaves, washed, drained and softened *(see page 21)*, stems removed

24 spinach leaves, washed, drained and softened *(see page 21)*, stems removed

1/2 cup of *Miti* *(see page 227)*

6 tablespoons dried, unsweetened coconut flakes, reconstituted *(see page 18)*

1 small onion, peeled and finely chopped

Smoke seasoning liquid (optional)

1. Preheat your oven to 350° Fahrenheit.

2. On your counter top or a large cutting board, spread out 6 12-inch squares of aluminum foil. First, lay a collard leaf on each aluminum square. Next, lay 4 spinach leaves on top of the collard leaf, alternating their position, to form a leaf bed that is thicker in the center.

3. Pick up each foil/leaf arrangement and, holding it in one slightly cupped hand, force your fist into the center of the leaves to form an indentation. Continue until you have formed a slightly concave receptacle in all the foil (and leaf) squares.

4. Deposit 2 tablespoons of the **Miti** and 1 tablespoon of the dried reconstituted coconut flakes in each leaf cavity. Sprinkle the chopped onion on each of the small pools of liquid. Add 1 or 2 drops of liquid smoke seasoning to each.

5. Carefully fold the leaves around the seasoned liquid filling to form a neat and compact package. (The moisture should help secure the package and you should tuck in any protruding corners; practice makes perfect.) Now, bend and fold the foil around each packet, crimping the edges to create a seal. Again, continue the process until all 6 packets are foil sealed.

6. Arrange the packets in a large baking dish and bake for 45 minute to 1 hour.

7. After the cooking time has expired, place the packets on a large, heatproof serving dish. Let them cool for several minutes and, then, carefully unwrap the foil on each to expose the contents. Serve at once.

ISLAND YAM, SWEET POTATO AND TARO BAKE

(MICRONESIA)

Although in Micronesia this casserole would be considered a main or primary dish, accompanied by smoked or dried reef fish and an anonymous green leaf vegetable, it can be an inspired side dish for a Western meal of roast turkey, duck or chicken.

Serves 8

1 teaspoon of salt

2 large sweet potatoes (about 4 cups), **peeled and cut into 1**^{1}/$_2$**-inch cubes**

1^1/$_2$ cups of yam, **peeled and cut into 1**^{1}/$_2$**-inch cubes**

2 large taro corms (about 2+ cups), **peeled and cut into 1**^{1}/$_2$**-inch cubes**

^{1}/$_4$ teaspoon of freshly ground black pepper

1^1/$_2$ cups of thick coconut milk *(see page 19)*

^{1}/$_2$ cup of Island Coconut Sauce *(see page 203)*,

2 tablespoons of dried, unsweetened coconut flakes

2 tablespoons of butter, cut into small pieces

1. Preheat your oven to 350° Fahrenheit.

2. Set a large saucepan of water on your range top, add the salt and bring the water to a boil over high heat. Add the sweet potato cubes and continue on the boil for about 8 minutes, or until they are just tender when pierced. (Do not overcook.)

3. Grease a large, deep casserole. Drain the sweet potatoes over the pan with a slotted spoon (leaving the water on heat) and place them in the casserole.

4. Add the yam and taro to the water, adjust the heat and let it return to a full boil. Cook the vegetables for about 10 minutes. Drain, as before, and add them to the sweet potato in the casserole.

5. With a fork, briefly mix all the root vegetables to an uneven mixture. Using gentle pressure, pack and force the vegetables together with a smooth top. Sprinkle in the pepper, pour in **1 cup** of the coconut milk and drizzle **one-half** of the **Island Coconut Sauce** over the surface. Cover with the casserole top or foil and bake in your oven for about 40 minutes.

6. Increase the heat in your oven to 400° Fahrenheit. Remove the casserole from the oven and uncover. Pour in the remainder of **both** the coconut milk and **Island Coconut Sauce.** Sprinkle with the coconut flakes, dot with butter and bake, uncovered, for about 15 minutes. Serve hot.

Note: This casserole may be made with only one of the root vegetables, increasing the proportions to allow for the replaced starches. Also, if you prefer this dish savory rather than sweet, omit the **Island Coconut Sauce.**

YOUNG TARO LEAVES IN COCONUT MILK

(OCEANIA)

This is a true pan-Oceanian dish that crosses both political and ethnic boundaries. It is present at most meal occasions, including feasts. I have sampled versions of this dish from New Guinea, through the South Pacific to Tahiti and from Hawai'i to Guam. In Rarotonga, in the Cooks, it was served with slices of firm, cooked taro as edible utensils.

The younger the taro leaves the lesser the amount of the irritating calcium oxalate crystals, which occur in varying concentrations in all parts of the plant. These crystals dissipate when subjected to the heat of cooking. Islanders in many areas prefer the young, unfurled leaves, also referred to as taro tops or shoots; they contain less of the crystals and can be cooked more quickly. In any case, taro leaves need to be cooked for between 20 minutes and 1 hour, according to their maturity.

Taro plant

If taro leaves are not available, spinach is the nearest and best substitute, and spinach has the advantage of reducing the cooking time.

Smoke seasoning liquid is my personal addition, for a mere drop of it imparts an almost indefinable hint of a dish having been cooked in a pot over a smoky fire in a remote Pacific village.

Serves 6

14 young taro leaves, thoroughly washed, stems and main ribs removed	the juice of 1 lemon
	1 teaspoon of salt
6 green onions, both white and green, finely chopped	$1/4$ teaspoon of freshly ground black pepper
1 tablespoon of fresh ginger-root, peeled and minced	1–2 drops of smoke seasoning liquid
$1/2$ teaspoon of turmeric	1 cup of thick coconut milk *(see page 19)*

1. Layer the taro leaves, one upon the other, into a neat stack. Tightly roll the stack, as you would a cigar, into a firm column. Slice the roll into $1/2$ -inch long cylinders.
2. Set a large saucepan of water over high heat and bring the liquid to a rolling boil. Add the taro leaves, reduce heat to simmer and let them cook for about 25 minutes. Remove the cooked leaves with a slotted spoon.
3. Now put the leaves into a large, non-reactive saucepan over a medium-low setting. Add the green onions, ginger, turmeric, lemon juice, salt, pepper and smoke seasoning. Simmer for about 5 minutes, stirring occasionally. Pour in the coconut milk and let the mixture heat through but not reach a boil.
4. Transfer the leaves in their sauce to a serving bowl and present immediately.

Note: If spinach is substituted, wash the leaves and remove the stems. Do not dry or drain the leaves. Coarsely chop them, eliminate the pre-boiling and begin the recipe at Step 3.

POI

Fresh Taro Paste (HAWAI'I)

Poi is merely a mixture of cooked, pounded or mashed taro corms and water, prepared to the consistency of a creamy purée or soft paste. The terms "one-finger" or "two-finger" refer to its consistency: one-finger sufficient to scoop out a respectable mouthful, two-finger a more liquid product.

The Hawaiians also made this creamy staple from breadfruit, *poi 'ulu,* and from bananas, *poi mai'a.* They fed freshly-made *poi* to infants and seniors. It is very nutritious but, preferring the aged and fermented version, they called the fresh *'ai ko 'eko 'e,* meaning to eat something bland and insipid.

When *poi* is mixed with water and left unrefrigerated, lactic acid bacilli reproduce, fermenting the mixture, and it assumes a characteristically sour taste. The acid preserves the mash and it can last for several weeks without refrigeration. In Hawai'i, *poi*—the preparation and consumption—has taken on almost mythic and religious dimensions. Many native Hawaiians adore the sour or aging version, calling it *'awa'awa.*

There are as many flavors and colors of *poi* as there are taro cultivars used in its preparation. Colors range from a steely blue to light gray, even a pinkish mauve.

Nowadays, most of the *poi* consumed in Hawai'i is commercially produced. It is sold in plastic bags and the commercial product varies in consistency between a thick paste, which requires the addition of water to further hydrate the mixture, to a more liquid version, like soup. The paste requires a water bath covering during refrigeration or it will dehydrate and harden when exposed to the cold air.

Some recipes mix *poi* in a blender with milk and sweeten it with sugar. This *poi malihini* (*malihini*, literally stranger or tourist) is more palatable to mainlanders; it almost resembles cream of wheat.

Poi contains respectable concentrations of vitamins A and B, together with calcium, phosphorus and iron.

This **Poi** is quick and easy to prepare using nontraditional cooking methods and appliances: a pressure cooker and blender. (I have prepared it from scratch in less than 15 minutes.) The fresh, homemade version has a mild, almost chestnut flavor, vastly superior to the commercial product—not your average library paste!

Yield: 2 cups

11 ounces of taro corms, peeled	**5^1/$_2$ ounces of water**

1. Place the corms in your pressure cooker and add the requisite amount of water. Pressure cook on a high setting (about 15 psi) for about 6 minutes.
2. After cooking, drain and rinse under cold, running water to help them cool.
3. Place the corms in a blender or food processor with a metal blade. Add the water and blend or process on low for a few seconds. Switch the appliance to the highest setting and continue for about 15 seconds, or until you have a smooth, uniform purée. Transfer to a tightly-covered, non-reactive bowl or container and refrigerate until needed.

THREE-BEAN SAUTÉ

(OCEANIA)

There were many occasions during my life and travels in the Pacific that I almost pinched myself to remind me that these sojourns in paradise were reality. One magical day comes immediately, almost unbidden, to my memory: Awakening before dawn in response to some subconscious signal, I glanced around the strange room in that post-dream dislocation that affects the mind when crossing too many time zones and political boundaries without allowing your circadian rhythms to adjust. I said out loud, "I'm really in Vanuatu!" laughed at my silliness and blundered out of bed to the sliding door in front of my balcony. It was destined to be another incredible Pacific daybreak and I wanted to be part of it. Climbing into shorts and a T-shirt, I slipped downstairs, past the slumbering guests behind their closed doors, and walked barefoot across a short stretch of grass to the beckoning water.

I stopped, standing on the firm, wet sand bordering Erakor Lagoon and, in the increasing pearly glow of the rising sun, watched the fishermen paddling their two-man, dugout, outrigger canoes. They glided silently across the water, cleaving sparkling wakes across the mirrored surface. Coconut palms kept guard on the windless sky, their fronds completely still. Suddenly birds flashed from tree to tree, singing a dawn chorus in a discordance of calls. The fishing village on the far side of the lagoon was almost obscured amid coconut palms, but the wood smoke of morning cooking fires rose in lazy curls among their trunks and soft voices called out across the water to welcome the fishermen as they drew near.

Strong French coffee and croissants broke my fast but, at lunchtime, seated before an open window overlooking the same lagoon (now azure, wind-ruffled and sparkling in the sunlight), I ordered reef fish and this accompanying dish of crisp, green mixed beans.

Yield: $2^1/_2$ cups (approximately)

1 cup of long beans, washed and cut into $1^1/_2$-inch lengths	1 tablespoon of peanut oil
	3 shallots, peeled and chopped
	1 heaped tablespoon of roasted, salted peanuts, crushed
$1/_2$ cup of hyacinth beans, washed and sliced on the oblique diagonal into about 1-inch lengths	
	$1/_4$–$1/_2$ teaspoon of dried chili pepper flakes
$1/_2$ cup of winged beans, washed and cut into 1-inch lengths	2 tablespoons of dried unsweetened coconut flakes

1. Almost fill a medium saucepan with salted water. Place the pan over high heat and bring the liquid to a rolling boil. Blanch all the beans together for less than a minute. Drain the beans in a sieve or colander and rinse under cold, running water to arrest the cooking. Set aside for use in Step 3.
2. Place a large skillet over medium heat and add the oil. When the oil is up to frying temperature, quickly stir and fry the shallots until they begin to darken.
3. Add the peanuts, pepper flakes and coconut flakes. Fry and stir vigorously for about 1 minute. Add the blanched beans and continue stir-frying for about 2 more minutes. Serve at once.

STUFFED SWEET POTATOES

(SAMOA)

All through the Pacific Islands, handsomely large vegetables beg to be stuffed and baked: yams, breadfruit, taro, sweet potatoes, eggplant, papaya, plantains—the list is really longer and the choices many. The preparation lends itself to traditional baking, either in the hot ashes of an open fire or within the tumulus of an earth-pit oven *(see page 127)*.

The fillings become a canvas for creativity. If fruits or curcubits are to be the receptacles, then there are always starchy roots or tubers to provide a comforting bulk to a mixture. Cooked rice is a definite possibility, particularly in Micronesia and parts of Melanesia. Grated coconut and chopped nuts contribute texture and flavor. Green vegetables lighten the mixture and refresh the combinations. Then there are the grace notes of fresh or smoked fish, chopped crustaceans or mollusks, chicken—even leftovers of pork, ham or corned beef. The permutations are almost endless.

This Samoan recipe for **Stuffed Sweet Potatoes** originally calls for taro leaves. We shall substitute spinach or a similar green leaf (please see page 21), unless you are provident and have a taro patch planted outside your back door. I confess that the addition of macadamia nuts is my idea. Try experimenting with other nuts. This recipe is only a Polynesian blueprint and infinitely adaptable.

Serves 8

4 **small** (approximately 10 ounces each) **sweet potatoes** (fairly oval), **scrubbed and dried**

2 **tablespoons of butter, softened**

1 1/2 **teaspoons of salt**

1/3 **cup of coconut cream** *(see page 19)*

3 **tablespoons of onion, peeled and minced**

3 **cups of fresh spinach leaves, washed, drained and finely chopped or about** 1/3 **cup of frozen spinach, defrosted**

1/2 **teaspoon of salt**

1/4 **teaspoon of freshly ground black pepper**

1/4 **teaspoon of freshly grated nutmeg**

2 **tablespoons of macadamia nuts, finely chopped**

3 **tablespoons of dried, unsweetened coconut flakes**

189

1. Preheat your oven to 400° Fahrenheit.

2. Rub the skins of the sweet potatoes with the butter and then sprinkle them with salt. Place them in a baking dish or pan and bake until they are soft when pierced, or about 50 minutes.

3. Meanwhile, place a medium saucepan over a medium-high heat and add the coconut cream. Add the onion and cook, stirring and modulating to just maintain the heat below a simmer, for about 6 minutes, or until the moisture begins to evaporate and the coconut oil begins to collect around the perimeter of the pan.

4. Introduce the spinach and season with the salt, pepper and nutmeg. Continue to cook and stir until the spinach is soft and most of the liquid has evaporated. When the spinach mixture is cooked, remove it from the heat and set aside for use in Step 6.

5. Remove the sweet potatoes from the oven and let them sit until they are cool enough to handle. When cool, halve them lengthwise and remove most of the pulp with a spoon (saving for use in the next step), leaving a 1/4-inch lining of skin and flesh, and set them aside for use in Step 8.

6. Place the spinach mixture from Step 4 in a medium mixing bowl. Add **1 cup** of the sweet potato pulp from above (discarding the remainder). Combine the spinach mixture with the sweet potato pulp and the macadamia nuts. Stir and mix to thoroughly combine all the ingredients for use in Step 8.

7. Increase the heat in your oven to 450° Fahrenheit.

8. Equally divide the sweet potato/spinach/nut mixture among the sweet potato shells (from Step 8) and heap them full. Sprinkle the tops of each with the coconut flakes and arrange them on a baking pan or dish.

9. Bake in the top shelf of your oven for about 10 minutes, or until the coconut topping browns and the sweet potatoes are heated through. Serve immediately.

FAFALO

Spiced Banana Bud with Walnuts (GUAM)

In one of those impetuous moments that many of us succumb to while food shopping, I bought a banana bud (see **Glossary,** page 252) in a food market on Guam. It was such a vibrant and warm purple, and so wonderfully shaped, that I swear it just leaped off the shelf and into my cart the moment I touched it.

I unpacked all the groceries. The banana bud just sat on the counter while I gazed at it. It promised culinary glory, but I had no idea where to begin. After researching several local recipes—they were universally unsatisfactory in their treatments—I gingerly took the first step and, after tearing off the exterior petals, cut a slice across the body. The interior was so intricately arranged in whorls, blobs and curls that it could have been one of Mandelbrot's fractals or a prize-winning graphic design. But no inspiration. Then I flashed to my grandmother cooking red cabbage. The banana bud was certainly the same color and almost the same firm texture. It didn't hurt to try. I had nothing to lose, except the possible purchase of another banana bud.

So I disregarded all island, banana-bud-cooking lore and treated it in a European manner. It cooked perfectly with Continental conventions but the color was eccentric, turning a rich, chocolate brown. Never mind, it needed color relief and contrast . . . well, you'll see what I've done with the recipe below.

For this and other recipes requiring banana buds, you can usually locate these exotic beauties in Latin American or Southeast Asian markets.

Serves 6

1 firm banana bud (with no brown edges), **exterior petals peeled and stemmed**	1 teaspoon of salt
	1/2 teaspoon of freshly ground black pepper
1 tablespoon of canola oil	1/4 teaspoon of allspice
2 tablespoons of butter	a pinch of nutmeg
1 large onion, peeled and coarsely chopped	1 small red bell pepper, cored, seeded and diced
1 large green apple, peeled, cored and diced	2 green onions, both white and green, finely chopped
1/4 cup of malt vinegar	1/4 cup of shelled walnuts, coarsely chopped
1/4 cup of water	
1 tablespoon of brown sugar	

1. Slice the banana bud crosswise into disks 1/2-inch thick. Further slice the disks into slivers and set aside for use in Step 3.
2. In a large, non-reactive saucepan, bring the oil and butter up to frying temperature over medium-high heat. Add the onion, stir and sauté until it is translucent.
3. Drop in the apple and banana bud slivers, stir and fry for about 2 minutes.
4. Pour in the vinegar and water, and season with the sugar, salt, pepper, allspice and nutmeg. Stir, cover and reduce heat to low to allow the mixture to simmer for about 10 minutes.

5. Uncover, add the bell pepper and cook for about 2 more minutes. Now stir in the green onions and walnuts, and continue to stir and cook until most of the moisture has evaporated.

6. Transfer to a serving bowl and use the *Fafalo* to accompany pork or any robust, grilled white fish, such as swordfish, shark, marlin, etc.

VEGETABLE MELANGE

(TONGA)

Although this uncomplicated recipe for mixed vegetables is from the Kingdom of Tonga, with subtle variations, it could be—with equal authority—said to be from any number of small atolls or villages where they enjoy a respectable vegetable harvest. Indeed, it brings to mind a time of gardening; walking along rows of plants with a basket on your arm, plucking a ripe specimen here, pulling another from the earth.

The small-plot farmers or gardeners in the Pacific Islands plant and harvest primarily to feed their families. The cooked food celebrates the prosperity and bounty of the individual plots. The townspeople have the luxury of choice when browsing the markets; villagers enjoy the quiet pleasure of reaping what they have sown themselves.

The ingredients for this **Melange** may be changed as long as the "island" balance is maintained by limiting substitutions to the spectrum of Pacific vegetables. (There is one exception: If green papaya is not available, substitute something equally crisp, such as chayote, plus a dash of lemon juice, or slices of sour, green cooking apple.)

Serves 6

3 tablespoons of canola oil

1 large onion, peeled and finely chopped

1 clove of garlic, smashed, peeled and minced

3 small (Oriental) eggplants, ends removed and cut into $3/4$-inch chunks

3 medium tomatoes, coarsely chopped

1 green papaya, peeled, seeded and cut into $1/2$-inch chunks

1 tablespoon of soy sauce

4 long beans, washed, ends removed and cut into $11/2$-inch lengths

1 green bell pepper, cored, seeded and sliced into thin strips

$1/4$ teaspoon of freshly ground black pepper

$1/4$ cup of freshly grated coconut or the equivalent dried, unsweetened coconut, reconstituted *(see page 19)*

1.   Place a large skillet or wok over medium-high heat, add the oil and let it come up to frying temperature.

2.   Add the onion and stir-fry for about 90 seconds, or until it is translucent. Put in the garlic and continue stirring and frying for 30 more seconds. Now add the eggplant, tomatoes and papaya. Continue cooking, stirring, for about 2 more minutes.

3.   Pour in the soy sauce, reduce heat to maintain a simmer, cover and let the mixture cook for 2 minutes.

4.   Uncover, add the beans and pepper and continue simmering, stirring, until the beans are just cooked but crisp. Stir in the coconut and cook for an additional 30 seconds. Transfer the **Melange** to a large serving bowl and present hot or warm.

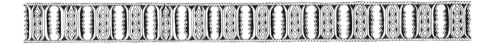

COCONUT RICE

(MELANESIA)

This **Coconut Rice** differs only slightly from the classic recipe. Yes, it has the rich coconut signature but, also, an almost indefinable overtone that hints of pots of rice being cooked over open smoky fires of coconut husks in a forest clearing somewhere in the Pacific. (Because of the concentrated coconut flavor, use this **Coconut Rice** to accompany dishes that do not contain coconut milk as an ingredient.)

Serves 4 to 6

1 tablespoon of peanut oil	1/2 teaspoon of salt
1 small onion, peeled and minced	3 cups of thin coconut milk *(see page 19)*
2 cups of long-grain rice	2 drops of liquid smoke seasoning
2 tablespoons of dried, unsweetened coconut flakes	

1.   Place a large, heavy saucepan (with a tight-fitting lid) over medium-high heat and pour in the oil. When a haze begins to form over the oil, add the onions and sauté, stirring until they become translucent.

2.   Pour the rice into the saucepan and fry, stirring, until all the grains are opaque.

3.   Add the coconut flakes and salt. Stir once, then pour in the coconut milk. Let it come to a boil. Immediately reduce heat to the lowest setting, add not more than 2 drops of the smoke seasoning and cover the pan.

4.   Let the rice cook for about 30 minutes. Remove the lid and stir. The liquid should be completely absorbed. (The test for doneness is, when you pinch a grain between your thumb and forefinger, it should squash with firm pressure. If there is too much resistance because the inside of the kernel is undercooked, re-cover the pan and let it remain on heat for an additional 5 minutes.)
5.   When cooked, uncover and transfer the rice to a serving platter.

Note: You may keep the rice warm until ready to serve by covering the (ovenproof) platter with a dampened tea towel and placing it in a low oven.

CHAMORRO RED RICE

(GUAM)

Red rice is the preferred accompaniment to Chamorro fiesta dishes, although other starches, such as taro and sweet potatoes, are also part of both fiesta and daily fare. The orange color of the dish is provided by the seeds of the annato plant (called *achiote* or lipstick tree by the Chamorros; see **Chapter 1**, page 15). The amber tinge is released from the rusty-red, hard annato seeds by soaking them in hot water or milk. Although island-style **Red Rice** is prepared simply by boiling the rice in water with the annato coloring, I prefer this more adventurous and flavorful version. (It received an enthusiastic reception whenever I brought it to local fiestas or parties on Guam.)

Serves 4 to 6

2 tablespoons of *achiote* seeds	1 cup of long-grain rice
1/2 cup of hot water	1 1/2 cups of water (including
2 slices of bacon, finely chopped	the *achiote* water from
1/2 medium onion, peeled and	above)
finely chopped	1/4 teaspoon of salt (optional)
1 clove of garlic, smashed,	1/2 teaspoon of freshly ground
peeled and chopped	black pepper

1.   Soak the *achiote* seeds in the hot water for about 15 minutes, rubbing occasionally with your thumbs and forefingers to help release their dye. Pour the colored liquid into a medium mixing bowl and discard the seeds.
2.   Place a non-reactive, medium-sized (about 2-quart) saucepan over a moderate heat. Immediately stir in the bacon. When the fat begins to sizzle, add the

onion and briskly stir and fry for about 30 seconds. Now, add the garlic and continue the stir-frying.

3.   While still on heat, add the rice to the saucepan. Stir vigorously and continue cooking until the rice kernels just begin to become translucent (about 2 minutes).

4.   To the cooking rice mixture, add the *achiote* liquid from Step 1 and all the remaining water. Modulate the heat, stir and let the mixture come to a full boil. Cover, reduce heat to low and gently simmer the rice for about 20 minutes, or until the rice is cooked (but still firm) and the water is almost completely absorbed.

5.   When you are satisfied with the consistency, transfer the **Red Rice** to an appropriate platter or dish for serving. Season with salt and pepper.

Chapter 10

Island Sweets and Treats

Desserts, Cakes and Breads

They had no means of boiling it, but were accustomed to put a quantity of the arrow-root powder with the expressed milk from the kernel of the cocoa-nut into a large wooden tray, or dish; and, having mixed them well together, to throw in a number of red-hot stones, which being moved about by thin white sticks, heated the whole mass nearly to boiling, and occasioned it to assume a thick, broken jellied appearance. In this state it is served up in baskets of cocoa-nut leaves, and is a very rich sweet kind of food, usually forming a part of every public entertainment.

William Ellis, 1831, *Polynesian Researches*

The fruits of Oceania . . . ah! One could write an ode to a freshly-picked, tree-ripened mango: fragrant, with its skin blushing pink to orange, shaded pale-green at its apex. Maybe there is a poem somewhere to a golden-green pineapple (its spiked crown of leaves, emerald, upright and perfect) straight off the truck jolting down the rough, earthen tracks from the fields to the town. Or, how about the bounty of a whole "hand" of bananas—tier after tier, all still attached to their central stem? The banana plant stands straighter after it is relieved of the enormous burden of its fruit.

In the pristine early morning of the Pacific, a little market opens on a sandy area by the sea. The perfume of banks of newly-harvested fruit rivals that of piles of flower leis on an adjacent table. Flower to fruit, the biological progression seems linked and relevant in the cool, fresh air just after daybreak.

Small boys scamper along the road by the market, sucking and munching on spears of pineapple. The juice runs down their chins and onto their bare, immature chests. A chain of drops splatters the footprints of their feet in the dust. A fat, jolly and dark-skinned matriarch sits under a striped beach umbrella. Her brilliantly-flowered, Mother Hubbard dress is a tent over her ample frame. Her teeth flash white in a broad smile as she squeezes oranges and watermelons into separate, large glass jars. The

refreshing juice will ease the parched throats of the market goers. A slip of a girl, about eight years old, stands alongside her, patiently waving away flies from the juice with a fan of woven pandanus grass.

Going Island Style

Life seems to slow down and simplify itself the longer one spends time in the islands. After a while in the South Seas, I left most of the clothes I had brought, hanging, unused, on bent wire hangers in the makeshift closet behind its curtain of unfortunately blue hibiscus printed on South Sea cotton. Instead, I walked freely in loose shifts purchased in the Solomons or Samoa, or wrapped in supple Tahitian *pareus*. My sandals remained in the suitcase; when I wasn't barefoot, I'd slide into a pair of rubber thongs. Flowers tucked behind either ear were my only accessory (I abandoned the concern with social convention about which ear should be favored; it varied from island to island and culture to culture).

Breakfast was coffee and papayas, occasionally rolls or croissants. Lunch often featured combinations of fish or chicken with island fruit; salads were always tempting and refreshing. Dinner ended with fruit compotes or local desserts. Beverages were almost exclusively island-style: fruit juice frappés or coconut water. In the evenings there was usually locally-brewed beer companionably quaffed with islanders at a friendly bar while catching up on local gossip. Conversations begun with strangers quickly became confidences between new friends.

One of the attractive customs in Oceania is that exercise is not a chore to be grimly and doggedly undertaken. Walking, swimming and dancing are as natural as breathing. Music is universal; seemingly talent is at every islander's fingertips. Coconut shells are bodies for homemade banjos and ukuleles. A packing crate, designed for shipping fruit, becomes the resonance chamber for a primitive string base. Voices rise in the natural harmony of island songs. They sing like angels and dance like devils.

Even for a while—time is, indeed, finite—worries and pressures disappear. Your mind embraces an island disposition and you quickly adopt a more relaxed mode. I found myself spending hours sitting in the shade of a tree regarding the majesty of the ever-changing Pacific. The days are lazy and long, yet slip by almost unnoticed. As an unrepentant sybarite, I once stood waist-deep in a secluded lagoon and, with a knife, proceeded to consume a large, juicy and messy mango. At the time, it seemed both practical and luxurious. I visited a shed factory in the jungle to observe the manufacture of coconut soap and perfumed coconut oil. It appeared to be intense and rigorous work. After about ten minutes, I wandered outside, sat on the grass and meditated on the flowers of a plumeria bush.

The Lore and Lure of Fruit

I learnt from the islanders. The inner side of the skin from ripe papaya could soothe my sunburn. I found that the Melanesians grate green papaya and mix it with coconut oil as a salve for sores. I discovered that the Cook Islanders use the slightly acidic sap of green banana stems to prevent burns from becoming infected. They infuse the leaves of yellow hibiscus and add the liquid to bath water to relieve muscle pains.

Local desserts and sweets were an endless delight. Many were permutations of starches, such as arrowroot or cassava, blended with coconut milk, sweetened and flavored with fruits. I brought Oceanian ways with fruit back home: I replaced vinegar with lime juice in salad dressings; blended lime juice with coconut cream into a island mayonnaise. I purchased an electric juicer and experimented with combinations of tropical fruits. These juice combinations flavored exotic ice creams and refreshing sherbets. I puréed fruits, whipped them with coconut cream into chilled desserts. I combined them with gelatin into jellied molds and decorated the dishes with slices of star fruit (carambola) and kiwi. I caramelized coconut cream and sugar into fudge sauces and toppings. Many of those island recipes follow—sweet seduction from Oceania.

PO'E 'I'ITA

Baked Papaya and Coconut Pudding

(MOOREA)

On Moorea, my friend Tépoé took me to an *arearea raa,* a Tahitian feast. She knew I wanted to see a genuine *ahima'a,* or earth-pit oven, in action. I had phoned her from Papeete and she suggested I take the ferry over and stay the night because the feast would last well into the evening, probably after the departure of the last ferry. (Before we go further, I must tell you that Tépoé is beautiful, one exquisite product of interracial marriages in the Society Islands. Tépoé, herself, is equal parts Tahitian and Chinese. Her husband is a mixture of Italian and Spanish. Their handsome young son, Dorian, is practically the United Nations incarnate.)

The site for the feast was by the beach, beginning just as the sun set and low, gray clouds hugging the coral pink horizon, reflected in the still lagoon like symmetric Rorschach patterns. We sipped rum punch as a group of musicians sang *ute* (impromptu, satirical Tahitian songs), accompanying themselves on ukuleles and *tita* (guitars). There was much laughter as the *taata pehepehe,* lead singer, gently mocked life on Moorea, the tourists, the cost of living and the government with equal emphasis.

When it was time to uncover the *ahima'a,* in the middle of a wide circle of bare earth, men began to push back wrappings, seemingly laid on the ground. They exposed layers of banana leaves beneath and, as these were gingerly flipped aside with sticks, clouds of escaping steam rose into the night air, filling it with mouth watering aromas of pork and vegetables.

The earth-pit oven was a permanent fixture with length and width dimensions of 6 feet by 4 feet. The oven was lined with cinder blocks and the bottom was filled to a depth of about six inches with heated stones. The food (some wrapped and some

Tahitian feast

exposed or raw) was contained inside a rectangular, wire mesh basket with loops of iron rebar welded at each corner as handles. Oiled muscles decorated with tattoos rippled in the light of the *flambeaux* as the men inserted iron rods into the "handles" and heaved the massive basket of food out of the pit. Randomly arranged in the mesh lining were whole fish and chicken, bundles of pork, taro, sweet potatoes, plantains (in their skins) and, in pride of place, a whole pig's head. Two leaf bundles were unwrapped. One was a large coconut cake (as it turned out, perfectly baked), the other was this traditional **Po'e 'i'ita,** or baked papaya and coconut pudding.

As we feasted, another group of musicians serenaded us. Their instruments came from the times of antiquity in the islands: *ofe tuapai*, bamboo bass, struck vertically against the ground to yield a deep, haunting, hollow resonance; *toere,* the Tahitian slit, hollow log drum, beaten with a stick; *vivo,* the bamboo flute; *ora ora,* coconut maracas and, of course, western guitars and ukuleles. Tahitian women in *aparima* (costumes of flowered *pareus* knotted low on their hips), garlands and head wreaths of *hei* flowers or *auti* leaves swayed like bamboo in the wind to a slow Tahitian hula. Torchlight, seawind from a dark ocean, music and song; I cannot eat *po'e* without remembering that night in Moorea.

Serves 8

4 cups of ripe papayas, skinned, seeded and mashed, or puréed in a food processor	**1 cup of sugar**
	1 teaspoon of vanilla extract
	1 cup of coconut cream *(see page 19)*
1 cup of tapioca flour (cornstarch may be substituted)	

1.   Preheat your oven to 375° Fahrenheit.
2.   Combine the papaya, tapioca flour, sugar and vanilla in a large mixing bowl and beat thoroughly to a smooth, uniform batter.
3.   Scrape the batter into a greased, 8-inch square baking pan, rapping the sides of the pan to even and level the batter.
4.   Bake in the oven for 45 minutes.
5.   Remove the pan from the oven and separate the pudding into 8 equal squares with the edge of a spatula or knife. Before the mixture cools, pour the coconut cream over the top.
6.   Let the pudding temperature reduce to warm, then, using the spatula from above, place the portions on individual serving plates.

FAIKAKAI

Taro Dessert With Coconut Sauce (TONGA)

This popular Tongan dessert and snack consists of squares of pounded and baked taro, soaked in **Island Coconut Sauce** and topped with coconut cream. The Tongans sometimes use breadfruit in place of the taro; in their version, it is called *faikakai-mei.*

Serves 6

1 pound of small taro corms, peeled and grated	2 tablespoons of sugar
1 egg, beaten	³/4 cup of Island Coconut Sauce *(see below)*
3 tablespoons of taro flour (tapioca flour or cornstarch may be substituted)	¹/2 cup of coconut cream *(see page 19)*

1. Preheat your oven to 250° Fahrenheit.
2. Place the grated taro in a food processor with a metal blade. (You may use a mixing bowl with a hand-held electric blender, also, for this exercise but don't expect the same uniform consistency.)
3. Add the egg and process on a high setting or beat until the ingredients are blended, about 30 seconds. Now, add the flour, 1 tablespoon at a time, processing or beating as necessary between each addition. Pour in the sugar and process or beat to a stiff but uniform batter.
4. Pour this batter into a greased, 8-inch-square baking pan. Cover with a loose tent of aluminum foil and bake for about 1 hour.
5. After the cooking is completed, remove it from the oven and set aside to cool for about 15 minutes. When the **Faikaki** is cool enough to handle and behave properly, use a knife or the edge of a spatula to cut the dessert into 1-inch squares.
6. Place all of the squares in a medium mixing bowl and drizzle the **Island Coconut Sauce** over them. Cover the bowl and refrigerate until ready to eat.
7. Just before serving, apportion the squares into individual serving bowls and top with the coconut cream.

Note: Nontraditional but delightful additions include adding 1 teaspoon of powdered ginger to the batter and including a soupçon of rum in the **Island Coconut Sauce.**

ISLAND COCONUT SAUCE

(OCEANIA)

Yield: 11 ounces (approximately)

1 cup of thick coconut milk (canned may be substituted or see page 19)	1 cup of sugar
	1 cup of brown sugar

1.   Pour the coconut milk into a medium saucepan. Stir in the sugars and place over medium-low heat.

2.   Heat and continue stirring to dissolve the sugars. As the liquid approaches a boil, immediately reduce the heat and let simmer.

3.   Cook, uncovered, without stirring until the mixture thickens and becomes dark brown (resembling a fudge sauce).

4.   Stir once and pour the sauce into a heatproof, glass bowl and let stand to cool.

5.   Transfer the sauce to a clean jar and tightly seal.

Note: The sauce will thicken upon cooling. If it separates, stir it before using. **Coconut Sauce** may be served over ice cream, cake, custard and other desserts.

THE TREE OF LIFE

Where tradewinds blow the seabirds high
    across Pacific skies
And boundless waters roll against the land;
Where tiny specks of coral build the isles of
    Paradise,
A coconut lies buried in the sand.

The craters of volcanoes catch the clouds
    amid their peaks.
The rainfall cuts its pathways like a knife;
Tumbling down the hillsides then combining
    into creeks
It brings the coconut the gift of life.

First tender spikes then branching fronds, the
    plant increases size
Through years of storm or sunlit, tropic calm.
Until one day its fruiting crown waves proudly
    'neath the skies;
An island jewel, the tree of life, the palm.

Its trunk a frame, its fronds for thatch, its
    attributes include
Material to build their sturdy huts.
Its water quenches natives' thirst, its meat
    provides their food.
The staff of life, Pacific coconuts.

                                        J.B.

PO'E MAPE
Polynesian Chestnut Pudding (TAHITI)

One of the most magnificent trees in Tahiti is the *mape* (pronounced "marpay") or Polynesian chestnut, which grows near the rivers in the wilder valleys. Its gray trunk is deeply grooved and solidly planted into the earth in a wide tangle of convoluted, knife-edged roots which curve and coil into the soil. Its green drupes contain large fleshy seeds with a flavor reminiscent of Western chestnuts. The Tahitians use the cooked drupes in a variety of dishes, such as this *po'e* or baked pudding.

Below is the traditional recipe, substituting Western chestnuts for *mape*, but I offer the following caveat: grating our smaller chestnuts is tedious and labor-intensive compared to the same task with the generous-sized *mape*. In the Note at the end of the recipe I offer an alternative; a short-cut that, while equally delicious, does not produce a *po'e* with the same consistency.

Serves 4 to 6

1 banana leaf, washed, drained and softened *(see page 21)*, stems removed or and 18-inch square of heavy-duty aluminum foil

1¹/₂–2 pounds of chestnuts (the extra ¹/₂-pound allows for discarding kernels that may be past their prime for grating)

5 cups of coconut milk *(see page 19)*
³/₄ cup of sugar
¹/₄ teaspoon of vanilla extract
¹/₂ cup of coconut cream *(see page 19)*

1. Preheat your oven to 375° Fahrenheit.
2. Line a standard loaf pan with either the banana leaf or foil, leaving a large, exposed margin to fold over the top.
3. Peel, skin and finely grate the raw chestnuts into a large mixing bowl. Stir in the **coconut milk,** sugar and vanilla.
4. Transfer the chestnut batter into the loaf pan and fold over the leaf or foil to seal tightly. Bake for 50 minutes to 1 hour, or until the mixture has the texture of a cake.
5. Remove the pudding from the oven and unwrap it. Invert it onto a wire tray to cool. Serve hot or warm accompanied by the **coconut cream.**

Note: As an alternative, you may boil the chestnuts before peeling and then mash the kernels into a floury paste. Mix in enough coconut milk to make a stiff batter, and beat in the sugar and vanilla. Bake, unwrapped, for about 20 minutes.

HAUPIA

Coconut *Lu'au Dessert* (HAWAI'I)

These little squares of firm, creamy-white coconut pudding are the traditional *lu'au* dessert; generally served in individual portions on leaf-lined plates.

Polynesian arrowroot (*pia*, see **Glossary,** page 206) was the original starch thickener for this dessert, however, cornstarch is now more commonly used.

Serves 16

2^1/$_2$ **cups of coconut milk** (*see page 19*)	**a pinch of salt**
5 rounded tablespoons of sugar	**6 tablespoons of cornstarch**
	2 tablespoons of dried, sweetened coconut flakes

1. In a double boiler, heat **2^1/$_4$ cups** of the coconut milk, reserving the remaining ^{1}/$_4$ **cup** for use in the next step. Add the sugar and salt, and stir until the sugar is dissolved.
2. In a small mixing bowl, combine the reserved coconut milk (^{1}/$_4$ cup) and the cornstarch, stirring, to make a cream. With a rubber spatula, scrape the coconut milk/cornstarch cream into the heated coconut milk above. Continue to stir, while still on heat, until the mixture becomes a thick custard.
3. After custard consistency has been achieved, pour the **Haupia** into an 8-inch-square baking pan, shake to level the mixture and set aside to cool.
4. When the contents of the pan have come down to about room temperature, sprinkle the surface evenly with the coconut flakes. Place the pan in the refrigerator to chill for at least 30 minutes.
5. After refrigeration, using a knife or the edge of a metal spatula, cut the dessert into 16 2-inch squares. Transfer each portion to individual serving dishes and present immediately.

FAIVKORN NA MANGGO SALAT

Carambola and Mango Compote

(PAPUA NEW GUINEA)

It is believed that carambola, or star fruit, were brought to Papua New Guinea from Indonesia. (This is not surprising since the other half of the large island of New Guinea, Irian Jaya, now belongs, politically, to Indonesia.) Apart from being a rich source of vitamin C, carambola brings an attractive and decorative dimension to any dish when sliced crosswise to form its trademark "stars." It lends a slight but refreshing tartness to this compote. Select only fruit that has ripened to a deep yellow.

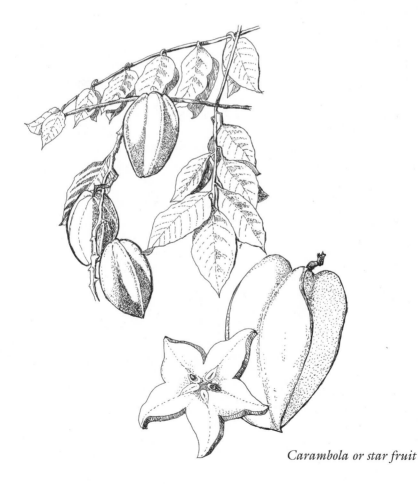

Carambola or star fruit

Serves 6

1 cup of sugar
1 cup of freshly squeezed
    orange juice
1 cup of water
3 carambolas, sliced across into
    stars (reserve the ends for
    use in Step 1)

4 ripe mangoes, peeled and the
    flesh sliced
1 tablespoon of Cointreau

1.   Set a small, non-reactive saucepan over low heat. Put in the sugar, orange
juice and water. Stir until the sugar is dissolved. Add the carambola ends,
increase heat and bring the mixture to a boil. Continue cooking and reducing, as
necessary, for about 4 minutes or until you have a thin syrup.
2.   Remove and discard the carambola ends. Now, introduce the carambola
stars, reduce heat and simmer for about 6 minutes, or until the fruit is tender.
Remove the cooked stars from the syrup with a slotted spoon and place them in
a shallow serving bowl.
3.   Check the syrup for consistency. (If it has begun to thin, increase heat and boil
for a minute or two.) Place the mango slices in the syrup, increase heat and allow
the syrup to boil. Briefly, for less than a minute, poach the mangoes. Again, remove
with a slotted spoon and deposit them on the carambola in the serving bowl.
4.   Increase the heat, as necessary, to boil the remaining syrup and reduce by
one-third. Strain the sauce into a 2-cup, heatproof measuring jug. Let the liquid
cool to room temperature and stir in the Cointreau.
5.   Pour about 3/4 cup of the syrup over the fruit in the serving bowl. (Reserve
any remaining fruit syrup for other desserts.)
6.   Chill the compote in your refrigerator for between 30 minutes to several
hours before serving.

Note: Peach Schnapps or gin may be substituted for the Cointreau.

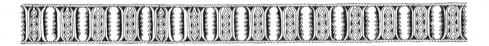

NUT-CENTERED BANANA BALLS IN PAPAYA PURÉE

(MELANESIA)

It seemed that, over most of Melanesia, whenever I flew between countries
I traveled on the same aircraft, no matter what the ticket stock said, no matter

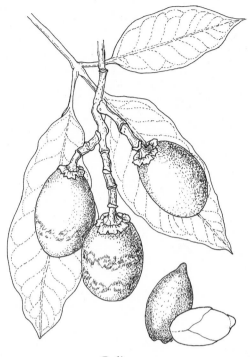

Galip nut

the crew uniforms, no matter the official name of the airline. Then I discovered the answer to this minor but puzzling question. Although all Melanesian countries have their own fleets of commuter planes for internal flights, few have the resources (at this time) to commit the significant expenditures necessary to acquire and operate a fleet of international turbojet transport aircraft. So, in a spirit similar to resort time-sharing, several sovereign countries communally invested in a new Boeing 737. They operate this airborne condominium with all the individual and collective national pride they can muster. (I never felt safer!)

I flew the *Guadalcanal* from Papua New Guinea to the Solomons, from thence, to Vanuatu and, as the flag carrier (Air Vanuatu) of that island republic, eventually down to New Zealand, seldom anywhere else enjoying such good in-flight food and personal attention.

At the end of the meal service between the Solomon Islands and Vanuatu, I was presented with a delicious but mysterious dessert. (Don't presume microwaved plastic trays of fodder; we're talking First Class service—linen and porcelain.) I asked my flight attendant what these morsels were. She didn't look bored and refer me to the menu. In measured tones with infinite goodwill and suffused with island pride, she explained it exactly:

"It's traditional throughout many of the islands. Do you know our local nut?" I said I did.

"Well, it is in the center and we wrap it in sago and banana, just like we make it at home. Then we make a sauce of papaya . . . that's what you are eating."

She smiled. I smiled back and felt pampered. Melanesian hospitality at 27,000 feet is exactly the same as it is at sea level.

The nuts in the center were *narngi* or *ngali*, depending on the region (see illustration of galip nuts, page 209).

Until we can import these galip nuts (see Glossary page 255) we shall substitute halved Brazil nuts.

Serves 6

4 ripe bananas, peeled and mashed	1 teaspoon of sugar
1 cup (or more, if necessary) sago or tapioca flour	1/2 teaspoon of fresh ginger-root, peeled and grated
9–12 Brazil nuts, shelled, skinned and halved	1 teaspoon of freshly squeezed lime juice
1 medium papaya, peeled, seeded and chopped	

1. In a large mixing bowl, combine the banana pulp and sago flour into a dough stiff enough to mold with your hands.
2. Scoop up enough dough to make a ball, about the size of a large walnut. Force a Brazil nut half into the center, then shape and mold the dough around it. Repeat until all the dough or nut halves are used.
3. Almost fill a large saucepan with water and place it over high heat. When the liquid reaches a full boil, carefully drop in the banana/sago/nut balls. After the water has returned to a boil, reduce heat and simmer the balls for about 20 minutes. When cooked, remove the balls with a slotted spoon and set aside for use in Step 5. Continue until all the balls are cooked.
4. Place the papaya, sugar, ginger and lime juice in a blender and blend on a high setting to a smooth purée.
5. Lay out 6 dessert plates. Pool equal portions of the papaya purée from Step 4 on each plate. Deposit 3–4 banana-nut balls in the center of each papaya pool and serve immediately.

Note: A soupçon of coconut cream may be drizzled over each serving, if desired.

BANANA-LIME-HONEY WHIP

(COOK ISLANDS)

It was sheer luck, not good planning on my part that I arrived in Rarotonga, capital of the Cook Islands, in the third week of November. This is designated as the Tiare (Floral) Festival week.

I proceeded to Avarua, the island township, on my first morning and found flowers everywhere. As I sat in the Cook's Corner Café, everybody was atwitter. All the women wore circlets of plumeria and hibiscus around their hair. They were clambering up and upon tables and chairs to wind garlands of flowers round pillars, down walls—anywhere imaginable. (Even the roadside take-out van was draped in garlands.) From my table, I watched the half-hourly arrival of the buses as they deposited their occupants and picked up fresh passengers for the journey around Rarotonga. There were fruit and vegetable stands on the sea side of the road and brightly-colored *pareus* for sale; flying from a line like flags in the wind.

After I wandered around the compact little town, explored and shopped, I indulged in this local sweet.

Serves 8

1 cup of whipping cream	4 ripe, firm bananas, peeled
1/2 cup of natural honey (New	and cut into chunks
Zealand honey would be	1 cup of coconut cream (*see*
politically appropriate)	*page 19*)
1 cup of sugar	2 tablespoons of dried,
1/2 cup of freshly squeezed	unsweetened coconut
lime juice	flakes, lightly toasted
1 teaspoon of unflavored	2 teaspoons of lime zest,
gelatin	grated
1/4 teaspoon of salt	

1. Place the whipping cream, the bowl (copper), beater, blades or whisk in the refrigerator to chill and for use in Step 4.

2. Place a small, non-reactive saucepan over medium heat and add the honey, sugar and lime juice. Stir to dissolve the sugar and adjust the heat to bring the mixture to a slow boil. Immediately remove the pan from heat and stir in the gelatin and salt. Set aside for use in Step 5.

3. Place the banana chunks in a large, non-reactive mixing bowl and mash to a smooth paste.

4.   Remove the cream and the implements from the refrigerator and whip the cream, slowly adding the coconut cream, until it is fluffy and will form peaks.

5.   Pour the honey/sugar/lime mixture into the bowl with the mashed bananas. Thoroughly blend to a smooth mixture. Fold in the whipped creams and gently mix to a uniform consistency.

6.   Spoon the whip into dessert glasses and sprinkle each with the toasted coconut flakes and lime zest. Chill until ready to serve.

BANANA CAKE WITH PASSION FRUIT ICING

(NIUE)

The cliff-girdled island of Niue, southeast of the Samoas and east of Tonga, has no rivers nor streams but its coral rock retains rainwater and its shallow soil is fertile. Sugar cane, limes, passion fruit, coconuts and bananas all flourish. This local cake recipe utilizes Niue's home-grown best.

Yield: 1 9-inch, double-layer cake

2¹/₄ cups of cake flour	1¹/₂ cups of ripe bananas,
2 teaspoons of baking powder	peeled, mashed and forced
³/₄ teaspoon of baking soda	through a sieve
¹/₂ teaspoon of salt	1 teaspoon of vanilla extract
1 stick (¹/₂ cup) of unsalted	¹/₄ cup of thick coconut milk
butter	*(see page 19)*
1¹/₂ cups of sugar	2 ripe (unblemished) bananas,
2 eggs	peeled and thinly sliced
	into disks

BANANA CAKE

1.   Preheat your oven to 350° Fahrenheit. Line the bottom of 2-9 × 1¹/₂-inch, round cake pans with circles of waxed paper, cut to fit.

2.   Sift the first 4 (dry) ingredients into a medium mixing bowl. Set aside for use in Step 5.

3. In a large mixing bowl, cream the butter then add the sugar, beating until the mixture is creamy. Beat in the eggs, one at a time, until the combination becomes fluffy and foamy.

4.   In a third mixing bowl, combine the banana purée, vanilla, and the coconut milk.

5. Beat about one-third of the sifted flour mixture into the sugar/egg/butter cream. When the mixture is uniform, beat in about one-third of the banana mixture. Continue beating, alternating additions, until all the ingredients are combined into a smooth batter.

6. Equally divide the batter between the 2 pans, rapping the sides of the pan so the batter forms a smooth layer.

7. Bake the layers for 30 minutes, or until the cakes begin to pull away slightly from the sides of the pans and, when a toothpick is inserted into the centers, it comes out clean.

8. Invert the cooked cakes on wire racks and let cool.

9. When cooled, layer the banana slices on top of one cake and place the other on top to form a banana sandwich. Ice the cake with the **Passion Fruit Icing.**

PASSION FRUIT ICING

$1/2$ **cup of sugar**
$1/2$ **cup of water**
the flesh and seeds from 6 passion fruits

3 tablespoons of unsalted butter
$2 1/4$ cups of powdered sugar

1. Place a small saucepan over medium heat and add the sugar and water. Dissolve the sugar in the water, stirring, and let the mixture come to a slow boil. Immediately remove from heat and stir in the passion fruit pulp and seeds. Set aside to cool and for use in Step 3.

2. Cream the butter and **one-half** the powdered sugar together in a small mixing bowl and set aside for use in the next step.

3. Force the passion fruit mixture through a sieve into a small mixing bowl. Add 3 tablespoons of the passion fruit syrup to the creamed butter/sugar and blend to a smooth paste. Continue adding sufficient powdered sugar to make a creamy icing.

Note: The additional, remaining passion fruit syrup may be refrigerated or frozen for later use in tropical fruit compotes, fruit pies or, diluted, as a beverage.

AUSTRALIA

Aborigines

The first peoples to move through and out of Southeast Asia to seek new lands across the seas were the original Australians, the aborigines.

In those far-off times, Australia was larger in area, lushly vegetated and populated by even more diverse species of fauna than it is today. However, as the weather patterns changed and the land became more inhospitable—particularly in the now arid center of the continent—the early aboriginal hunter-gathers were obliged to adopt ecological practices that ensured the renewability of their resources. They learnt to understand, revere and preserve their beloved land and all it contained. They abstained from wanton killing and hunted only for food. They began to comprehend the importance of preserving vegetation and burnt only to renew the vigor of fresh plant growth, and to attract animals to the new-growth shoots and leaves.

Aboriginal society encompasses the longest continuous cultural traditions on earth. Much of their culture was codified into their religion; the concept of the Dreamtime, or the Dreaming, called by them *tjukurpa*. To all aboriginal tribes it signifies the era of creation, a time when the earth was barely formed and the great ancestral spirits traveled across the land, creating rivers, rocks and forests, and dedicating plants and animals to be specially reserved for their descendants.

The aborigines still believe that features of the landscape are metamorphosed ancient beings and are therefore held as sacred sites. While this concept seems far-fetched in the abstract, there is no doubt that eerie, spiritual, emotional and, almost supernatural, but tangible sensations can catch you unaware when you visit certain areas within Australia. Two that I can personally testify to are Lake George, between Sydney and Canberra (a dark and silent body of water, now thought to possibly contain some of the earliest sites of human habitation) and Hanging Rock, outside Melbourne. (Hanging Rock was the location for Peter Weir's haunting film *Picnic at Hanging Rock* and approached by a road that, in one section, seems to defy gravity and confuse your senses; upslope appears down and vice versa.) Then, of course, there is the almost metaphysical formation, Ayers Rock, called *Uluru* by the aborigines. It looms alone in the center of endless plains, defying explanation; a center of the continent and of the tribes' religious beliefs. This is the closest simile I can summon: it is as if you are walking within the precincts of a vast cathedral left by an unknown civilization from another planet; the same landmark fixation captured by Steven Spielberg in *Close Encounters of the Third Kind*.

The vibrant and powerful paintings and rock carvings of the aborigines record their religious beliefs. The Rainbow Serpent, Kalarrbirri, the supreme female spirit, cuts wide swaths through the earth to form the rivers of northern Australia and the barramundi fish's thrashing makes the rivers bend. Wet season man, Barra, is even now called upon to fight the dry season man, Jinaroo; to battle for the annual time of the "Great Wet," when the rivers spill their banks and the land becomes fertile again. This is a continuing and everlasting supplication to the forces of nature that they may renew the earth and nourish some of its oldest inhabitants.

This unity with nature permeates the philosophy of the aborigines with regard to food. There is no element of bloodlust nor sport to their hunting. They hunt only to eat and employ an extraordinary range of skills: stalking; camouflage and disguise; speed;

(Continued.)

animal calls; ruses and tricks; and, finally, accuracy. Myths, taboos and totems protect both animals and plants at certain times for conservation. A plant will never be stripped of all its leaves or fruit, nor will an entire yam or other tuber be dug up (the top of the yam is left attached to a tendril in the ground so it will grow again). Neither are all the eggs in a turtle's nest removed.

As the men are hunters, so are the women the gatherers. In times of drought, the men may return empty handed. The women are always foraging for food, overlooking nothing edible. Their botanical knowledge is comprehensive. The children accompany them to watch and learn. Tubers, roots and shoots are harvested, seeds are gleaned. Nuts, berries and fruits are picked. *Witjuti* grubs, honey ants (their abdomens distended into amber balloons with collected nectar), certain species of moths (described as sweet-tasting and walnut-flavored after heads and wings are removed and they are cooked) and grasshoppers, are all items for the meal. At the seashore, crustaceans and shellfish are caught and gathered. The women never return empty handed. But the roles of the genders in obtaining food are not absolute. The women may hunt lizards and "possums" on occasion. The men may gather plant food if they have failed to locate an animal or have spared one with which they have a totemic relationship.

Of the bush foods gathered, the method of preparation depends on the type of food. Some plants or portions thereof are poisonous unless treated with heat and/or processed. Others need painstaking preparation before they can be eaten. Large roots and tubers are either roasted or, if requiring processing, are grated, washed and the starch extracted, in the manner of tapioca or cassava. Small roots are steamed. Some roots are roasted, peeled and their starch hammered or mashed to a paste, mixed with water and used as a dough. In Northern Australia, taro, yams and Polynesian arrowroot are staples on the continental side of the Torres Strait and along the east coast of Cape York. The coconut grew there in prehistoric times, probably through random dispersal and flotation of the nuts from Papua New Guinea. It does not appear that the aborigines ever ate or cultivated it.

Grass seeds are laboriously collected and ground wet into a paste, which is then eaten or milled dry and used as flour. That flour is made into "dampers" or bush bread which is baked in the ashes of an open fire. Nuts are also ground into flour but are mostly eaten raw or roasted. Fruits and berries are consumed in their natural state. The seeds of leguminous shrubs are either steamed in the pods, split open and eaten, or dried, heated and then ground into flour. Seeds of certain herbs and ferns are ground into flour. The seeds of cycads, which are toxic, are rendered harmless by aging or are roasted and mashed, or sliced then leached in running water. They are either eaten raw, wrapped in bark and baked, or made into flour that produces light, fluffy bread when a leavening is added.

The aborigines also eat edible flowers, use some pollen for bread and suck the nectar as a sweet from other blossoms. Edible gum is also consumed.

Earth ovens are constructed in shallow depressions in the ground by letting a fire, prepared in the hole, burn down to hot ashes. The animal to be cooked is placed directly upon the ashes and covered with a further layer of embers and then earth. Heated stones or pieces of ant heap are also heaped on the fire to help contain the heat. Often leaves are placed in a layer over the stones and an additional layer packed down over the food before the oven is sealed with earth. If leaves are used, water is

(Continued.)

frequently added to create more steam. Bush foods steamed in earth ovens include bush carrots, bush onions, shellfish, freshwater eels and kangaroo steaks. *Witjuti* grubs and small lizards are merely baked in hot ashes. Shellfish (bivalves) are set, hinge end upright, in tight rows in the sand and a brief fire of twigs, set to burn for no more than ten minutes, is laid above them.

Fire was essential to the aborigines, not only for cooking and warmth, but for illumination during night ceremonies, for frightening and flushing game and for constructing weapons by melting types of gum from the spinifex plant. A smoldering fire stick of hardwood was carried from one camp to the next so that fire was always available.

Because the knowledge of locating food and gathering or hunting it, then apportioning it, was so important to the aborigines, the lore was incorporated into paintings on bark using mineral ochre and plant dyes. Many of these works of art symbolically indicate the habitat of animals and the location of plants, such as yams. Some depict the animals anatomically, in x-ray fashion; others show how they are to be butchered.

The main events of tribal life are celebrated by rituals and ceremonies. Some, which are concerned with maintaining the natural species or to do with death and afterlife, are sacred exclusively to fully-initiated males within the tribes. Other rituals are within the secret and sole province of the females. However, general festivals of dance, known a "play-abouts" or *corroborees* are common to all and take place almost nightly. The men sing and beat clap-stick boomerangs while the deep, sonorous drone of the didgeridoos penetrates the air. The firelit figures dance old

"X-ray" bark painting of a barramundi from the Northern Territory of Australia

stories of the tribe, imitate antics of animals or recreate the frenzy of the hunt. The women dance in the shadows, often with sleepy children perched on their shoulders. The forms cross and re-cross, bobbing up and down in hypnotic rhythm, intermittently lighted by the flickering fire as they dance the Australian night away.

The Australian, bush-food recipes in this book feature local ingredients. While substitutions may be made, it is hoped that the "down under" ingredients may soon be available in other parts of the world. There is good "tucker" (Aussie idiom for food) to be found in the wild Australian countryside and the aborigines have always known it.

DAMPER

(AUSTRALIA)

Aborigines all over Australia make this native bread, which is traditionally baked in the hot ashes of a fire. While tribal names for bread are *wikki, myhee, nurong* or *krepauwe,* damper was so christened by Aussie stockmen because it "dampened the appetite."

The bread was originally made from the seeds of wild grasses, portulaca or *Portulacaceae,* the scientific name for purslane. Some dampers were even made from ground nuts. The seeds were winnowed in a *coolamon,* the aboriginal carved wood food dish—a process they called *yandying*—before being ground with water. Nowadays, dampers are mostly baked from flours, either white or whole-wheat. In the bush, the Australians serve damper with wild honey or golden syrup (the thick, English cane-sugar syrup) and accompany it with a cup of strong, black tea, brewed in a "billy can."

Serves 3 to 4

3 cups of self-rising flour (plus additional flour for shaping and kneading the dough)	**$^2/_3$ cup of instant** (powdered) **milk**
1 teaspoon of salt	**$1^1/_4$ cups of cold water**

1. Preheat your oven to 400° Fahrenheit.
2. Lightly grease a cookie sheet and set it aside for use in Step 5. Dust your working surface with a sprinkling of the flour.
3. Sift all the dry ingredients into a large mixing bowl. Make a well in the center and pour in the water. Using a pastry spatula, lightly and briefly mix the ingredients to a smooth, moist dough.
4. Turn the dough onto your floured working surface and knead it once into the shape of a ball. Force and pat the ball to flatten it into the shape of a disk, approximately the size of a dinner plate (8–10 inches).
5. Transfer the dough to the cookie sheet and make two, shallow, parallel incisions on the top of the dough. Dust the top with flour and bake the bread for about 20 to 30 minutes, or until a toothpick, when inserted into the center, comes out clean.
6. Serve hot or warm, sliced and buttered.

Note: Variations on dampers include using whole-wheat flour or adding 2 tablespoons of finely chopped fresh herbs to the dough. (If you include the herbs to make the bread more savory, omit the honey and/or golden syrup.) Other additions could include finely chopped nuts or wattle seeds.

REWENA PARAOA

Maori Bread (NEW ZEALAND)

The traditional starter, called *rewena,* was made from potato water, flour and sugar; it contained no yeast. For that reason **Maori Bread** was often nicknamed potato bread. This more modern starter uses yeast in addition to the potato water.

STARTER

Yield: Sufficient for 2 loaves

1 medium potato, peeled and cubed	1 $1/4$-ounce packet or $1/2$ tablespoon of active, dry yeast
2 cups of water	
1 cup of unbleached white flour	1 teaspoon of sugar

1.   Boil the potato in the water until it is just tender but not falling apart. Pour off and measure 1 cup of the potato water. (You may reserve the vegetable for later use in another recipe.) Set the liquid aside to cool and for use in the next step.

2.   Select a heatproof glass or ceramic bowl and rinse it with boiling water. Pour in the flour, yeast and sugar. Stir in the potato water from above and lightly mix to a smooth cream. (Do not over beat.)

3.   Cover the bowl with plastic wrap and pierce it with several, small holes to help release the accumulating gases. Place the **Starter** in a warm, dry, draft-free location for 2 days. Stir several times a day and recover. After about 48 hours, cover and refrigerate until ready to use.

PARAOA

The *rewena* Starter from above, allowed to return to room temperature	$1/2$ cup of milk
	1 tablespoon of salt
	1 teaspoon of baking powder
5 cups of unbleached white flour (plus additional flour for kneading)	2 tablespoons of melted butter

1.   Pour the Starter into a large, non-reactive mixing bowl. Gradually stir in **1¹/₂ cups** of the flour and **¹/₄ cup** of the milk. Beat vigorously for about 1 minute.

2.   Add the salt, baking powder, **1 more cup** of flour and the **remainder** of the milk. Stir to thoroughly combine all the ingredients into a dough. Place a clean tea towel moistened with hot water over the bowl and return it to a warm environment to rest for about 30 minutes.

3.   Spread the remaining **2¹/₂ cups** of flour on a large board or marble slab. Turn the rested dough from Step 2 onto the center of the board. Use your hands to mix and knead the flour into the dough. Vigorously knead the dough for about 8 more minutes, using additional flour as necessary to prevent it sticking to either your hands or the board.

4.   Grease 2 bread loaf pans. Divide the dough equally and, with the heel of your hands, flatten one portion into a large rectangle. (The width of the dough rectangle should approximately equal the **length** of your pans. The length of the dough should approximately equal 3 × the **width** of your pans.) Fold the longer ends of the dough into the center, in thirds, one end over the other. Knead the dough ends to seal them. Repeat the flattening, folding and kneading with the second dough portion.

5.   Place each in their respective pans, cover both, again, with the moistened tea cloth (wrung out in hot water) and let them rise for about 45 minutes, or until they have individually almost doubled in volume. (While the dough is rising, continue with Step 6.)

6.   Heat your oven to 350° Fahrenheit. When the dough has risen, remove the cloth, brush the tops of the dough with melted butter and bake for about 55 minutes, or until the loaves respond with a hollow thud when tapped.

7.   Turn the cooked loaves onto a wire rack and allow to cool before serving or storing.

Chapter *11*

To Complement the Meal

Unusual Island Relishes, Condiments, Sauces,
Dressings and Beverages

As a condiment to the breadfruit they use mitiaro, *or*
grated cocoa-nut kernels, sprinkled with salt water and
carefully fermented. It possesses a rich and sharp taste,
which may be compared to cheese.
Edward Dodd, 1976, *Polynesia's Sacred Isle*
(from the journals of Dr. Frederick D. Bennett, written in 1833)

Traditional Oceanian condiments, relishes and sauces remind me again of how many totally different effects can be achieved from so few ingredients by sheer ingenuity. I marvel at the islanders' knowledge of the process of fermentation, which they use with skill to produce nuances of flavor in side dishes. They understand—almost inherently—exactly the length of time required, the appropriate temperature and humidity without scientific measuring. In this, they are the brethren of European or Asian country folk; harvesting, pickling and fermenting their grains, fruits, vegetables and milk in the ways of their ancestors.

Knowledge, Skill and Pleasure are up to the Diner

Those casual visitors to the Pacific Islands who complain about the bland food should look more closely at the total balance of dishes within a large Oceanian meal or feast: the pairing of soothing starches with spicy preparations; of rich with plain; of oily or fatty with astringent; of fresh with preserved. Except for the diets and meals of subsistence eating on the most remote islands—seldom on the itinerary of most visitors—flavor, texture and tastes are balanced, albeit not so delicately as they are in Asia. The saltiness of *lomi* salmon is offset by the blandness of *poi* in Hawai'i. In most of Polynesia, the nourishing fiber of cooked root vegetables or breadfruit is enlivened by spiced, salted dry dips, or sour, tangy fermented relishes. The essence of the "pointy" bite and aroma of hot chili peppers, lemon juice and onions (the top note, created by the volatile oils) is measured and counterpointed with the accompaniment of plainly-cooked but impeccably-fresh fish.

Fresh fruit frequently offers a flavor balance. It may be used, green and sharp with acidity, to marry with an oily or fatty fish, or as a ripe and mellow vehicle of sweetness and perfume (the floral note) to accompany chicken or pork.

In Pacific custom, all dishes are brought to the eating area at the same time. The diner is encouraged to experiment with the properties, consistencies, textures and balance of one dish with another. There are no rules, save those of pleasuring the mouth, the palate and stomach. (At an island feast, you will often see a native with a piece of fish in one hand and a banana in the other.)

As we in the West have learned to appreciate the contrasts of pears with Brie or tart, vinegared pickles with cold meats, so the islanders esteem pickled, fermented fish with cooked breadfruit. (Consider the Roman predilection for *garum,* fermented fish; the British partiality for anchovy based pastes to spread on bread. Or, ponder on the Southeast Asian use of spicy fermented fish and shrimp sauces as dips for spring rolls, stuffed rice-flour pancakes, or beef, rolled in bundles of lettuce and fresh herbs.)

Grace Notes of Fresh Ambrosia

Evolutions and trends in food are cyclical and tend to be recursive. In the current state of many international cuisines, the role of fruit in savory dishes has grown closer to its import in medieval times. Oceania produces a cornucopia of tropical fruits with which to experiment and, throughout its cities and capitals, local chefs and good cooks are partnering fruit together with meats and fish in exciting new combinations. (I encourage you to explore similar amalgamations and permutations.)

Salsas, or fresh relishes of mixed fruits and vegetables, bring out the superb flavors of *ono* (wahoo), *'opakapaka* (snapper), *mahi mahi* (dolphin fish) and *aku* (skipjack or bonito) in Polynesian-inspired fish dishes. Fruit-based chutneys and dips are transformed into intriguing sauces or used to enrich gravies.

Delectable conserves of coconut and/or fruit become benedictions upon desserts, compotes, puddings, ice creams and more. A coconut sauce from your kitchen can elevate commonplace desserts. Also, consider using it for flans and tarts or as an ingredient in cookies. (Fill layered cakes with it, etc.)

Pacific Island Coolers, Thirst Quenchers and Mood Changers

Island beverages run the gamut from refreshing nonalcoholic blends of fruit juices and coconut—together with sparkling waters or flavored sodas—to tourist-oriented time bombs; usually served in stemware or coconut-shell halves and mixed with 151-proof rum. (Please garnish this image with any number of tropical fruits and the requisite paper parasol.)

I shall leave you at the mercy of island bartenders for exponential variations on alcohol-based drinks. I would like to invite you here to

Adapted from a lithograph by J.A. Pellion from the Louis de Freycinet visit to Guam in 1818. On the left is a hotno, an outdoor oven. In front, bottom left, is a wooden mortar for threshing rice. At right, they are making palm toddy.

explore the infinite arrangements of tropical fruits (and their juices) translated into liquid refreshment. Then, of course, there are the islanders' local and traditional celebratory libations; occasionally disabling on a tropical night in the company of good people on a special occasion.

Although alcohol was not historically drunk in Oceania before contact with Westerners, palm toddy is now consumed on many islands. Micronesians tap the coconut flower stalk for a liquid that may be drunk fresh and sweet or fermented into powerful liquor called *tuba*. A local custom on Guam is to backstop it with beer chasers. Devastating. This dual insult to your body is often the most commonly served beverage at a Chamorro wedding or christening.

'*Okolehao* is the Hawaiian distilled spirit made from the baked roots of the ti plant. The Tahitians are producing a variety of "interesting" spirits distilled from breadfruit, ginger and other plants. I bought some bottles from a Society Island equivalent of a wine-tasting store in the Paea area. (A very inebriated Tahitian, happy in his state, with floating robes and a crown of flowers around his frizzy, dyed hair, supervised the tasting. The experience was surrealistic—definite echoes of a Tahitian *La Cage aux Folles*—at once both fun and poignant.)

In addition to the recipes in this chapter, you will find other sauces and dressings throughout the book, usually attached to their complementary dish. All of them can comfortably change partners and create a new theme or link. Mix and match according to your mood and inspiration. It's island style!

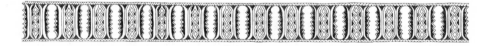

ROUGAIEDE DE COCO

Coconut Relish (NEW CALEDONIA)

This side dish is both relish and condiment, and is generally served in coconut shell halves beside each diner's place at feasts. It is best made with freshly-grated coconut meat but reconstituted, dried unsweetend coconut may be substituted (see Chapter 1, page 19)

Serves everybody

1 1/2 cups of freshly grated coconut or reconstituted dried, unsweetened coconut flakes	1/2 teaspoon of salt 1/4 teaspoon of freshly ground black pepper
1/4 cup of parsley, minced	2 teaspoons of lemon juice 1 tablespoon of canola oil

1. Combine all the ingredients and stir until the salt dissolves. Cover and refrigerate until ready to serve.

Note: The **Rougaiede** should be made on the same day you plan to serve it.

'INAMONA

Kukui Nut Condiment (HAWAI'I)

This ancient Polynesian condiment uses candle nut (known in Hawaiian as *kukui*). Although *'inamona* has a delightful flavor, only small amounts are indicated because of the laxative properties of the nut. (For those who do not live in the Fiftieth State, substitutions are given in the Note.)

Yield: 1/2 cup (approximately)

36 or more fresh, unshelled *kukui* nuts	**2 green chili peppers** *(Serrano* or *Jalapeño),* **seeded and**
1 tablespoon of *'alae* salt	**minced**

1. Preheat your oven to 275° Fahrenheit.
2. Place the *kukui* nuts in a large baking pan and roast them for about 2 hours. Turn the nuts occasionally. To check for doneness, crack one of the nuts open. The kernel should be brown.
3. Shell the nuts and mash the kernels into a coarse paste. (You may use a mortar and pestle but a food processor is more convenient.)
4. Add the salt and chili peppers. Stir to thoroughly combine the latter ingredients. Serve in a decorative bowl with your *lu'au* food.

Note: An equivalent amount of roasted Macadamia nuts may be substituted. Rock, kosher or sea salt may be substituted for the *'alae* salt. *'Inamona* may be refrigerated in a tightly-capped jar and can be kept successfully for up to 2 months.

FINADENE

Chamorro Hot Sauce (GUAM)

Pronounced "fin•a•den•ay," this simple but incendiary sauce accompanies *every* Chamorro meal on Guam. *Finadene* and/or Tabasco Brand Pepper Sauce are the two hot and spicy components without which no self-respecting Chamorro (Guamanian) would consider eating, regarding most food bland and, therefore, inedible without one or the other.

When dining out, the Chamorros rely on Tabasco for spice, because *finadene* is always freshly prepared at home but seldom served in restaurants. Sitting in a coffee shop in Guam at breakfast time, watching a Chamorro shake Tabasco over his fried eggs until they are obliterated by the orange/red veil, is a sobering experience.

The hotness of *finadene* is easily modulated to personal taste by adjusting the ratio of hot peppers to liquid. On Guam, the chili pepper of choice is the "boonie" pepper, which now grows wild over much of the island. The large family of hot peppers has now crossbred to such an extent that it is difficult to identify the species. Sufficient to say, the native pepper is about $1^1/_2$- to 2-inches in length, $1/_4$-inch thick and is invariably eaten at the fully-ripened stage of maturation of fire-engine red.

The legacy of long association with the U.S. has bequeathed to Guam the term "boonies" for the colloquial "boondocks" (a term coined by G.I.s garrisoned in the Philippines prior to World War II, from the Tagalog *bundok*, meaning mountain) and it refers to the surprisingly wild interior of Guam (particularly in the south of the island). Groups of eager enthusiasts regularly engage in the pastime of "boonie stomping" or wilderness hiking and, just as regularly, someone gets lost.

Although Guam is a relatively small island, its size is deceptive. Its jungled areas enabled one of the last World War II Japanese soldiers to hide on the island, unaware the war had ended 27 years before. He visits Guam almost every year and has become a legend. While taking the island road (Marine Drive) south, you might stop in at the Guam Museum and peruse Sergeant Shoichi Yokoi's survival exhibit, as well as other displays of Island history.

Finadene sauce is most commonly eaten with fish but may accompany any Guamanian savory recipe.

Serves everybody

1/2 cup of white onion, finely chopped	1/3 cup of soy sauce
1–6 *Jalapeño* chili peppers (depending on your heat tolerance), **sliced into disks**	2/3 cup of freshly squeezed lemon juice

1. Combine all the ingredients and save. (Leftover sauce may be refrigerated for up to a week.)

MITI

Coconut Cream Sauce (FIJI AND SAMOA)

The Fijian term for coconut milk and cream is *lolo*. Traditional dishes that are prepared with coconut milk and cream use the *–lolo* suffix. For example, *ika vakalolo: ika* is the generic term for fish and *vakalolo* denotes that it is cooked in coconut milk.

Miti is a coconut sauce made with thick *lolo*. The traditional recipe, requiring freshly grated coconut, follows. See the Note at the end for a shortcut recipe.

Yield: 1³/₄ cups (approximately)

the meat from a freshly grated coconut *(see Chapter 1, page 19)*	**1/2 onion, peeled and finely chopped**
1 lemon, coarsely chopped	**1/2 cup of hot water**
2 green chili peppers *(Serrano or Jalapeño)*, **seeded and minced**	

1.   Combine all the ingredients in a medium, non-reactive mixing bowl. Let the coconut meat and the other ingredients steep in the hot water for at least 1 hour.

2.   Line a large sieve or colander with muslin or several layers of cheesecloth. Place the lined sieve over another large, non-reactive mixing bowl. Pour in the contents of the bowl from Step 1.

3.   Gather the corners and edges of the cloth and squeeze vigorously and repeatedly to express all the liquid.

4.   Use the resultant *Miti* at once or store it for one day (maximum), unrefrigerated, in a tightly sealed container.

Note: *Miti* can be used as an ingredient or a stand-alone dish. By adding a teaspoon of cornstarch or similar thickening agent and cooking it, the result, for instance, is a very refreshing dip. The shortcut recipe is not as concentrated as the traditional recipe and yields about 1/2 cup of sauce. In a small, non-reactive mixing bowl, combine the following: 1/2 cup of thick coconut milk; the juice of 1 lemon; 1/4 teaspoon of salt; 1 small green chili pepper, seeded and minced; 1/4 cup of onion, finely chopped. Cover and refrigerate until use. If the green chili peppers are omitted from either recipe, the *Miti* becomes the Samoan *niu*.

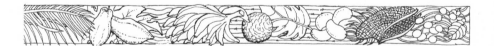

SWEET AND HOT
CHILI-PINEAPPLE SAUCE

(OCEANIA)

This sauce is an Oceanian cousin to the chili sauces of Southeast Asia; a titillating combination of sweet, sour and spicy. Dilute it with additional pineapple juice for marinades, whip it into mayonnaise, use it for dips or as an accompaniment to fritters, fish, meats, etc.

Yield: approximately 35 ounces

2 tablespoons of cayenne
2¹/₂ cups of pineapple juice
1¹/₂ cups of white vinegar
1 cup of sugar
¹/₂ cup of pineapple chunks,
    minced

6 cloves of garlic, smashed,
    peeled and minced
2 teaspoons of salt
1¹/₂ tablespoons of fresh gin-
    gerroot, peeled and
    minced

1. Sterilize 1 or 2 suitably-sized jars or bottles with tight-fitting caps.
2. Place a medium, non-reactive saucepan over high heat and add all the ingredients. Stir until the sugar dissolves and let the mixture come to a boil. Reduce heat to medium and let the mixture cook for about 20 minutes.
3. Remove the pan from heat and let it cool for several minutes.
4. When cool enough to handle, pour the sauce into your blender and blend on a high setting for about 45 seconds. Pour the sauce into the jar(s) or bottle(s) you have prepared.
5. When the sauce has cooled to room temperature, cap it tightly and refrigerate until serving.

Note: The jars of sauce will keep for at least 6 months to 1 year with refrigeration.

SPICY BANANA-GINGER-ONION DIP

(VANUATU)

This double-hyphenate recipe can be separated into two different but equally exciting accompaniments: one, as a stand-alone dip, to be served with deep-fried taro or sweet potato chips or, two, without the mayonnaise, a fruity chutney to accentuate curries, pork dishes, cold meats or fish steaks.

Yield: 2 cups

1$^1/_2$ tablespoons of peanut oil
$^1/_2$ large onion, peeled and
    finely chopped
1 teaspoon of garlic, smashed,
    peeled and minced
1 packed tablespoon of fresh
    gingerroot, peeled and
    minced
2 medium-ripe bananas, peeled
    and cut into chunks
$^1/_4$ cup of freshly squeezed
    orange juice

the juice of 1 lemon
$^1/_2$ teaspoon of lemon zest,
    grated
$^1/_4$ teaspoon of salt
$^1/_4$ teaspoon of freshly ground
    black pepper
$^1/_4$ teaspoon of turmeric
$^1/_2$ teaspoon of *garam masala*
    (Indian sweet spice mix)
1 cup of mayonnaise

1.   Place a small, non-reactive saucepan over a medium-high heat. Pour in the peanut oil and modulate the heat to achieve a frying temperature; when a haze just forms over the oil.

2.   Add the onion, reduce heat by a fraction and fry, stirring, for about 2 minutes. Add the garlic and continue stirring and frying for about 30 more seconds. Drop in the ginger and continue the process for about an additional 90 seconds.

3.   Now add the bananas, orange juice, lemon juice and lemon zest and season with the salt and spices. Adjust the heat to produce a low simmer and cook for about 15 minutes, stirring occasionally, until the mixture has reached the texture and consistency of applesauce; the liquid has almost completely evaporated.

4.   Remove the saucepan from the heat and set aside to cool. (After cooling, you may place the conserve in a container with a tight seal and refrigerate until required.)

5.   When cool, combine the banana mixture from the above step in a non-reactive mixing bowl with the mayonnaise. Mix and stir to combine all the ingredients. Serve at room temperature as a dip.

Note: The dip may be refrigerated, covered, for up to 24 hours. The chutney may be kept longer under refrigeration and has more broad applications.

KAVA

Kava, also variously known as *'awa, yaqona, sakau,* etc., in the Pacific Islands, is the preeminent and traditional drink through most of Oceania. It is prepared from the roots and stems of *Piper methysticum,* a member of the Piperaceae family of pepper plants. The multi-branched shrub with heart-shaped leaves probably originated in the archipelago of Vanuatu but was taken with the ancient migrants and planted as far afield as Tahiti and Hawaii.

    The drinking of *kava* has ritualistic, mystical and social significance in the Pacific: the ceremony of its drinking takes place at feasts, special events (such as the harvest

(Continued.)

of the first fruits of the season) or at mere pleasant, social gatherings. In some areas, only men are allowed to drink *kava* and to prepare it. In others, young females concoct it for the chiefs. On other archipelagoes, both men and women may imbibe. In Vanuatu, *kava* is usually drunk in mens' *nakamals,* or huts that serve as men-only clubs or bars for the exclusive purpose of gathering socially and drinking *kava.* Special carved wooden bowls

Pounding kava (sakau) roots with water to make the beverage and Piper methisticum vine leaves.

(usually multi-legged) and vessels are dedicated exclusively to holding the prepared beverage and drinkers use cups made of coconut-shell halves.

The root, branch and stem of the *kava* vine have many applications in traditional Oceanian medicine. *Kava* contains several alkaloids and has analgesic and tranquilizing properties. It is also an antibacterial and anti-fungal agent. In the villages, the mildly narcotic drink is made by grinding or scraping the root and squeezing the resultant pulp through fibers into a bowl, then combining it with water. Nowadays, *kava* powder is packaged and can be mixed into an instant beverage.

In historic Oceania, because of *kava's* mood-altering properties, the European missionaries attempted to ban its consumption. This prohibition only caused an increase in the drinking of alcohol and drove the *kava* culture temporarily underground.

Visiting the Fiji Museum in Suva, as I walked into the entrance hall, I was surprised to see three men in tapa-print shirts seated on a grass mat around a large, four-legged wooden bowl containing a muddy-looking liquid. It transpired that they were museum staff, enacting a *yaqona*-drinking ceremony (and enjoying the process enormously).

"Tavolea mada!" They asked me to join them. Unsure of the protocol, I took my shoes off, knelt on the mat and edged forward. I knew already that, in many places, the ancient ceremony was exclusively a male preserve but, since the invitation had been extended, I merely made sure that I kept my head lower than theirs (an Oriental custom—can't go wrong).

The leader in the middle picked up a coconut half-shell and passed a full scoop of the *kava* to the man on his left who clapped his hands once, accepted the libation with both hands, drained the contents of the shell, then clapped thrice. We all clapped three times and said *"mbula"* (also spelled *bula,* meaning health or life). The principal then dipped the scoop into the bowl again and passed it to me. I drained it down. It had the color and consistency of powdery cocoa with a slightly bitter, earthy taste. The ceremony was repeated around the circle of four; each person duly

(Continued.)

applauding. Later, my Fijian friend, Paul, told me that the hand clapping is used instead of *"vinaka,"* or thank you. Apparently, it becomes tiresome to repeat "thank you" each time you drink.

Many *kava*-drinking occasions later, I came to the conclusion that the *kava* in Vanuatu is definitely more potent that that of Fiji. The reaction of each person to the potion varies from a slight fuzzy-headedness to mild euphoria, depending on the volume consumed.

The beverage is an acquired taste. The effects after one small cup produce a slight numbing of the lips and tongue. After two cups, the speech can become slightly thick, the head remains clear but noise is magnified. Three cups is a respectable limit.

Kava drinkers don't talk too much; the beverage shifts the drinker into an inner communication with himself, called "listening to the *kava*." F. W. Christian wrote in 1899 of the effects of drinking three or more cups and attempting to get up and go home: "One leg struggles south while the other is marching due north."

Basically, *kava* drinking has a pacifying effect; it is useful in peacemaking ceremonies between rival tribes. The beverage tends to act as an appetite stimulant and is generally taken before eating. Personally, I prefer it mixed with coconut milk.

VAI NITA

Papaya Cooler (COOK ISLANDS)

A refreshing new spin on a non-alcoholic beverage.

Serves 6

ice cubes (sufficient for 6 glasses)	1 teaspoon of ginger juice
the flesh of 2 papayas, puréed in a blender	2 tablespoons of freshly squeezed lime juice
	36 ounces of ginger ale

1. Fill 6 tall (Collins) glasses with the ice cubes.
2. In a non-reactive mixing bowl, mix together the papaya purée, ginger juice and lime juice. Then apportion the juices equally among the glasses.
3. Fill each to the top with ginger ale, stir and serve.

HIBISCUS-GINGER NECTAR

(BELAU)

One of the joys of living in the tropics is the constant visual treat provided by the profusion of exotic flowers, particularly the hibiscus. Single blossoms, double blossoms; scarlet, pink, white and yellow. They garnish food, they grace a table and make it instantly festive. One tucked behind the correct ear is all the adornment an island female needs.

Few know that the flower is edible. For this nectar, use the ordinary, single scarlet blooms.

Yield: 3$^1/_4$ quarts (approximately)

40 single, red hibiscus flowers, gently washed (checking for ants) **and drained until dry**	**3 quarts of water**
	1$^1/_2$ cups of sugar, or to taste
6 tablespoons of fresh gingerroot, peeled and minced	**1$^1/_2$ cups of freshly squeezed lime juice**

1. Inspect each hibiscus flower carefully and remove the green calyx.
2. Pour **1$^1/_2$ quarts** of the water into a large saucepan and place it over medium-high heat. Add the ginger and sugar. Let the mixture come to a boil, stirring to dissolve the sugar. Reduce heat to low, cover and simmer for about 10 minutes.
3. Uncover and deposit the flowers in the simmering liquid. Remove the pan from heat, occasionally stir and force the flowers under the liquid. Set aside and let the mixture steep and cool to room temperature.
4. Line a sieve with cheesecloth and strain the liquid into a large (4-quart), non-reactive container.
5. Add the remaining water and lime juice. Decant the nectar into clean bottles or jugs and refrigerate until needed.

Note: If it's your pleasure, you may spike individual servings of the nectar with a soupçon of rum.

THE FEAST

On the islands of Oceania, almost any event is an excuse or an indication for a feast. There are feasts of welcome to visitors, feasts of parting and farewell. Feasts to honor the accession of a new chief (lavish and of major import), feasts to celebrate the construction of community centers, feasts to mark the first fruits of the season, feasts to observe the Christian saints' days, feasts to heal inter-village feuds. Then there are births and marriages to be celebrated, and wakes to be commiserated. Akin to our harvest festivals of thanksgiving, our community or block parties, our receptions and banquets, Pacific feasts are major ritual occasions wherein the sharing of food is a sign of group identity and solidarity. They are also great fun. Traditional foods prepared with age-old recipes are at the center of every occasion.

Just as in Western society, sometimes the feasts are hosted by a prominent and wealthy patron; other times they will be the result of the combined efforts and contributions of several families or even an entire village.

There are those feasts created expressly for tourists. While understandably artificial, these still conform to the basic dynamics of the occasion. The "visitors" usually donate money rather than food. The locals provide the comestibles, preparation and entertainment. (Natives are entertained when they succeed in persuading visitors to get up and attempt the local dance, generally an occasion for much mirth.) Except for the most commercialized productions with jaded and overexposed participants, the majority of Pacific Islanders take pride in the opportunity to share their cuisine and showcase their dancing and musical skills. The social interaction between people of widely differing cultures at such events also generates the spark of mutual interest, reciprocal discovery and consequent enjoyment.

The sonorous echoes of a blown conch or the penetrating pounding of a wooden slit drum (the latter in Melanesia) cut into the evening air, alerting the participants and guests to the start of the festivities. With an air of subdued excitement and anticipation, clusters of people converge toward the feast site. You obey the summons and move amid them, drawn by lights hanging from the trees leading to a grassy clearing amid coconut palms by the sea. As the sun slips beneath the water on the horizon, a lambent sky of orange and rose eclipses the pale yellow of the lanterns.

Several paces off to the right, a trio of musicians, heads crowned with wreaths of green ferns, softly beat on drums and pluck the strings of coconut ukuleles.

You *are* hungry. All day you have seen men and women moving to and fro, carrying bundles of food, baskets of fruit, suckling pigs slung by their feet from bamboo poles. You have heard laughter, the staccato of chopping, the thud of pestles meeting mortars. You wished you could participate. You are no stranger to food preparation but you are a guest. This feast is partially in your honor.

A long train of large finely-woven pandanus mats has been laid down the center of the clearing. A four-foot wide swath of banana and ti leaves forms the "table" surface down the center of the mats. Feathery green palm fronds, decorated with scarlet hibiscus, yellow hibiscus, creamy-white and rose-red fragrant plumeria complete the setting. However, you hardly notice the blossoms. Your attention is focused almost exclusively on the profusion of food arrayed down what seems to be the endless green expanse; wooden platters jostle woven palm serving dishes, bamboo baskets, coconut bowls and containers fashioned from banana leaves. Chunks of purple taro contrast with bone-white sweet potato. Yellow yam slices punctuate green leaf cradles filled with

(Continued.)

The roast suckling pig

young taro tops, steamed in coconut milk. Scarlet coconut crabs loom over dishes of the little, brown reef crabs, humble but no less delicious.

Whole, cooked reef fish, mouths agape, lie supinely on banana leaves. Bowls display chunks of larger, white game fish, marinated until "cooked" in lime juice, speckled with a confetti of green onions, scarlet chili peppers and dressed with coconut cream. Platters of chicken pieces lie alongside curved ribs of barbecued pork. Bound bundles of heat-browned banana leaves contain young taro leaves wrapped around a steamed filling of coconut cream, lemon, onions and shredded beef. Other leaf-wrapped "puddings" feature taro, sweet potato, yams, plantains, all mixed in a melange of coconut cream, seasonings and steamed in the earth oven.

Bowls, holding mounds of sliced pineapple, papaya, mangoes and bananas, are set at intervals in this magnificent array. Your attention is inevitably drawn to the pièce de résistance: bamboo racks which support two whole suckling pigs, skins glistening caramel brown, still steaming since their recent extraction from the earth oven and releasing their own seductive odors to mix with the aromatic medley.

You are bidden to your allotted place by the hosts. You sit down a little awkwardly but are pleasantly surprised to discover the mats are soft and springy from the mattress of turf below. Bowls of coconut water (for drinking), fresh fruit juices and smaller receptacles of relishes, such as sea salt, pulverized and dried seaweed, sea water, and fermented coconut, flank your personal eating space. Platters, lined with leaves, are in front of each diner. There are no eating utensils. Fingers are the order of the evening. Firm-cooked slices of taro are used like spoons to scoop up the softer foods. Fingers select pieces of fish, hold pork ribs, chicken, open shells, remove shreds of crab and tear off succulent and juicy pieces of the tender, smoky earth-oven pig.

There are speeches, of course; lengthy but full of passion. (It seems as if the orators studied in drama school.) The audience is appreciative.

To signal the end of the serious presentations and announce the beginning of the festivities, more musicians strike up. Drums pound. Fingers blur over strings. Pan pipes provide a haunting over melody. You may have heard or heard of—but not seen—a

(Continued).

235

washtub or packing-crate bass. Now you are nodding with the basso resonance of the primitive instrument.

Island voices, sweet and harmonious, take up the melody. The harmony is close and natural. Some obviously gifted dancers rise and move to the irresistible beat. Others follow. You find yourself on your feet. Everyone is dancing.

The white moon sails serenely above the dark sea. The waves splash like brushes on a snare in gentle counterpoint to the rhythm.

The hours slide by unnoticed. Coolers of beer and other, stronger libations have appeared for the dancers. Old men are sitting in a group, sepia bent lumps, happily recounting the past.

You realize you are tired, replete and sleepy. It is time to leave. You look for your hosts. They're difficult to locate among the dancers and bystanders silhouetted against the lanterns and moonlit sky. As you walk away over the grass, the diminishing percussion still reverberates; its beat will accompany your dreams.

Recipe Directory
and Menu Suggestions
(By Region)

Following is first a listing of recipes sorted by principal ethnic regions (Polynesia, Micronesia, Melanesia) and Australia (bush-food). I have used the convention of placing a superscript "V" preceding those recipes that are traditionally or exclusively vegetarian, except for the obvious beverages and desserts, for instance. (Of course, many recipes may be converted to vegetarian by deleting or substituting ingredients.) For those recipes that are leaf-wrapped and classically cooked in an earth-pit oven, I have used a superscript "W."

Polynesian Recipes

Pacific appetizers, hors d' oeuvres and **pupus**

[V]Toasted Coconut Chips (Tuvalu) . . . 26
Reef Caviar on Toast, *Palolo* (Samoa) . . . 28
Hawai'i-Thai Pork and Shrimp *Dim Sum* . . . 33

Different soups . . . almost stews

Fish Soup Gauguin, *Soupe Des Poissons Gauguin*
 (Marquesas) . . . 41
Breadfruit and Taro Soup, *Fai Sua a 'Ulu i le Talo*
 (Samoa) . . . 43
Carrot, Mango and Pumpkin Soup (Hawai'i) . . . 48

Tropical salads of meat, fish, fruit, vegetables and seaweeds

[V]Avocado, Mango and Orange Salad with Honey-Sesame-Lime
 Dressing (Hawai'i) . . . 54
[V]Auckland Kiwi Waldorf Salad with Tropical Mayonnaise
 Dressing (New Zealand) . . . 58

Micronesian Recipes

Melanesian Recipes

Familiar meats of Oceania

Island vegetables and grains in main and side dishes

Desserts, cakes and breads

Unusual island relishes, condiments, sauces, dressings and beverages

Australian (Bush-Food) Recipes

Different soups . . . almost stews

Pacific Ocean fish offerings

Familiar meats of Oceania

Desserts, cakes and breads

POLYNESIAN MENU SUGGESTIONS

LUNCH FOR SIX

Carrot, Mango and Pumpkin Soup
(page 48)

•

Takia Ni Tao Painaviu
Chicken in Pineapple Canoes
(page 155)

•

Stuffed Sweet Potatoes
(page 189)

•

Banana Cake with Passion
Fruit Icing
(page 212)

•

Via Nita
Papaya Cooler
(page 232)

DINNER FOR SIX

Palolo
Reef Caviar on Toast
(page 28)

•

Fai Sua A 'Ulu I Le Talo
Breadfruit and Taro Soup
(page 43)

•

Tournedos Pomare
(page 166)

•

Vegetable Melange
(page 192)

•

Po'e Mape
Polynesian Chestnut Pudding
(page 205)

PARTY BUFFET
FOR SIXTEEN

Hawai'i-Thai Pork
and Shrimp *Dim Sum*
(page 33)

•

Avocado Sea Foam with Cucumber
Outrigger Canoes and a Cargo
of Shrimp and Lobster
(page 81)

•

Poulet Avec Des Limettes
Chicken with Limes
(page 157)

•

Auckland Kiwi Waldorf Salad with
Tropical Mayonnaise Dressing
(page 58)

SUPPER FOR SIX

Soupe Des Poissons Gauguin
Fish Soup Gauguin
(page 41)

•

French Bread

•

Pork, Apple and *Kumara*
Casserole
(page 147)

•

Fresh Fruit

Banana Cake with Passion
Fruit Icing
(page 212)

•

Banana-Lime-Honey Whip
(page 211)

•

Via Nita
Papaya Cooler
(page 232)

MICRONESIAN MENU SUGGESTIONS

DINNER FOR FOUR

Marcel Ukoy
Fish, Shrimp and Vegetable Fritters
(page 36)

•

Mal
Purple Taro Salad
(page 63)

•

Merizo Chicken *Tinola*
(page 152)

•

Fafalo
Spiced Banana Bud with Walnuts
(page 190)

•

Fresh Fruit

DINNER FOR SIX

Trochus Chowder
(page 46)

•

Curried Sweet Potato, Banana
and Brazil Nut Salad
(page 64)

•

Shrimp in a Garlic, Banana
and Chili Sauce
(page 86)

•

Chamorro Red Rice
(page 194)

•

Fresh Fruit

LUNCH BUFFET FOR TWELVE

Tuna *Sashimi* Rolls Tumon-Style
(page 131)

•

Kelaguen Mannok
Marinated Salad of Chicken
(page 67)

•

Tinaktak
Braised Beef in Lemon Juice with Vegetables and Coconut Milk
(page 168)

•

Island Yam, Sweet Potato and Taro Bake
(page 183)

•

Young Taro Leaves in Coconut Milk
(page 185)

•

Banana-Bud Paella
(page 76)

•

Fresh Fruit

•

Hibiscus-Ginger Nectar
(page 233)

MELANESIAN MENU SUGGESTIONS

LUNCH FOR SIX	DINNER FOR SIX
Crab and *Nama* Salad (page 157)	Sweet Potato and Taro Chips (page 34)
•	•
Point Cruz Tiger Shrimp and Papaya in a Peanut, Garlic and Coconut Sauce (page 178)	Spicy Banana-Ginger-Onion Dip (page 229)
•	•
Coconut Rice (page 193)	*Rourou Supsup* A Soup of Mixed Greens (page 45)

Faivkorn Na Manggo Salat
Carambola and Mango Compote
(page 207)

Vuaka Kei Na Ura Tavuteke
**Pan-Fried Fillets of Pork
and Shrimp with Asparagus,
Broccoli and *Vudi* in
Orange Sauce**
(page 145)

•

Three-Bean Sauté
(page 187)

•

**Nut-Centered Banana Balls
in Papaya Purée**
(page 208)

LUNCH BUFFET FOR TWELVE

Dalo, Vainaviu Ura Kei Vuaka Sa Vakamasimataki
Taro, Pineapple, Shrimp and Bacon
(page 30)

•

Kokoda
Marinated Fish and Shrimp Salad in Coconut Cream
(page 68)

•

Sweet Potato and Shrimp Cakes with Tomato-Orange Sauce
(page 90)

•

Vila Curried Papaya Salad
(page 61)

•

Chili-Garlic Chicken with Mangoes
(page 154)

•

Coconut Rice
(page 193)

•

Vegetable and Peanut Stew
(page 180)

•

Sweet Potato and Taro Chips
(page 34)

•

Fresh Fruit

AUSTRALIAN MENU SUGGESTIONS

DINNER FOR FOUR

Kangaroo Tail Soup
(page 49)

•

Emu *Satay* with a Citrus Honey Glaze
(page 170)

•

Seared Barramundi Fillets with a Macadamia
and Bunya Bunya Nut Crust on Quandong Purée
(page 112)

•

Damper
(page 217)

•

Fresh Fruit

OCEANIAN FEAST SUGGESTIONS

MELANESIA	MICRONESIA	POLYNESIA
Kokoda Marinated Fish and Shrimp Salad in Coconut Cream (page 68)	*Kare Jetaar* Curried Red Snapper (page 106)	*Kalua* Pork in Your Oven (page 142)
Makira Yam and Savory Fish Pudding (page 125)	Chamorro Red Rice (page 194)	*Laulaus* Leaf-Wrapped Fish and Pork Bundles (page 116)
Kovu Vonu Turtle Baked in Banana Leaves (page 84)	*Finadene* Chamorro Hot Sauce (page 226)	*Kamano Lomi* *Lomi* Salmon (page 105)
Laplap Baked Beef and Coconut Milk in a Starch Paste, Wrapped in Leaves (page 162)	*Tinaktak* Braised Beef in Lemon Juice with Vegetables and Coconut Milk (page 168)	*Poisson Crû* Tahitian Marinated Fish Salad (page 70)
Miti Coconut Cream Sauce (page 227)	*Kelaguen Benado* Marinated Salad of Venison (page 59)	*Fai ʻUlu Pisupo* Stuffed Breadfruit (page 163)
Young Taro Leaves in Coconut Milk (page 185)	Merizo Chicken *Tinola* (page 152)	*Poʻe Tʻita* Baked Papaya and Coconut Pudding (page 200)
Fresh Fruit	Shrimp in a Garlic, Banana and Chili Sauce (page 86)	*Haupia* Coconut *Luʻau* Dessert (page 206)
	Fresh Fruit	

An Eclectic Glossary

The Exotic Foods of Oceania

To walk through the markets of the islands of Oceania is to enter an unusual but fascinating world of food. Colors are vivid, the shapes are different, the smells fantastic. Your mind is assaulted, teased and your senses seduced by the strangely familiar, the uncommon and the completely bizarre. You find yourself muttering over and over, "What *is* that? I *think* I know this one," or "this reminds me of . . . ." It is a realm where many objects defy Western categorization: fruits are used as vegetables; nuts may be fruits; greens for the table can be leaves or shoots from plants that, themselves, could never—even remotely—be grouped as vegetables.

Large slabs of red/brown flesh repudiate our notions of butchers' cuts. Tails lie like a row of bullwhips. They are too slender for oxtails. (It turns out they are wallaby or kangaroo tails.) Rows of small game are paraded in an orderly still life. Fresh-caught fish, hung in bundles by twine, gleam like tropical butterflies' wings. Dark crabs are trussed like heroines in a silent movie. Lobsters are corralled in reed baskets and their antennae wave feebly through the slits.

Not for the fainthearted, the markets are, at once, a botanist's dream, a carnivore's challenge, a fisherman's adventure and a neophyte cook's nightmare.

This Eclectic Glossary provides brief descriptions of the principal foods of Oceania, with particular attention to the strange and unfamiliar. They are alphabetically listed within approximate categories, relevant to their location in markets. With the increasing variety of exotic foodstuffs coming to our local stores, we shall soon be able to locate and recognize many of the items listed below. (Ethnic markets are currently your best source for the more esoteric ingredients.)

251

Honiara Market, Solomons

Vegetables, Fruits and Nuts

Aibika

Melanesian pidgin name for two botanically separate plants that look
and cook like spinach. *Abelmoschus manihot* is used as a soup green.
Amaranthus sp. is lightly steamed. Substitute spinach or beet greens.

Banana Bud (*Musa* spp.)

The dark-purple inflorescence apex of the banana plant, it forms at
the end of a long stem, springing from the center of the leaves.
Bananas grow in radiating clusters above the blossom. The bud is
the male part of the inflorescence; tulip-shaped, purple and large—
up to twelve inches in length. Cut away the outer bracts (petals).
The interior is more pale and, when sliced crosswise, reveals wonderful whorls of tightly packed young bracts. Banana buds can be thinly
sliced for salad, dressed with coconut milk and spices. Reminiscent
of red cabbage when cooked but with an earthier flavor, the bud
may be boiled and then sauced, or spiced with vinegar, salt, sugar
and a dusting of cayenne before being sautéed until crisp but tender.
The transverse slices of cooked banana buds have a strong visual

appeal as a vegetable accompaniment to fish or meat. (See illustration, page 76)

Breadfruit (*Artocarpus altilis*)

A large, knobbly-skinned, green fruit, about the size of a football. When baked in its skin, the cream-colored flesh develops a firm, bread-like texture with the aroma of a fresh baguette. An important island starch, breadfruit may also be boiled, steamed or roasted as a vegetable. (Its large seeds are roasted and eaten as snacks.) (See illustration, page 164)

Bunya Pine (*Araucaria bidwillii*)

This mountain tree is found throughout southeastern Australia. Its large cones divide into many segments, each containing a delicious kernel or nut, approximately one inch in length. The pines were called *bun yi bun yi* by the aborigines who prized the sweet, immature nuts, eating them raw, and would climb the trees to collect the green cones. The ripe nuts from fallen cones were either crushed and eaten, or roasted in the ashes of a fire. The flavor of the cooked nut is reminiscent of chestnut but with a hint of pine. Since "bush food" is increasingly popular in Australia, the nuts are now available commercially and are incorporated into many recipes.

Bunya nuts

Candle Nut (*Aleurites moluccana*)

Also known as *kukui,* these nuts are familiar to visitors to Hawai'i in the form of the brown/black *leis*. The roasted kernels were traditionally strung on coconut midribs and burned as candles. They are currently used to make the ancient Hawaiian condiment, *'inamona.*

Carambola (*Averrhoa carambola*)

Known also as a star fruit and in Melanesia as "five corner," carambola is a waxy-skinned, yellow fruit with five ridges, between two- and five-inches long. The flesh is crisp and tart-sweet. Fully ripened, it is included in fruit salads and other desserts. The green, unripe fruit is used as a vegetable; pickled or sautéed, as a garnish for fish or meat. (See illustration, page 207)

Cassava (*Manihot esculenta*)

Another important Pacific starch food, cassava is usually available in Hispanic markets under the names of either *yuca* or *manioc*. The tuber is large and tapered with a skin like bark and firm, white flesh. As versatile as a potato, cassava is baked, boiled or fried. It is also used to thicken soups and stews. Cassava is also the source for the manufacture of tapioca.

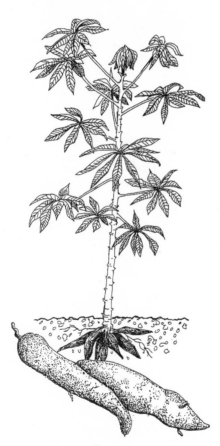

Cassava

Coconut (*Cocos nucifera*)

The coconut is so essential to Oceania's existence that, if it were to disappear, life, culture, food and many customs on most of the islands would change or cease to exist. The maxim in the Pacific is: "He who plants a coconut tree, plants food and drink, vessels and clothing, a habitation for himself and a heritage for his children." Coconut milk is the universal and traditional liquid medium used in Oceanian cooking. The coconut has a culinary use at every stage of maturation. The flesh of the young, unripe nut is like jelly; an easily digestible snack for young children and invalids. When the outer shell darkens and firms, the jelly-like lining of the inner shell is thin and soft: the texture and color of a three-minute egg white. This is the "drinking" coconut, containing up to 20 liquid ounces of coconut water. The mature nut is what we generally find in our markets. The meat is firm and liquid can still be heard sloshing around inside when the nut is shaken. In the islands, the flesh is grated and soaked in its own liquid, water or milk to produce coconut milk. The flaked and desiccated meat is incorporated in innumerable dishes, from soups to main dishes, baked breads and desserts. The sun-dried flesh of the mature nut—called copra—is used for the extraction of coconut oil. When the nut is planted and sprouting, its embryo is fluffy, spongy and sweet, like cotton candy. It is considered a treat for children. See Chapter 1 for the preparation and storage of coconut. (See illustrations, pages 24 and 227)

Davidson's Plum (*Davidsonia pruriens*)

The fruits of a rain-forest tree growing in semitropical Queensland and northern New South Wales, the Davidson's plums are large with a dark bluish-purple skin and juicy, sour, scarlet flesh. Popular with the aborigines, the plums lend themselves to jams, fruit sauces and desserts, and are currently used in many "bush-food" recipes.

Galip Nut (*Canarium indicum*)

Known as the *ngali* nut in the Solomon Islands and as *narngi* is Vanuatu, the galip nut has a hard shell and an almond-shaped kernel, about $1^1/_2$ inches in length. Its delicate but rich flavor is a cross between a Brazil nut and a macadamia. Unshelled, the galip stores at room temperature. Because of its delicious flavor, appealing texture, favorable nutritional values and long shelf life, health food stores in Australia and Hawai'i are preparing to market the nut. In Melanesian cuisines, the nuts are ground and added to taro and cassava dumplings and pastries, or incorporated in soups and cakes. I tasted an excellent galip-nut pesto on Éfaté, the principal island in Vanuatu. French bakers on that island have used the nut flour for cakes. The galip nut is a marvelous addition to casseroles and stir-fries and can be partnered with fish and vegetables. It can also be combined with grains in pilafs and cereals or as a garnish for desserts. We look forward to its importation, soon. Meanwhile, substitute Brazil nuts or macadamias. (See illustration, page 209)

Hyacinth Beans (*Lablab purpureus*)

There are several different cultivars of this bean. Some resemble broad beans. Others look like large green beans with thin, tapered ends. In Melanesia, the leaves are cooked as greens and the pods are eaten as vegetables. Hyacinth bean seeds are sold in U.S. seed catalogs as ornamentals. You may look for them in ethnic markets, otherwise, substitute Western green beans.

Kau-kau

There are two botanically different plants called by this name in Melanesia. One is *Ipomoea aquatica,* also called water *kau-kau,* and, sometimes, swamp cabbage. It has hollow stems and spear- or spade-shaped leaves, which have a slightly astringent and sharp taste after cooking. It is widely available in Chinese and Southeast Asian markets; it is illegal to be sold in Florida. The other is *Ipomoea batatas,* the leaves of the sweet potato. Only the young leaves are cooked, traditionally steamed with meat or root vegetables. Substitute turnip tops or any other slightly bitter green. Their flavor is well balanced when they are poached in coconut milk.

Lillipilli (*Acmena smithii; Syzygium* spp.)

Found all over eastern Australia, the tree, *Acmena smithii,* bears white flowers, then clusters of small, white, pink or purple fruit; round and lightly lobed with thick, sour flesh. The lillipilli berries were eaten raw by the aborigines and made into jam by the early European settlers. Species of *Syzygium* fruit (rose or bush apple, scrub cherry, etc.) were also referred to as "lillipilli." The fruits of all lillipillies are made into jams and deserts.

Mango (*Mangifera indica*)

While the ripened mango is one of the best-known of the tropical fruits, eaten fresh or used in endless dishes, the green, unripe fruit is also popular in Oceania. Tart and crisp as a green apple, it is shredded raw and eaten with salt, sugar and sprinkling of hot pepper flakes. Slices of the fruit are also dipped in soy sauce and then dusted with granulated sugar, and served as a snack or relish. Green mangoes are made into pickles and chutneys, particularly in Fiji. In Melanesia, the green fruit is chopped and added as a vegetable to

stews. Look for firm,
unripened mangoes in ethnic
markets.

Mountain Apple (*Syzygium malaccense*)

Also called Malay apple, this
little fruit—2 to 3 inches in
length—has a thin, deep-rose-
colored skin and crisp, white,
juicy flesh. It grows throughout the South Pacific and is
the native equivalent of our
apples. Generally eaten fresh,
the mountain apple is also
incorporated in salads and
fruit cocktails. Its juice makes
a refreshing drink. In some
places it is cooked into a

Mountain apples

sweet, spiced pickle. Substitute small apples or crabapples.

Pandanus (*Pandanus* spp.)

Like the coconut (ibidem), the pandanus plant is a provider of all the
essentials of island life: food, shelter, clothing and an almost endless
catalog of related uses. Growing by the seashore, it resembles a small,
multiple-branched palm; each branch terminating in a crown of
spiked leaves and a trunk buttressed by a cage of aerial roots plunging
into the ground (usually sand) around the main stem. Its fruits form
the center of each star burst of leaves; superficially similar in size and
form to pineapples. Together with the coconut, it is one of the few
plant species that has disseminated itself throughout Oceania. The
seed-bearing segments of the fruit are buoyant. They are also attractive to birds. It is the fleshy base of these drupes that is eaten. In
some species, they are covered in a sweet orange pulp that can be
made into a beverage. In other varieties, the drupe is firmer, cooked
and pounded, and mixed with coconut milk and flesh to make cakes.
These cakes are also dried and pounded into a flour for cooking. The
Tahitians roast the young tips of the aerial roots. Similar to yams in

257

Pandanus

flavor, they are eaten as a starch vegetable. In the highlands of Papua New Guinea, the seeds or kernels of some species taste like coconut and are often smoked to preserve them. Yet another Melanesian species is known as *marita*. Its elongated and very large fruits are red or orange in color. Their juicy segments are boiled then scraped of fiber and strained to make a thick scarlet sauce that, like tomato sauce, goes well with meats and vegetables.

Papaya (*Carica papaya*)

Also known as "pawpaws," ripe papayas are a familiar item on our produce counters. However, in Oceania, both the papaya plant and its fruit have additional culinary uses. Meat is wrapped in mature papaya leaves for an hour or so to tenderize it. The Melanesians boil young papaya leaves in two changes of water and consume them as slightly bitter greens. Unripe, green papayas are treated like squashes, being steamed, boiled or baked, or added to soups and stews. Raw, green papaya is peeled and shredded, then eaten as a piquantly-sour salad or relish, after being dressed with soy or fish sauce. It is also sliced for pickles or transformed into sweet chutneys. The peppery seeds of the ripe fruit taste somewhat like nasturtium seeds. They can be crushed to flavor salad dressings and sauces. Look for green, unripe papayas in ethnic markets.

Passion Fruit (*Passiflora edulis, Passiflora* spp.)

Although fairly recently introduced to Oceania, the passion fruit is now growing semi-wild in Papua New Guinea. It is also popular through the

South Pacific and in Hawai'i. The
size and shape of a large lemon,
with dusty purple-brown or
yellow-orange skin, the fruit pre-
sents a somewhat unattractive
appearance. Looks aren't everything. Inside the cardboard-like
rind nestle a mass of tiny teardrop-
shaped capsules; each containing a
seed encased in pulp with an
intense, perfumed flavor. The
essence of tropical fragrance, it is,
at once, both fruit and flower
combined: evocative of gardenia,
honey, limes and jasmine. The
pulp may be strained, and both the
whole fruit and the pulp freeze
well. (Because of the concentrated
essence, I recommend only small
measures be used.) Cooked
or uncooked, combine the
pulp with other blended
fruits into sorbets, ices, cus-
tards and creams. Solo, it
provides fruit syrups for
desserts, or may be used in
cakes and cookies. Try the
fruit sauce with baked
chicken. The imaginative
cook will find almost endless applications for this
robust flavoring.

Papaya

Pit-pit

In Melanesia, this name
refers to shoots that are
the tender inside stems
of two species of wild
grasses, *Saccharum edule*

Passion fruit

(a relative of sugar cane) and *Setaria palmifolia* (palm grass). *Pit-pit* is also called Pacific asparagus. *S. edule* plants have red stems; *S. palmifolia's* stalks are green. The outside leaves and coverings are stripped off and the shoots eaten raw, or are steamed/baked. They taste like a cross between sweet corn and asparagus. Substitute the stems of mature asparagus (usually discarded), peeled and steamed until tender.

Plantain (*Musa ✕paradisiaca*)

Through the many Latino and Asian immigrants to our shores, we are becoming acquainted with the thick-skinned, starchy, cooking bananas, called plantains. They are another primary source of starch throughout Oceania, where they are baked in their skins in earth-pit

Polynesian arrowroot

ovens or amid the hot embers of cooking fires. They are also peeled and boiled in salted water. Mashed, their cooked interior is baked into cakes or fermented for preservation. Thin slices are fried into chips, like our potato chips. Plantains are also cut into chunks and steamed in packages fashioned from banana leaves. Look for them in Hispanic markets under the name *plátano*. After peeling, plantains can be wrapped in plastic and frozen. Substitute green, unripe sweet bananas (*Musa acuminata*).

Polynesian Arrowroot
(*Tacca leontopetaloides*)

Arrowroot is the generic name given to certain starchy tubers, rhizomes or root stocks from different plant families that are processed to a fine powder and used for thickening gravies, desserts and sauces. In the

Hawaiian, Society and Cook Islands, the Polynesian arrowroot is the thickener of choice and is known as the *pia* plant. The Polynesians combine cooked arrowroot with fruits, such as papaya, banana or pumpkin for their traditional baked desserts. These are called *p'oe* in Tahiti and *poke* in the Cook Islands. Similarly, the Hawaiians cook a pudding, called *haupia*, enriched with coconut cream and thickened with *pia*.

Polynesian Chestnuts (*Inocarpus fagifer*)

This tall, handsome tree with glossy leaves and tangled buttresses of aboveground roots grows throughout the South Pacific. Its green drupes produce large, fleshy seeds, between 3 to 5 inches in length. In Tahiti, both the tree and its nuts are called *mape* (pronounced "marpay"). The nuts are hulled and the kernels grated raw, then mixed with coconut milk and sugar to make a baked dessert, *po'e mape*. The nuts may also be boiled for about 30 minutes and then eaten as a starchy vegetable or incorporated into cakes, croquettes, pies or stews. We can substitute our chestnuts in the ratio of one (*mape*) to five (chestnuts).

Quandong (*Santalum acuminatum*)

Also known as a native peach, but closer in proportions to an apricot, quandongs grow over wide areas of Australia; the trees standing singly or in clumps in arid bush country. The fruit is spherical, approximately 1 inch in diameter, and, when ripe, is bright red. It contains a central stone, the kernel of which is high in calories, protein and fat. Dried quandongs are stewed with sugar and lemon juice; the citric acid preserves their color. The aborigines pick them dried from the trees and, after removing the stone, pound their flesh into a paste.

Sago (*Cycas circinalis*, also *Metroxylon* spp.)

Sago starch is extracted from the edible pith of two completely different plants. In Asia and parts of the Pacific, species of cycads, the venerable plants that have existed since the age of the dinosaurs, yield their edible pith that is processed into sago. In Melanesia, the source of sago is a palm that grows mostly in low marshy areas. When the palms are about fifteen years old, they flower for the first and only time, stimulating their trunks to fill with a nutritional starch. At this

Sago palm and processing sago

stage, they are felled and their trunks split open to extract the pith, which is then crushed, grated and washed to form a starch paste. Slightly dried, this is the form of sago eaten in Melanesia. For export, the paste is forced through sieves to form pellets that are then dried and packaged. In the trade, these are referred to as pearl sago or bullet sago, according to size. The Melanesians use the sago meal for puddings (both savory and sweet), as a thickening for soups and stews, and for cake flour. We can find the palm sago, imported from Thailand, in Southeast Asian stores in the U.S. Tapioca is a suitable substitute.

Sweet Potato (*Ipomoea batatas*)

Confusion in common names still exists in the U.S. between the sweet potato and yam. Sweet potatoes are storage roots whereas the yam is a tuber. When cut, the exposed surfaces of the sweet potato discolor, while those of the yam are sealed over by the juice of the tuber. Sweet potato skins are generally smooth, whereas most yams have hairy outer surfaces. The sweet potato, that the world outside the U.S. recognizes as such, has a white or pale yellow flesh, is less sweet than our orange-fleshed variety and, when cooked, its texture is rather creamy. A favorite starch veg-

Sweet potato

etable in Oceania, it is prepared in every way imaginable, but the most common and popular is to bake it in its skin, in the hot ashes of a fire or in an earth-pit oven. The skin becomes deliciously crusty and the vegetable assumes a delicate, smoky flavor. To be authentic in your Oceanian cooking, look for the true variety in Hispanic stores and markets under the names of *boniato, camote* or *batata*.

Taro (*Colocasia esculenta*)

Taro is an ancient plant. The most popular starch and green vegetable in Oceania, scientists have recently proved that the natives of New

Guinea were harvesting and processing it some 30,000 years ago. When you first come upon a taro patch—broad, spade-shaped leaves nodding in the sunlight from sturdy stems—it seems familiar. Indeed, the taro is related to the tropical garden plant we call "elephant ears." The taro corm is as ugly as the leaves are handsome, looking like some kind of dark and dirty, hairy and ridged potato. However, this homely underground stem is the source of delicious and easily digestible starch, tasting, after cooking, like a cross between potatoes and chestnuts. When thoroughly mashed, it becomes the popular purée called *poi* by the Hawaiians. Taro corms can be steamed or boiled, added to soups and stews, pan- or deep-fried, or mashed before incorporating into fritters and soufflés. In island cuisines, the young leaves are boiled in coconut milk and become similar to spinach in flavor and texture. The shoots and runners of the plants are also cooked as vegetables. (See illustration page 185)

Ti or Ki *plant*

Ti or *Ki* (*Cordyline fruticosa*)

The ti plant (called *auti* in Tahiti and *ki* in Hawai'i) is known and used throughout Oceania. Its shiny green leaves are used as wrappers for cooking. Traditionally, the Polynesians prized the plant equally for its large, fibrous tuber that is rich in carbohydrates. They baked the tubers in large, communal earth-pit ovens to produce a sweet, brown, syrupy, candy-like confection. The first Europeans arriving in the islands fermented the tuber for beer. In Hawai'i, after the introduction of distillation, the resultant liquor from the ti root was called *'okolehao*. (For details on the use of leaf wrappers, see Chapter 1.)

Vegetable Shoots and Leaves

Shoots and leaves from a wide variety of plants, which we would probably not consider as vegetables, are all used as such in Oceanian cuisines. The long list includes pumpkin tips, papaya leaves and shoots, taro leaves (*lu 'au* in Hawaiian); bean leaves (such as those of the lima and hyacinth beans), wild fig leaves, ferns, bamboo shoots. Explore your ethnic markets for some of the above-mentioned, or expand the range and use of the leaves and shoots from edible plants in your garden.

Winged Beans (*Psophocarpus tetragonolobus*)

Also known as the asparagus bean, this fancifully-frilled legume is a common sight in the markets of Hawai'i and Melanesia (from Papua New Guinea to Fiji). Four ruffles decorate its entire length and give it its exotic appearance. The vine on which it grows is equally attractive and culinarily useful; producing edible flowers, leaves, shoots, tubers, pods and seeds; all full of flavor and protein-

Winged beans

rich nutrition (in varying concentrations). Boiled or steamed briefly, winged beans are crunchy with a true bean flavor. Try slicing them crosswise or diagonally for a decorative addition to soups and stews, or cook them in stir-fries. Serve them, cooked quickly and chilled, in mixed salads, or individually, tossed in a coconut-based dressing. You will find winged beans in Asian markets. Select them fresh, green and snap-crisp, under 5 inches in length.

Yam (*Dioscorea alata, Dioscorea* spp.)

There are six species of yam within the tropical Pacific Islands. This tuber, generally an underground swelling of the stem of a vine, is

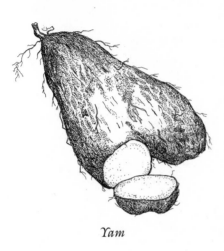

Yam

seasonal; requiring sunshine, humidity and rich soil. However, unlike sweet potatoes—with which it is often confused—the yam has a long storage life. Varying in shape and size according to their species, yams can range from the elongated and tubular to the multi-branched and misshapen, or the bulbous and grotesque. The skin of the yam is usually hairy. The color of the flesh ranges from white or cream to pink or purple. Large yams are actually practical purchases because pieces can be cut off for cooking when

needed: the tuber's juices conveniently seal over any exposed surfaces. Used as the basic starch vegetable in Melanesian cuisine, the yam's cooked texture varies according to the method of preparation; fluffy and dry when baked, as waxy and bland as a new potato after boiling. Grate yams raw or boil and purée their flesh for breads, cakes and puddings. Also grate raw and form into rissoles or fry as fritters. Thinly-sliced and deep-fried, yam makes delicious snack chips. A panoply of yam species can be found in Hispanic and African markets.

Yard-long Beans (*Vigna unguiculata* subspecies *sesquipedalis*)

Related to the black-eyed pea, these lanky legumes are appearing more frequently in ethnic produce markets in the U.S. However, although many of us have seen them, fewer buy them or understand their culinary use in Pacific cuisines. These tropical beans are slender and flexible, and can grow up to three feet in length (hence the name). In Oceania, yard-long beans are cut into short (eating) lengths and briefly simmered in coconut milk. (Try adding a dash of curry powder.) They shine in stir-fries and dry sautés, becoming both crunchy and chewy in texture. Cooked and chilled, they are a welcome ingredient in salads. The islanders also put them in stews or partner them with chicken, pork or fish. Look for firm, resilient beans with no rust-colored spots. Purchase only the younger legumes, 18 inches in length or less.

Sea Vegetables (Seaweeds)

Following are a few of the principal seaweeds eaten in Hawai'i and other Pacific Islands. For ease of identification, where there is no common, English name, Hawaiian and scientific names are given, together with their label in any other language, where applicable.

Limu 'ele 'ele (*Enteromorpha prolifera* spp.)

The long, grass-green strands of this hair-like seaweed grow wherever fresh water and sea water mix; at the estuaries of streams and under-water springs. One species, *E. intestinalis* is found throughout the world. *Limu 'ele 'ele, E. prolifera,* becomes very dark when mixed with salt and allowed to stand. (This coloration accounts for its picturesque Hawaiian name, *'ele 'ele,* meaning black or the color of native Hawaiian eyes.) After being "ripened" in salt, it is traditionally eaten at island feasts as a condiment. This prepared sea vegetable has an attractive, nutty flavor and is also popular in stews, with Oriental noodles and as a condiment with raw fish.

Limu kohu (*Asparagopsis taxiformis*)

A seaweed with a pungent, peppery flavor that is primarily used in small amounts as a seasoning, *limu kohu,* is also referred to as *limu lipa 'akai* from the sea salt in which it was traditionally preserved. Described as "supreme," *kohu* was associated with Hawai'i nobility *(ali'i)* because of its rose-red color. The sea plant has fuzzy plumes that resemble

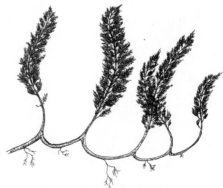

Asparagopsis taxiformis (limu kohu)

those of the land-based, scarlet "cockscomb" flower. After salting, this seaweed keeps indefinitely under refrigeration. It is used to spice food and is added to meat or fish stews. *Kohu* is a traditional ingredient of *lomi* (massaged) salmon.

Limu manauea (*Gracilaria coronopifolia*) and **Ogo Nori** (*G. parvispora*)

These two species are used as food interchangeably, but are structurally different. *G. coronopifolia,* more stubby in appearance, though similar in taste and color to *G. parvispora,* is more appreciated by modern Hawaiians. They both resemble translucent branches of gracefully curved twigs. The former ranges in hue from deep rose to gold; the latter from a pink to a yellowish-green. Traditionally, they both were chopped and salted, then mixed with fish or chicken. (Usually only freshly chopped and combined with raw fish, they are also favored by the Japanese-Hawaiians in *namasu,* a fish salad.) They have the property of thickening liquids when cooked and are popular in soups and stews. They are pickled, incorporated in salads and dips, battered and fried (Japanese-style) for *tempura;* even candied. Their mild flavor makes them an ideal introduction to seaweeds for the novice.

Gracileria coronopifolia (limu manauea) *and* Ulva fasciata (limu palahalaha)

Limu mane'one'o (*Laurencia nidifica*)

This sea vegetable is also known as the "chili pepper seaweed," and is called *mane'o* for its itchy or peppery effect in the mouth. It is small and bushy, with numerous knobbed branches and varies in color from pink to red. Only the young plants are harvested because they are more tender and with a pronounced pepper flavor. Try it as a spicy,

fresh relish in combination with cooked, chopped vegetables in a
miso- based sauce, for instance. Alternatively, add it to the mixture for
fish cakes. It is also used, traditionally, as a relish with raw fish in the
dish called *poke* in Hawai'i.

Limu pahe'e (*Porphyra vietnamensis*)

Pahe'e means "slippery" or "satiny" in Hawaiian and refers to the flat,
smooth blades of this sea vegetable, related to the European "laver"
and the Japanese *nori*. Islanders also call it *lu'au* because the blades
resemble cooked taro leaves. In its natural state, the seaweed is a deep
purple but lightens to violet when exposed to the sun. Prized by
Hawaiian nobility, *pahe'e* was eaten with limpets or salted and combined with raw fish. It may be sun-dried or frozen for future use but,
currently, is almost superseded in island cuisines by sheets of
imported *nori* from Japan. It may be used as a wrapper for *sushi* or
other ingredients, cooked in soups or incorporated, fresh, in salads.
Together with lemon juice and olive oil, cooked and drained *pahe'e*
makes a satisfying spread or dip. Fresh blades of the seaweed may be
thoroughly dried and then deep-fried into snack chips.

Sea Grape (*Caulerpa racemosa*)

Known in the Philippines as *arucip,* this sea vegetable has no native
Hawaiian name although it grows off O'ahu. It is eaten throughout
the remainder of Polynesia as a relish, chopped and mixed with
coconut cream or freshly grated coconut. The Filipino-Hawaiians
combine it into a salad with tomatoes and onions. This seaweed
resembles a creeping vine with tiny bunches of roots along its length
and small, erect clusters of "grapes." A brilliant green, it has a spicy
flavor and crunchy texture.

Sea Lettuce (*Ulva* spp.)

Known as *limu palahalaha* in Hawai'i, the well-known green seaweeds of this genus are eaten on both our Atlantic and Pacific coasts.
In Hawai'i, two species are used in foods: *Ulva expansa,* which is very
broad-bladed, and *U. fasciata,* the blades of which are more ribbon-
like. The Hawaiians eat sea lettuce mixed with other seaweeds, chili
peppers and onions as a relish. It is also pickled alone and, consistent
with the strong Japanese influence on the islands' cuisines, is often
fried for *tempura.* Try it with small shellfish, such as winkles, or with

escargots cooked in a butter-garlic-shallot-parsley sauce. Sea lettuce may also be dried, powdered, then mixed with salt for a store-cupboard seasoning. (See illustration, page 268)

Seafood, Fish and Reptiles

Chiton (family Chitonidae)

These strange-looking mollusks are often referred to as "coat-of-mail shells" because the armor on their backs is formed by eight overlapping platelets. The shape of these pieces caused the Australian aborigines to nickname them "toenail shells." The Chamorros on Guam call them *tagula* and look for them at low tide when they are exposed on the sides of rocks close to the shore. The foot of the chiton—the edible part of the mollusk—is flat and acts as a suction cup. Like abalone, chiton must be taken unaware; usually by a single, quick prying action of a large screwdriver or tire iron. If the first attempt is unsuccessful, their suction exerts such pressure that they will be mutilated before separation from their anchor. The more tender foot of the younger chitons is preferred. Otherwise, prolonged soaking and boiling are the only recourse before completing a recipe. On Guam, chiton meat is often sautéed and sauced with lemon juice, soy and chili peppers. In other regions of Oceania, coconut milk provides the sauce base. Abalone or other footed mollusks may be substituted.

Coconut Crab (*Birgus latro*)

Also known as the "robber crab" because it is a coconut thief, this large, clanking, amphibious crustacean weighs in at upwards of four to five pounds (including its armor plating). Closely related to the hermit crab—because it shelters in empty shells during its juvenile stage—the adult *Birgus latro* will graze on almost anything in its path. However, it is particularly addicted to coconuts, which it tears open with its large and powerful pincers; easily rivaling those of the biggest New England lobster. While the coconut crab is found throughout most of Oceania, it is becoming scarce in parts of Melanesia and Micronesia because the flavor and texture of its meat make that of most other crabs pale into insignificance. I have eaten this giant crustacean stewed on Guam, cur-

270

ried on Guadalcanal in the Solomons and sauced in garlic and coconut cream in Port Vila, the capital of Vanuatu. Its meat lends itself admirably to most crab recipes but its delicate flavor of coconut calls for simplicity of preparation. Scientists are now examining the viability of crab farms for this monster delicacy. (See illustration, page 89)

Conch (family Strombidae)

While the West Indian species of this family of mollusks is familiar to us through the cuisines of Florida and the Caribbean, conchs are also very poplar throughout most of Oceania. Locally known as *kibi* in the Motu language of Papua New Guinea, for instance, those natives often eat the meat raw, or boil it or bake it in ashes. In other parts of Melanesia, Micronesia, and, as far as Tonga in Polynesia, conch is generally cooked in coconut milk or sauced, after sautéing or boiling, with coconut cream, green onions and other herbs. It is also a popular component of Pacific seafood soups and stews.

Crocodile (*Crocodylus porosus*)

The Indopacific (sometimes erroneously known as the estuarine or saltwater) crocodile is probably the most feared and ferocious of all reptiles in Oceania. Reaching a length of 20 feet or more, this omnivore lurks in freshwater rivers and lakes, as well as estuaries, but it is also able to swim hundreds of miles out to sea. (Some individuals have been found with barnacles attached to their scales.) It is the largest living reptile, justifiably feared and considered a man eater. The females emerge from the sea to lay their eggs in the sand and both genders like to bask in the sun. Woe betides the unwary villager who disturbs one; *C. porosus* is able to run swiftly on land. Hunted for their valuable skins, meat and eggs, the numbers of these dangerous reptiles have fallen sharply. They are now being bred on farms in Papua New Guinea. Crocodile meat tastes somewhere between firm white fish and veal. It is often baked in an earth-pit oven or broiled over a fire. The meat may be stewed and is surprisingly good when sauced with coconut cream, green onions and wild herbs. (I have eaten crocodile filets breadcrumbed and deep-fried in restaurants in Japan.)

Eel (order Anguilliformes)

Eels are eaten throughout Oceania and were traditionally much prized. The ancient Hawaiians only ate saltwater eels, and salted and dried their flesh before broiling or steaming (wrapped in ti leaves) in an earth-pit oven, *imu*. It was said that the chiefs and nobility (*ali'i*) considered eels more choice than wives! The Maoris preferred freshwater varieties (family Anguillidae), trapping them in *hinaki*—woven traps set in specially constructed weirs, called *pa tuna*. Moray eels (family Muraenidae) are hunted for food all over Oceania, but only the smaller ones are taken since the larger specimens are frequently ciguatoxic.

Giant Clam (family Tridacnidae)

The royalty of all bivalves must be the members of this family. All ten members are eaten by the Pacific Islanders. The largest is *Tridacna gigas*, whose shells have four deeply indented ribs. Though these gargantua have been known to reach 5 feet across and weigh over 580 pounds, smaller sizes are more common. The flesh of the giant clam is thoroughly enjoyed in Oceania, the most flavorful being the border meat or skirt at the edge of the shell. The huge adductor muscle is often boiled and then dried for use in soups and stews. The shells are much sought after outside Oceania. The conservation of Tridacnidae is now of the greatest importance, since the species have been decimated by overharvesting.

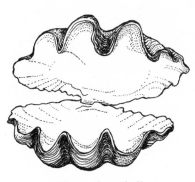

Giant clam shell

Limpet (*Cellana exarata* and *C. sandwicensis*)

Also known as Chinaman's Hat from the conical shape of their shells, these two species of limpets are called *'opihi* in Hawaiian. Traditionally, these little sea creatures were eaten raw and given a *lomi* (massage) in salt. Current preparation techniques include marination in soy sauce.

Mangrove or Mud Lobster (*Thalassina anomala*)

This strange crustacean is a compulsive digger; it probably eats as it burrows and the large mounds of soil it excavates signal its presence to its hunters. The mangrove lobster is considered a pest in Southeast Asia and the islands of the West Pacific because it tunnels through the dykes of rice paddies and aquaculture ponds. The Fijians, however, call it *mânâ* and rate it as a delicacy *par excellence*. They catch it by placing traditional snare traps at the mouths of its tunnels. In Fiji, virtually tons of *T. anomala* are sold in the main market of Suva, the capital, during its trapping season, December to July. The mangrove lobster's meat is sweet and delicate, interchangeable in recipes between and among that of other lobster species.

Mantis Shrimp (*Harpio squilla*)

These outsized crustaceans are often referred to as "mantis prawns" because they average 9 to 10 inches in length; the largest measuring 1 foot. They are not, in fact, shrimp at all but are of a different biological order, Stomatopoda, and, within their family (Squillidae), there are 200 different species. They can be found along both coasts of the U.S., as far south as Mexico, as well as in European waters and, of course, much of the Pacific. The Hawaiians call them *'alo 'alo* and a handsome, striped and variegated variety on Tahiti is known as *varos*. Their meat is delicate and finely textured, needing little adornment; however they are difficult to capture and, at this writing, not commercially viable. Mantis shrimps do not stand up to freezing well so they must be caught and cooked almost immediately.

Mud Oyster (*Batissa violacea* and *Polymesoda coaxans*)

The aborigines on the northern, tropical coast of Australia eat two species of bivalves they call "mud oysters." Found beneath the surface mud of the mangrove swamps, they are about the size of the palm of your hand. The aborigines never eat the oysters raw but place them, closed (hinged-end upward), in rows set in clean sand. A brief, flaming fire of dry twigs is made over them for about ten minutes. The ashes are brushed off the shells, the oysters opened and the succulent meat consumed in its own juice.

Octopus, Squid and Cuttlefish (class Cephalopoda)

All of these "head-footed" creatures are hunted with spear or special hooks throughout the coastal waters of the Pacific Islands and provide a good and regular source of food. Although baby squid and cuttlefish may be merely cleaned and, then, cooked in a liquid or fried, the larger of the species will benefit from a 2- or more-hour marinade in a bath consisting of $2/3$ salted water to either $1/3$ lemon juice or vinegar. In the Marianas, octopuses are traditionally boiled until tender; the more senior and larger, the longer the cooking time. The Chamorros on Guam have adapted modern technology to the tenderizing task: they have been known to place all tough cephalopods in a top-loading washing machine and let the paddles flog them for a few hours! Throughout Oceania, octopus is often cooked in a rich soup with coconut milk. *Estofas* is a traditional Guamanian dish wherein chunks of cephalopods are cooked in vinegar and onions, seasoned with sugar, soy sauce, black pepper and herbs. Squid is often pickled in vinegar, chili peppers, ginger, garlic cloves, bay and sage for at least 24 hours, then simmered (in the marinade), drained and stir-fried.

Palolo (*Leodice viridice*)

A relatively small area of the South Pacific, encompassing the islands of Vanuatu, Fiji and Samoa, is home to a minute and rare sea creature known to the islanders as "the coral worm." Locally called *palolo* or *balolo*, it is actually a tiny annelid of the class Polychaeta. They swarm to the surface of these tropical, coastal waters once a year during the last part of the lunar cycle falling in October or November. Their brief annual breeding is akin to the running of grunion: hectic, frantic, swarming. Triggered by subtle environmental stimuli, the reproductive parts of these tube-dwelling annelids separate and shoot into the water, where their fertilization and subsequent adolescent development occur. When the tide is full at the midnight of *palolo* rising, the islanders, who follow the lunar calendar, wade out in droves through the turbulent sea and scoop the millions of tiny ($1 1/2$ to 2 inches long), threadlike creatures into fine-mesh nets from the waters over the coral reefs. *Palolo* have a wonderfully delicate sea flavor, like malossol caviar. They are a gourmet's dream. The islanders feast on them, raw or fried briefly in oil. Having been fortunate to visit Western Samoa at the time of *palolo* rising, I can attest to their excellence. They were presented to me, lightly sautéed on toast. The more sophisticated diners may garnish them like roe of sturgeon, but their superior taste needs little adornment. *Palolo* freeze and defrost well, and it is hoped devoutly that a food processing company will import this special delicacy to our tables in the near future.

Paua (*Haliotis iris*)

The Maoris of New Zealand eat an abalone, which they call *paua*, that has black meat. The inside of the *paua* shell is a brilliant, iridescent blue-green, shot through with flashes of silver. Traditionally, they fashion it into jewelry and use pieces for the reflective eyes of carved wooden figures of chiefs and ancestors. Once the "foot" meat of a live abalone is removed from its shell, it is wrapped in a cloth and bludgeoned with a mallet to tenderize it. The Maoris are particularly fond of the soft roe (*pewa*) of the *paua*, although it has a concentrated and, some find, off-putting flavor.

Pipi (*Paphies autralis*) and *Pipipi* (family Neritidae)

Pipi is the Maori name for a white-shelled mollusk; a small bivalve, between 1^1/$_2$- and 3 inches across. Found in muddy sand, it was traditionally consumed by the bushel; raw, dried, cooked over hot coals, or boiled by briefly suspending a plaited basket containing the mollusks into a volcanic steam hole. Maori males used the empty shells for shaving or plucking facial hair. In a direct linkage of the Polynesian language, food and culinary practices, the Hawaiians seek out and glean similar small mollusks that they call *pipipi*. They are also consumed raw as well as cooked.

Sea Cucumber (family Holothuridae)

For such a homely creature, the sea cucumber, or bêche-de-mer, belongs to an enormous clan of approximately 1100 species and boasts a commercial history within which the fortunes of both Occidentals and Orientals have been made. This warty sea dweller, with a cucumber-shaped body, litters the beaches and shallow waters throughout the Pacific. The Chinese have historically esteemed its boiled, dried and smoked meat (known as *trepang*) as an aphrodisiac. Rich in protein, the fresh sea cucumber provides a variety of dishes for the islanders of the Western Pacific. Its five, internal, long, white muscles are the edible part, being cooked after briefly tenderized. Two species are popular on Guam. Locally called *balate*, their white, inner strands are fried. The flavor is that of a mild-tasting clam. The Palauans cook the innards of one species, *Stichopus variegatus* (which they call *ngimis*), with coconut cream in a soup. We can substitute our West Coast, large, red sea cucumber, *S. californicus*, found from Alaska to Mexico. The American

Indians of the Northwest preserved them for food by hanging and drying the inner muscles.

Sea Urchin (class Echinoidea)

There are some 700 species of sea urchin worldwide but not all are edible. Some species also have toxic spines for self defense and should be handled, literally, with kid gloves. The sea urchin takes its common name from the old English meaning of "urchin," a hedgehog; the land dweller that, when curled up to defend attack, resembles this echinoderm. It is also called sea egg because, in much of the world, only its five, star-shaped, yellow-orange roe or coral are eaten. In some parts of Oceania, the meat (generally cooked) is consumed. Urchins are usually harvested during their breeding season, when their eggs are plump and yellow. The eggs are scooped out and eaten raw. The Maoris say, "When the *kowhai* tree is blooming, the roe of the *kina* will be as golden as its flowers." The Australian aborigines put sea urchins on a fire until the spines burn off, then crack the shells and eat the steaming meat in its juices.

Shark (order Lamniformes)

Shark eaten in Oceania include the requiem (family Carcharchinidae), the hammerhead (family Sphyrnidae) and thresher (family Alopiidae). These cartilaginous or non-bony fish have always played a large part in the lore and superstitions of the Pacific Islanders. Clans would adopt a shark name for protection and their members would not kill nor eat shark meat. In Hawai'i, sharks were said never to harm but, frequently, protect those who petted and fed them. Tales were told of certain species who rested their heads on the outriggers of fishing canoes and were loved and stroked by the fishermen. Shark-calling ceremonies are still enacted in the Solomon Islands. In Polynesia, shark meat was skinned, salted and dried, then broiled or cooked in an earth-pit oven. It was alternatively soaked in brine overnight to remove the ammonia before being cooked.

Slipper Lobster (*Scyllarides* spp.)

A cousin, related to the Pacific crayfish, the slipper lobster is well known and esteemed in Oceania. It is a comical crustacean, looking as if the Creator had taken shears to a conventional (*Homarus ameri-canus*) lobster, after stomping it flat. Pincers or claws are reduced to serrated, flat paddles. It lacks antennae and makes curious, cricket-like noises in the water. Vernacular names reflect people's attempts to describe this strange, small ($5^1/_2$ to 10 inches in length) decapod. It is also called shovel-nosed, bulldozer and sand lobster. Tail meat is all that this ugly creature yields. It is generally used in Pacific soups and stews.

Trochus (family Trochidae) **and Turban** (family Turbinidae)

Top shells, or trochus, are conical—shaped like a toy top—with a strongly marked pattern; russet brown or purple. When the shell's outer layer is polished away, a lustrous mother-of-pearl is revealed. Both trochus and turban shells are called *alileng* by the Guamanians and are traditionally broiled in their own juices in the embers of a fire. (Unfortunately, this cooking process destroys the mother-of-pearl.) Both shells may also be boiled to force their meat from the helix shells. Trochus meat is comparable to abalone in flavor and texture. (On Guam, scuba-diving friends would arrive at our door, still dripping in their wet suits from hunting on the ledges of the reefs, and ask if I would cook a chowder or stew for them with their freshly caught trochus.) (See illustration, page 46.)

Turtles (order Testudines)**: Sea Turtles** (families Cheloniidae and Dermochelyidae)**; Snake-necked Turtles** (family Chelidae)

There are only seven extant species of sea turtles inhabiting the seas of the world. Most are hunted for their delicious meat, their eggs or their beautiful shells. The two most commonly hunted species are *Chelonia mydas,* the green turtle, and *Eretmochelys imbricata,* the hawksbill turtle. The meat and eggs of both are consumed, however the hawksbill has concentrations of toxins in the flesh that make it less than desirable. The green is the star of the classic turtle soup; the scutes of the hawskbill provide the decorative tortoiseshell prized in the jewelry trade. The eggs of the huge leatherback (*Dermochelys coriacea*) are taken because they are believed to be an aphrodisiac. As a result of previously unrestrained harvesting, the leatherbacks are endangered and protected. (For some isolated peoples, they are an important source of dietary protein.) Currently, the largest breeding populations are in Mexican-Pacific waters. The Australian aborigines regard the snake-necked turtles

(*Chelodina* spp.) as a culinary delicacy. (They belong to the same family as most land and freshwater Australian turtles, Chelidae.) After decapitating them the aborigines roast them, upside down, on an open fire. After cooking, they eat the meat directly from the shell. Sea-turtle eggs are now being incubated on beaches under protective wire barriers. (Their Pacific-island breeding grounds were tabooed by chiefs.) The hatchlings—no more than 3 inches long—are now being cared for by students, under experimental programs until they are old enough to head to the sea. With conservation becoming a priority in the Pacific, it is my sincere hope that the world's turtle population will be restored. (See illustrations, pages 74 and 84)

Meats

Cuscus (families Phalangeridae and Pseudocheiridae)
and Possum (families Acrobatidae, Burramyidae and Petauridae)

Cuscus and possums are small marsupials that range through the tall tropical forests of New Guinea, the Solomons and Northern Australia. Cuscus have small ears, and their heads are rounded and covered in woolly, dense fur, similar to, but smaller (in diameter) than that of baby seals. Clinging to branches with both hands and feet and often using their prehensile tails for balance, they have been called "marsupial monkeys." They eat mostly leaves and fruit but will also stalk insects, small lizards and even birds. Both are very distant "cousins" to the opposum, only in that they are also marsupials. The Australian and New Guinean possum has a longer snout than the cuscus, and its tail tends to be bushy. Cuscus and possum are hunted for meat; sometimes for their fur. The Australian aborigines may singe the fur off before cooking the smaller marsupials in hot ashes. The islanders of Papua New Guinea and the Solomons will usually skin the animals before cooking them; either over a fire or, wrapped in leaves, in an earth-pit oven. The texture and flavor of the meat are reminiscent of rabbit.

Emu (*Dromaius novaehollandiae*) **and Cassowary** (*Casuarius* spp.)

The flesh of animals that we are just discovering in our more progressive meat markets is that of creatures with pedigrees dating back over 100 centuries. The emu came in second in the sweepstakes for the "Largest Flightless Bird." (The cassowary was show.) There are no more species extant. The emu is the sole, remaining member of its family, Dromaiidae. (The white settlers in Southeastern Australia had a "fair go" at turning the emu's ancestors into the equivalent of the dodo bird.) The cassowary is reduced to three family members. However, the emu has not only survived but thrived, primarily due to its swimming ability and land-running speed (with foot strides of almost ten feet, they have been clocked at between 25 to 30 miles per hour). The bird is agile, tricky, destructive to crops, often bad-tempered and hostile (the latter traits are ones to which I can personally attest!). The cassowary is said to be even more aggressive. Their meat makes lean and healthy eating for us carnivores. (For those whose delicate sensibilities can be easily assuaged by historical precedents, the aborigines have hunted the birds *selectively* over countless centuries.) The flesh tends to be tough because it is well exercised. Consider marination before cooking, or use the equivalent of the native earth-pit oven method; slow, covered cooking at a constant temperature. (See illustration, page 171)

Fruit Bat (family Pteropodidae)

Shortly after arriving on Guam, I found out that fruit bat was considered a local delicacy by the Chamorros. There are some 154 species in the family, of which the flying foxes (*Pteropus*) are the largest in size. *Pteropus mariannus,* the Guam fruit bat, is actually a flying fox (no, not a fox with wings). Down in the South Pacific, specifically Fiji and Vanuatu, I encountered the dog-faced bat, Rousettus. This is the only member of the family that uses rudimentary echolocation to navigate in their dark caves. All of them fly nocturnally but the

Flying fox (fruit bat)

rest of the species rely on their large eyes for "head-up" flying. During the daytime, most fruit bats hang around, upside down, from tree branches, moving occasionally along a branch to locate and munch on fruit. This diet gives their flesh a delicate sweetness—unfortunately militating the depletion of the species in Micronesia. (Their numbers are proliferating in Melanesia.) I discovered that the Chamorros cook the whole bat—fur and all—in coconut milk. The idea of eating soggy fur is daunting, at least, and I did not experiment with these esteemed chiropterans until I visited Vanuatu. (In the former New Hebrides, because of their previous Anglo-French colonial heritage, English speakers call the bat "flying fox," the French "*rousette*.") Suitably dressed, cooked in a *sauce Bordelaise* by an accomplished *chef de cuisine*, the *rousette* resembled a small game bird and was delicious.

Goanna (family Varanidae) **and Iguana** (family Iguanidae)

Lizards are eaten in Melanesia and some other regions of Oceania; generally on remote islands, in the wilder areas of more populated islands and in the Australian outback. These reptiles are a rich source of protein for isolated tribespeople. The exceptions to this minor culinary role are the large saurians encompassing members of the monitor lizard and iguana, families Varanidae and Iguanidae, respectively. Some members of these families can reach over six feet in length and yield substantial meals for several people. The cooked meat is white, somewhat chewy and tastes like fried chicken without the skin. Central Australia is the home of the perenty (*Varanus giganteus*), which grows to almost 7 feet long. These "goannas" are a feast item for the Australian aborigines. In both Australia and Papua New Guinea, goannas are seared over hot flames to crisp their skin, then cooked in earth-pit ovens. The Papuans wrap them in large leaves before burying them to slow-cook to perfection. One genus of the iguana family, *Brachylophus*, is found in Fiji and some other of the Western Pacific Islands.

Kangaroo and Wallaby (family Macropodidae)

Presented as a national symbol for the continent Down Under (along with another marsupial, the koala), the kangaroo bounds through the open forests and grassy plains of the country. Three of the largest species are the red (*Macropus rufus*), the common gray (*M. canguru*) and the euro (*M. robustus*), also known as the wallaroo. Unfortunately, one man's pet may be another man's pest, and 'roos qualify, alas, under the latter category since they graze voraciously on almost any herbage they find and compete with commercial livestock. They also breed prolifically and now have to be culled through hunting. Fortunately, as the aborigines already knew, their meat is attractive to humans, slightly tougher than graded beef and with a hint of game flavor. To me, the flesh is similar to venison, particularly after a bath in red wine, spices and herbs, before cooking. Kangaroo steaks are deli-

Kangaroo

cious. Kangaroo tails are similar to oxtail; succulent in soups and stews. Wallabies (*Macropus rufogriseus, M. elegans,* etc.), the smaller cousins of the family, also provide traditional meat for aborigines, together with tree kangaroos (genus *Dendrolagus*). Species of both, together with a few of the large kangaroos, are also hunted in Papua New Guinea—where they are a common game animal—found in the markets fresh, or smoked and dried.

Megapode (*Megapodius freycinet*)

Also known as the mound builder, or incubator bird, the megapode is a rather bizarre creature with nesting habits even more strange that those of the cuckoo. Of the order Galliformes—which includes chickens, turkeys, pheasants, etc.—12 species inhabit a large area: from Australia and Papua New Guinea, the Solomons and Vanuatu, to the Carolines and Marianas in the northern Pacific. The bird has large legs, a small head, short, rounded wings and strong breast muscles. It clucks and cackles in the daytime but makes mewing sounds at night. I first became aware of this unusual bird while I was in the Solomon Islands and locals told me I had to taste megapode eggs. When I asked where I could get them, I was told to go to

Savo Island (across a narrow strip of water from Guadalcanal). They then informed me that the birds laid their eggs under mounds of sand and let the heat from the volcano hatch them. Further inquiries indicated that I could take the eggs up the hill and fry them on the ground (volcanically heated). I was convinced I was the victim of the age-old game "get the visitor (or tourist)." I ended up buying my megapode eggs at Rove Market, by the beach. They were slightly reddish, rather like duck eggs in flavor, but a more dominating yolk. Later, I found that these species will bury their eggs in holes dug almost 3 feet down in the sand, relying either on solar or volcanic heat to hatch them. Others, jungle dwellers, will form huge mounds of fermenting plant matter—like compost—over the eggs to incubate them. When the eggs hatch, the chicks dig upward and run off on their own, flying within two to three days. Megopodes are a protected species in all areas, but their eggs may be taken in limited quantities.

Muttonbird (genus *Puffinus*)

In New Zealand, the early Maoris used to trap the young chicks of the sooty shearwater (*Puffinus griseus*) or muttonbird. They called them *titi* and relished their fat, rich meat. Muttonbird is still eaten but the flesh is an acquired taste with a flavor somewhere between fish and wild duck. Current recipes for it include pies and croquettes but, in all instances, the meat is first boiled in three changes of water; presumably to mitigate its strong, fishy essence. In Australia, *Puffinus tenuirostris,* the short-tailed shearwater, is called muttonbird and its chicks are also taken for their meat and oil.

Spiny Anteater (*Tachyglossus aculeatus*)

Called echidna (pronounced "a-KID-na"), this Australian and New Guinean, long-nosed monotreme is egg-laying and completely unrelated to the hedgehog and porcupine, although its back is covered with spines and fur. About one foot in length, the echidna is of the same order as that zoologic anomaly, the duckbilled platypus. A second member of the family Tachyglossidae is *Zaglossus bruijni;* a larger, more porcine, spiny anteater that inhabits the island of New Guinea. Echidnas live in forests, scrub land and deserts, burrowing into the earth vertically when disturbed. Prized for its delicious flesh by the aborigines, the spiny anteater was also a source of succulent, chicken-like meat for the earliest white settlers in Australia. Both the aborigines and New Guineans bake the animals; first burning off their spines or skinning them.

Wild Pig (*Sus scrofa papuensis*)

Probably introduced into New Guinea around 6000 years ago, the pig was valuable cargo on the canoes of the migrants to the Pacific Islands and continues to play a central role in Pacific ceremonies and feasts. After the advent of the Westerners to Oceania, the feral pig became an ancestor of mixed breed, domesticated porkers now raised in Oceania. Called *pigpig* in Vanuatu Bislama, or pidgin, the direct descendant of the original wild pig can still be found all over Melanesia. These little, long-snouted island pigs are smal
ler, thinner, more bristly and agile than their stolid Western cousins. Their meat has a flavor of wild boar. With native directness, the Melanesians refer to foreign, imported porkers as *sot fes,* meaning short-faced. However, in any shape or form, pig ends up in the large earth-pit oven, carefully wrapped and insulated in layers of leaves and slow-cooked to a succulent, tender and delicious feast item. (See illustration, page 136)

Witchety Grub (family Cossidae) and Sago Grub (*Rhyncosphorus ferringinlus*)

Although the name, witchety grub, embraces the grubs of moths of The Cossidae family, it refers primarily to the fat larvae of the carpenter moth (several species of *Xyleutes*) and also encompasses those of the ghost moth (family Hepialidae); both of the latter are popular food in Australia.

The common name, witchety, is more properly spelled "*witjuti*"; thus called by the aborigine Arabana tribe after their name for two species of *witjuti* or wattle shrubs (*Acacia kampeana* and *A. ligulata*) that act as hosts and

Roasted witjuti (witchety) *grub*

feeding grounds for the grubs. An important food item to the aborigines, the grubs are eaten raw (reputedly tasting like peanuts) or

283

roasted in ashes, whereupon they become similar to herbed sausage, both in texture and flavor. The witchety grub has now become a fashionable delicacy, served in the increasingly popular bush-food restaurants in Australia. In Papua New Guinea, the larvae of a beetle, *Rhyncophorus ferrugineus,* is eaten. Known as the sago grub, this plump creature feasts on the pith of the sago palm (ibidem). You can often find these in local, open-air food markets, spitted and grilled like *satay.* If one cavils—as I did—at eating these larval-stage insects, you might know that they feed only on an exclusive diet of vegetable sap (sugar) and pulp, giving them a sweetness and purity of flavor. (Contrast this with the diet of scavenging sea insects, such as lobster and shrimp.) As a final endorsement, their nutritional rating is excellent: rich concentrations of protein, fat and sugars, calcium and iron.

Ingredient Sources

It is possible to cook almost every recipe in this book with ingredients purchased at your local supermarket and, for those that are problematic, substitutions are recommended. However, a wider range of authentic ingredients may be found by visiting Hispanic, Southeast Asian or Chinese markets. (The best results are always obtained by befriending enlightened purveyors and, when necessary, gently urging them to greater efforts on your behalf.) Of course, if you have the acquaintance-ship of a Pacific Islander, ask them where they shop.

By their nature, some of the ingredients listed are not currently available in the West. This may change—who knows? (My motives for including some esoteric ingredients are to induce familiarity and insinuate the possibility of importation.)

Australian bush "tucker" is not, at this time, beyond our grasp. Most of the ingredients in my recipes, as well as other bush foods, products and information can be obtained from Bush Tucker Supply Australia Pty., Ltd., Post Office Box B103 Boronia Park, New South Wales 2111, Australia. (Telephone: +(02) 817-1060; facsimile +(02) 817-3587.)

Bibliography
and Additional Reading

A Lady (Mary Wallis). *Life in Feejee*. Suva: Fiji Museum, 1983.

Abbott, Isabella Aiona. *Limu—An Ethnobotanical Study of some Hawaiian Seaweeds*. Lawai: Pacific Tropical Botanical Garden, 1984.

Abernethy, Jane Fulton and Tune, Suelyn Ching. *Made in Hawaii*. Honolulu: University of Hawaii Press, 1983.

Abo, Takaji, Bender, Byron W., Capelle, Alfred, and Debrum, Tony. *Marshallese-English Dictionary*. Honolulu: University of Hawaii Press, 1976.

Allardice, R. W. *A Simplified Dictionary of Modern Samoan*. Auckland: Polynesian Press, 1989.

Allen, Gerald R. *Fishes of Western Australia*. Hong Kong: T.F.H. Publications, 1985.

Amesbury, Steven S., Cushing, Frank A. and Sakamoto, Richard K. *Fishing on Guam—Guide to the Coastal Resources of Guam—Vol 3*. Guam: University of Guam Press, 1986.

Amesbury, Steven S. and Myers, Robert F. *The Fishes—Guide to the Coastal Resources of Guam: Vol. 1*. Guam: University of Guam Press, 1982.

Ashby, Gene. (compiler and editor) *Never and Always—Micronesian Stories of the Origins of Islands, Landmarks, and Customs*. Ponape: The Community College of Micronesia, 1983.

Ashby, Gene. *Ponape—An Island Argosy*. Ponape: Rainy Day Press, 1983.

Bermann, Richard A. *Home from the Sea—Robert Louis Stevenson in Samoa* (translated by Elizabeth Reynolds Hapgood). Honolulu: Mutual Publishing Company, 1939.

Bonnemaison, Joël. *Vanuatu* (translated by William Reed and Jane Philibert). Singapore: Les Editions du Pacifique, 1986.

Bounds, John H. *Tahiti—Oasis of the South Pacific*. Bend: Maverick Publications, 1978.

Brower, Kenneth. *A Song for Satawal*. New York: Penguin Books, 1983.

Burchett, Wilfred G. *Pacific Treasure Island—New Caledonia*. Melbourne: F. W. Cheshire Pty. Ltd., 1942.

Burgess, Warren and Axelrod, Herbert R. *Pacific Marine Fishes*. Hong Kong: T.F.H. Publications, 1972.

Burgess, Warren and Axelrod, Herbert R. *Fishes of the Great Barrier Reef*. Hong Kong: T.F.H. Publications, 1976.

Capell, A. (compiler) *A New Fijian Dictionary*. Suva: Government Printer, 1991.

Cherikoff, Vic. *Uniquely Australian—A Wild Food Cookbook*. Gladesville: Bush Tucker Supply Australia Pty Ltd., 1992.

Cherikoff, Vic and Isaacs, Jennifer. *The Bush Food Handbook*. Balmain: Ti Tree Press, c. 1989.

Clairmont, Leonard. (compiler) *Say It in Tahitian.* Los Angeles: Tahiti Musique.

Craig, Robert D. (editor) *The Marquesas Islands—Their Description and Early History by Reverend Robert Thomson.* Laie: The Institute for Polynesian Studies, Brigham Young University—Hawaii Campus, 1980.

Crowley, Terry. *An Illustrated Bislama-English and English-Bislama Dictionary.* Vila: Pacific Languages Unit and the Vanuatu Extension Centre of the University of the South Pacific, 1990.

Davidson, Alan. *Seafood of South-East Asia.* Singapore: Federal Publications, 1977.

de Bisschop, Eric. *Tahiti-Nui* (translated by Edward Young). New York: McDowell, Obolensky, 1959.

Diolé, Philippe. *The Forgotten People of the Pacific* (translated by J. F. Bernard). Woodbury: Barron's, 1976.

Dodd, Edward. *Polynesia's Sacred Isle.* New York: Dodd, Mead & Company, 1976.

Douglas, Norman and Ngaire. *Pacific Islands Yearbook.* North Ryde: Angus & Robertson Publishers, 1989.

Ellis, William. *Polynesian Researches: Polynesia.* Tokyo: Charles E. Tuttle Company, Inc., 1977.

Escoffier, Auguste. *Ma Cuisine.* London: The Hamlyn Publishing Group Ltd., 1965.

Eustis, Nelson. *Aggie Grey of Samoa.* Adelaide: Hobby Investments Pty. Ltd., 1989.

Finney, Ben R. (compiler) *Pacific Navigation and Voyaging.* Wellington: The Polynesian Society Incorporated, 1976.

Flood, Josephine. *Archaeology of the Dreamtime.* Honolulu: University of Hawaii Press, 1988.

Fox, Charles E. *The Story of the Solomons.* Sydney: Pacific Publications, 1975.

Furnas, J. C. *Anatomy of Paradise.* New York: William Sloane Associates, Inc., 1937.

Gassner, Julius S. (translator) *Voyages and Adventures of La Pérouse.* Honolulu: University of Hawaii Press, 1969.

Gill, William Wyatt. *From Darkness to Light in Polynesia.* London: William Clowes and Sons, Limited, 1894.

Gould, Richard A. *Yiwara—Foragers of the Australian Desert.* New York: Charles Scribner's Sons, 1969.

Grimble, Arthur. *A Pattern of Islands.* London: John Murray (Publishers) Ltd., 1952.

Hill, Paul J. and Mavis A. *The Edible Sea.* New York: A. S. Barnes and Company, 1975.

Hinz, Earl R. *Landfalls of Paradise—The Guide to Pacific Islands.* Ventura: Western Marine Enterprises, Inc., 1981.

Howe, K. R. *Where the Waves Fall.* Honolulu: University of Hawaii Press, 1988.

Isaacs, Jennifer. *Bush Food—Aboriginal Food and Herbal Medicine.* Sydney: Weldon Publishing, 1989.

Kane, Herb Kawainui. *Voyagers.* Bellevue: WhaleSong, Incorporated, 1991.

Kawaharada, Dennis. (editor) *Hawaiian Fishing Legends.* Honolulu: Kalamaku Press, 1992.

King, Michael. *Maori—A Photographic and Social History.* Auckland: Heinemann Reed, 1989.

Kuper, Jessica. (editor) *The Anthropologists' Cookbook.* New York: Universe Books, 1977.

Kyselka, Will and Lanterman, Ray. *North Star to Southern Cross.* Honolulu: University of Hawaii Press, 1976.

Kyselka, Will. *An Ocean in Mind.* Honolulu: University of Hawaii Press, 1987.

Langdon, Robert. *Tahiti—Island of Love.* Sydney: Pacific Publications Pty. Ltd., 1979.

Lewis, David. *We, the Navigators.* Honolulu: The University Press of Hawaii, 1969.

Makereti. *The Old-Time Maori.* Auckland: New Women's Press, 1986.

Malinowski, Bronislaw. *Argonauts of the Western Pacific*. New York: E. P. Dutton & Co., Inc., 1922.

Maretu. *Cannibals and Converts—Radical Change in the Cook Islands* (translated and edited by Marjorie Tuainekore Crocombe). Suva: Fiji Times Ltd., 1987.

Marshall, Donald. *Ra'ivavae*. Garden City: Doubleday & Company, 1961.

Martini, Frederic. *Exploring Tropical Isles and Seas*. Englewood Cliffs: Prentice-Hall, Inc., 1984.

Maude, H. E. *Of Islands and Men*. Melbourne: Oxford University Press, 1968.

May, R. J. *Kaikai Aniani—A Guide to Bush Foods Markets and Culinary Arts of Papua New Guinea*. Bathurst: Robert Brown & Associates, 1984.

McClane, A. J. *The Encyclopedia of Fish Cookery*. New York: Holt, Rinehart and Winston, 1977.

McDermott, John and Bobbye. *How to Get Lost and Found in the Cook Islands*. Honolulu: ORAFA Publishing Co., Inc., 1986.

Mead, Margaret. *Coming of Age in Samoa*. New York: William Morrow & Company, Inc., 1928.

Miller, Carey D., Bazore, Katherine and Bartow, Mary. *Fruits of Hawaii*. Honolulu: The University Press of Hawaii, 1981.

Mitchell, Donald D. Kilolani. *Resource Units in Hawaiian Culture*. Honolulu: The Kamehameha School Press, 1982.

Moorehead, Alan. *The Fatal Impact: The Invasion of the South Pacific 1767–1840*. Sydney: Harper & Row, Publishers, 1987.

Motteler, Lee S. *Pacific Island Names*. Honolulu: Bishop Museum Press, 1986.

Muller, Kal. *Indonesian New Guinea—Irian Jaya*. Berkeley: Periplus Editions, Inc., 1991.

Murphy, John J. *The Book of Pidgin English*. Carina Old: Robert Brown & Associates, 1989.

Myers, Robert F. *Micronesian Reef Fishes*. Guam: Coral Graphics, 1991.

Mytinger, Caroline. *Headhunting in the Solomon Islands—Around the Coral Sea*. New York: The Macmillan Company, 1942.

Nordyke, Eleanor C. *The Peopling of Hawaii*. Honolulu: The University Press of Hawaii, 1977.

Oliver, Douglas L. *The Pacific Islands*. Honolulu: The University Press of Hawaii, 1979.

Osborn, Fairfield. (editor) *The Pacific World*. New York: W. W. Norton & Company, Inc., 1944.

Parnwell, E. C. *Oxford Maori Picture Dictionary*. Hong Kong: Oxford University Press, 1988.

Parsons, Claire D. F. (editor) *Healing Practices in the South Pacific*. Honolulu: The Institute for Polynesian Studies, 1985.

Pollock, Nancy J. *These Roots Remain—Food Habits in Islands of the Central and Eastern Pacific since Western Contact*. Laie: The Institute for Polynesian Studies, 1992.

Price, Willard. *America's Paradise Lost*. New York: The John Day Company, 1966.

Price, A. Grenfell. (editor) *The Explorations of Captain James Cook in the Pacific as Told by Selections of His Own Journals 1768–1779*. New York: Dover Publications, Inc., 1971.

Pukui, Mary Kawena and Elbert, Samuel H. *Hawaiian Dictionary*. Honolulu: University of Hawaii Press, 1986.

Reed, A. W. *Aboriginal Words of Australia*. Balgowlah: Reed Books Pty. Ltd., 1991.

Ruhen, Olaf. *The Tongans*. Sydney: Pacific Publications Pty. Ltd., 1978.

Savage, Stephen. *A Dictionary of the Maori Language of Rarotonga*. Wellington: Institute of Pacific Studies, University of the South Pacific in association with the Ministry of Education, Government of the Cook Islands, 1990.

Schenck, Earl. *Come unto these Yellow Sands*. New York: The Bobbs-Merril Company, 1940.

Schneider, Elizabeth. *Uncommon Fruits & Vegetables—A Common Sense Guide*. New York: Harper & Row, Publishers, 1986.

Semper, Karl. *The Palau Islands in the Pacific Ocean*. Guam: Micronesian Area Research Center, University of Guam, 1982.

Sinclair, James. (editor) *Papua New Guinea Handbook and Travel Guide*. Sydney: Pacific Publications Pty. Ltd., 1980.

Stair, John B. *Old Samoa or Flotsam and Jetsam from the Pacific Ocean*. Papakura: R. McMillan, 1897(?).

Stanley, David. *Tahiti—Polynesia Handbook*. Chico: Moon Publications, Inc., 1989.

Stanley, David. *South Pacific Handbook*. Chico: Moon Publications, 1989.

Stanley, David. *Micronesia Handbook—Guide to an American Lake*. Chico: Moon Publications, 1985.

Stevenson, Robert Louis. *In the South Seas*. Honolulu: The University Press of Hawaii, 1979.

Stoddard, Charles Warren. *South-Sea Idyls*. New York: Charles Scribner's Sons, 1899.

Strandberg, Olle, *Tigerland and South Sea* (translated by M. A. Michael). New York: Harcourt, Brace and Company, 1953.

Te Rangi Hiroa (Peter H. Buck). *Arts and Crafts of Hawaii, Section I, Food*. Honolulu: Bishop Museum Press, 1964.

Theroux, Paul. *The Happy Isles of Oceania—Paddling the Pacific*. New York: G. P. Putnam's Sons, 1992.

Thurn, Everard Im and Wharton, Leonard C. (editors) *The Journal of William Lockerby, Sandalwood Trader in Fiji 1808–9*. Suva: Fiji Times & Herald Ltd., 1982.

Tinker, Spencer Wilkie. *Fishes of Hawaii*. Honolulu: Hawaiian Service, Inc., 1991.

Titcomb, Margaret. *Dog and Man in the Ancient Pacific with Special Attention to Hawaii*. Honolulu: Bernice P. Bishop Museum, 1969.

Titcomb, Margaret. *Native Use of Fish in Hawaii*. Honolulu: University of Hawaii Press, 1972.

Trager, James. (editor) *The People's Chronology*. New York: Holt, Rinehart and Winston, 1979.

Turner, George. *Samoa—A Hundred Years Ago and Long Before*. Suva: Institute of Pacific Studies, University of the South Pacific, 1984.

Wagner, Warren L., Herbst, Derral R. and Sohmer, S.H. *Manual of the Flowering Plants of Hawaii, Volume 1* and *Volume 2*. Honolulu: University of Hawaii Press and Bishop Museum Press, 1990.

Weiner, Michael A. *Secrets of Fijian Medicine*. Berkeley: University of California, c. 1975.

Wells, Marjorie D. *Micronesian Handicraft Book of the Trust Territory of the Pacific Islands*. New York: Carlton Press, Inc. 1982.

Wendt, Albert. *Flying-Fox in a Freedom Tree*. Auckland: Penguin Books, 1988.

Wyban, Carol Araki. *Tide and Current: Fishponds of Hawaii*. Honolulu: University of Hawaii Press, 1992.

and

The indispensable Lonely Planet Guide Books (travel survival kits) from Lonely Planet Publications, Hawthorn, Victoria, Australia; Berkeley, California, U.S.A.; Chiswick, U.K. Following are the titles I used: *Australia, Fiji, Micronesia, New Caledonia, New Zealand, Papua New Guinea, Rarotonga & the Cook Islands, Samoa, Solomon Islands, Tahiti & French Polynesia, Tonga, Vanuatu.*

General Index

Culinary Index

Japan

Northern
Marianas
Islands

Guam

Philippine
Islands

Belau

Federated States
of Micronesia

Papua
New
Guinea

Indonesia

Solom
Isla

Vanua

New
Cale

Australia

Tasmani